THE COMPLETE ENCYCLOPEDIA OF COCKTAILS

THE COMPLETE ENCYCLOPEDIA OF COCKTAILS

Cocktails old and new,
with and without alcohol

SIMON POLINSKY

This 2nd edition reprinted 2004

Text: R&R, Australia
Production: R&R, Australia
Cover design: Minkowsky Graphics, Enkhuizen, The Netherlands

ISBN 90 366 1498 8

Contents

1. History of Spirits and Distillation

In the middle ages spirit was known as "aqua vitae", a term which survives today in Swedish and Norwegian aquavit and Danish Akvavit. This was symptomatic, because the name means "water of life."

In ancient Greece, Aristotle wrote: "Sea water can be rendered potable by distillation. After it has been converted into humid vapours it returns to liquid." A Greek is said to have discovered this simply by noticing how steam condensed on the inner lid of a dish.

The principal remedies of the ancients were, as we know, wine and herbs. From the time of the Egyptians, great use was made of flowers, plants, and spices cooked, macerated or infused for pharmaceutical or culinary purposes. The healing perfumed liquid was preserved in airtight jars with wine or water. The science of distillation, if not continuously practised, crops up again and again in history. The distillates, as far as we know, were water and scents. The discovery of the distillation of alcohol was made by the Arabs in the early Middle Ages. In the tenth century, the philosopher Avicenna produced a complete description of the alembic, but did not mention alcohol - although it must have been discovered about that time. Like alchemy, the word "alcohol" derives from the Arabic.

A certain black powder was liquified, converted to vapour, allowed to solidify again, and then used as eye paint by the harem beauties. This was "kohl", which is in use throughout the Arab world today. And when the spirit of wine began to be distilled, the Arabic name for this distilled powder - "Al Koh'l" - was adopted, because of the similarity of the process.

In fact, we inherited the Arabian science of distillation by way of alchemy, which played a larger part in the medieval world. The earliest name of genuine importance in distillation is that of Arnau of Vilanove (d 1313), a Catalan professor at the University of Montpellier. He was probably the first to write about alcohol and his traits on wine and spirits was a handbook of the time. His pupil, Rainumdo Lulio (or Raymond Lull), was a philosopher and chemist who carried on with the experiments.

"Eau-de-vie", Lulio wrote, is "an emanation of the divinity, an element newly revealed to men but hiden from antiquity, because the human race was then too young to need this beverage, destined to revive the energies of modern decrepitude." Arnau was more ecstatic. To him, the liquor was the long-sought panacea, the elixir of life itself, the dream of the alchemists. Although they never found what they were looking for - the secret of transmuting base metal into gold, or the elixir of everlasting life - the alchemists discovered a great many other things in the process. They developed the science of chemistry; and while they did not discover "aqua vitae", they used it extensively and bequeathed its uses to us.

To the general public, "aqua vitae" was a medicine and tasted like one. Another name for it was "aqua ardens" - firewater. The fruit and herbs with which the spirits were doctored helped to hide the taste as well as to heal the patients. When, later on, people began to think of brandies and liqueurs primarily as drinks, there was much experimenting with different plants to improve the flavor; and except in such favored regions as Cognac, Frenchmen were still tackling the same problem at the end of the eighteenth century. Then, in 1800, Adeem invented the process of rectification of rectifying - that is, a redistillation which removed the "mauvais gout." Unfortunately, it removed all taste, good as well as bad, and the French, who had been adding herbs and fruit concoctions to hide the nasty taste, had to restore them again to give flavor to the neutral spirit.

"Aqua vitae" was on sale in Italy in the Middle Ages. At about the same time, or a little earlier, it appeared in Ireland, gaelicized into "uisge beatha" and distilled from a barley beer. Variants of this name for the "water of life" persisted throughout the centuries, but in the end it was unquestionably whisky.

Scotch whisky originated in the Highlands. By the fifteenth century, it was a familiar drink there and was purely malt whisky. Gradually it seeped through to the Lowlands and the Scottish court.

The English at first preferred the fine French Cognac brandies miraculously distilled from the thin sharp wines of Charente. In early days, ships from the north used to put in at La Rochelle, principally to pick up salt. Then the inhabitants began to sell their wine as well; and afterward, to save space in the ships - and perhaps to avoid taxes - they began to boil down the wine, which travelled much better when it was thus metamorphosed. At first the idea was to restore the wine by adding water when it reached land again, but it was soon discovered to taste better as it was. A gentleman called Croix-Maron, who is supposed to have had a lot to do with the boiling down of the wine, is said to have remarked: "In cooking my wines, I have discovered their soul."

A report from 1688 says that very little wine of the Charente region could be sold abroad, both "when the white wines are converted to 'eau-de'vie', which is the customary thing, then the English and Danish fleets come to the ports of the Charente in search of it." So, by the date, the brandy of Cognac was established. The name "brandy" may well have come from the Germanic "Branntwein" - burnt wine. There are mentions of "brand wine" in English in 1622 and 1650.

It is interesting that much of the early distilling was done in the house, and the politest ladies were proficient in this domestic art, as common as cooking. Scotch whisky was at first almost entirely made at home: the best was for the Highland chiefs; the crofters mashed their surplus grain into whisky. When, in that mountainous and inaccessible country, the domestic stills were banned by the Hanoverian kings, and heavy taxes and duties began to be placed on the spirit, the distillers quite naturally took to the hills.

It is estimated that of the roughly half a million gallons of Scotch whisky being made annually in 1800, the amount made legally was approximately nil. Some 300,000 illegal gallons are said to have eluded the excise men and flowed down over the border into England year after

year. At one time there were two hundred illicit stills in the famous glen of Glenlivet, where perhaps the finest unblended whisky in the world is made today.
The Scottish distillers were defiant men who brewed their illegal potions quite openly. All that was necessary was to choose a defendable glen, and then go about armed to the teeth. In 1823, the English government lowered the duty on whisky in order to encourage the open and legal distillation of good spirit. Yet the illicit stills were so well established that when a daredevil named George Smith came to Glenlivet itself and set up a legal distillery, he was considered to have shown great effrontery. His memoirs tell nothing of how he made his whisky, but they do tell the secret of his success. He hired the toughest men he could find, and by standing watch in turn with them around the clock he saved his still from being burned out, the fate that befell the few others as bold as himself. Smith's foothold in Glenlivet was the beginning of the end. The sad decline in illegal distilling can be read in the statistics of illicit stills detected in Scotland; in 1834, 177; in 1854, 73; in 1864, 19; in 1874, 6. Whisky-runners were a dying race, like the romantic highwaymen of the previous century.
American whiskey (the word is spelled whisky in Canada, England and Scotland, whiskey in the United States and Ireland) began to be made in the eighteenth century. Distilling of rye and barley grains had become so strong a habit by the year 1794 that such interferences as taxation and control were resented to the point of armed revolt - this was the year of the Whiskey Rebellion in Pennsylvania. The distillers, losing the fight, moved west in large numbers, preferring the Indians to revenue men. A few years before, in Bourbon County, Kentucky, they had started making corn whiskey; with the arrival of the refugees from the east, the trade prospered. At first corn whiskey was made to reduce the carrier's load; the pack-horses winding down the narrow mountain trails of Kentucky could carry only 4 bushels of corn each; when the corn was distilled to whiskey, they could carry the equivalent of 24 bushels. This corn whiskey took the name "Bourbon" from Bourbon County.
There was another incentive for home distilling, and that was the whisky price in Kentucky. In 1782, about the time when the first Bourbon stills were set up, the price fixed by the court in Jefferson County, Kentucky, was 15 dollars a half-pint and 240 dollars a gallon. The Indians had already set the example, making a corn spirit they called Nohelick (the Apaches, further west in undiscovered territory, were brewing their Teeswin from boiled corn), and the settlers pitched in. The first may have been Elijah Craig. At any rate, that intrepid Baptist preacher "considered it as honourable a business as any. Even preachers did not deem it derogatory to their high calling to lend their countenance to its manufacture and engage in it themselves, or drink a little for the stomach's sake."
Adam's process of rectification eventually set off a complete revolution in the manufacture of spirits. Cognac (which even now is

never rectified, but is pot-distilled by the ancient method derived from the alembic) changed its manner of exportation some three-quarters of a century ago as a consequence of the growing competition from rectified spirits. Traditionally shipped in barrels, it began to be exported in bottles, so that the distillers and shippers could be sure of having full control over the liquid they were selling - sent abroad in casks, it was increasingly likely that it would be stretched and adulterated at the end of its journey. One important consequence was that the brandy began to be called after the little rivertown from which it was shipped, and for the first time it was known as Cognac.

Rum - the sugar-cane spirit of the West Indies - had a riotous history in those islands. It was the traditional drink of the fighting men along the sea lanes of the empire-builders - and if the sailors did not get their issue of rum, there was danger of mutiny. The blaxing cane-juice brew was also the drink of the western American Colonies and, in one sense, fired them to revolt and form an independent United States - for England's taxing of rum was resented at least as bitterly as her taxing of tea. Even more romantic was the connection of rum with the pirates of the Spanish Main. In the coves of Barbados, Jamaica, and the other islands, the privateers hove to for concealment - and a fresh load of rum.

We drink - by and large - rather tamed rum today. Once again it is rectification that has brought about the revolution. By repeated redistilling, all by-products can be eliminated from any base liquid - in many a light modern rectified rum little of the lustiness of the pungent cane is left. These light rums are the Puerto Rican and Cuban - different from the heavier, pungent, sweeter liquors of Demerara and Jamaica, and more to the modern taste.

It is in the vast popularity of gin and vodka that the true effects of rectification appear. Both are, fundamentally, spirits made neutral by rectification, then - in the case of gin - reflavored. The persisting predilection for gin may be called "the vogue of the Martini." During Prohibition, complex mixtures of alcohol appear all over North America and spread their influence over the world. These mixtures were known as cocktails. Evolving perhaps from cold punches or mint juleps, they certainly developed and multiplied as they did because illicit synthetic "bath tub" gins needed to be well-disguised by other, less disgusting flavors. Nowadays the cocktail - once so complex - grows simpler and simpler.

The overwhelming preference is for the Martini - simply gin with a touch of vermouth, a concoction which is only possible when the basic ingredients are good.

Vodka is the latest craze. Originally a Russian, Polish, Balkan, Lithuanian and Estonian spirit, it is now made from grain in the United States and in England, France and elsewhere in Europe. The Smirnoff vodka formula bought by an American firm in 1939 from a White Russian refugee started this post-war fashion.

2. Distillation Process

Spirits are made in specially designed machines called stills.
As the base liquid in the still warms up, the first vapor that forms is methyl alcohol. Because alcohol boils at a lower temperature than water, it is possible to vaporize nearly all the alcohol in the base liquid leaving mostly water behind. This is the type of alcohol used in substances such as fuel anti-freeze. It's lethal stuff and modern distillation methods first remove all the methyl alcohol.
After all the vaporized methyl alcohol is removed, ethyl alcohol - the alcohol in the spirits you drink - begins vaporizing along with some water. The vaporized mixture is carefully collected by rapid condensation until the later stages of distillation, when it becomes more water than alcohol.
Typically, distillers must re-distill the base liquid at least once and sometimes 3 or 4 times.
Besides alcohol and water, base liquor contains many other aromatic and flavorful elements called 'congeners'. These add richness and complexity to a finished spirit. It's the distiller's challenge to capture them without including any undesirable impurities.
If the spirit is to have a neutral taste, as in Vodka and Gin, the condensed vapor - called the distillate - must be re-distilled or rectified after collection. Rectification is simply a technical term for repeated distillation that removes all traces of flavor from the pure spirit.

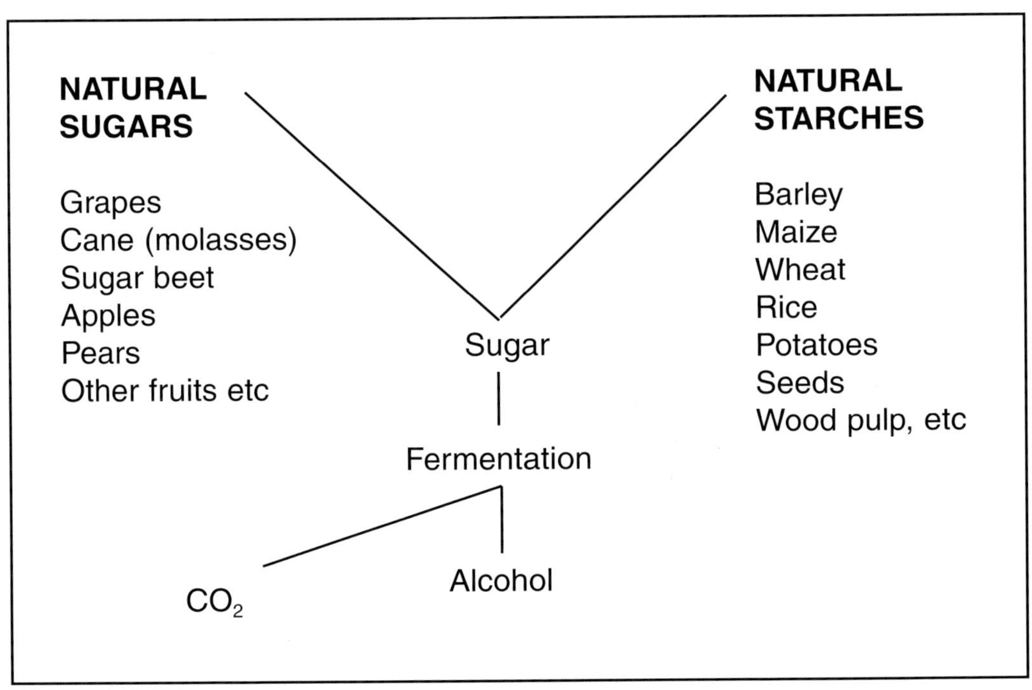

3. Types of stills

THE POT STILL

The POT STILL is the traditional tool of the distiller. Its basic design has changed little since the days when medieval monks distilled spirits for medicinal purposes. It's usually made of copper in the shape of an onion.

Even today, the pot may be heated by a fire burning below it. More often, however, it is encircled by gas operated warming coils. The heated liquid inside the still vaporizes and passes through a spout to a condenser, where the spirit is liquefied and collected. The process is slow because only small quantities are made at one time in each pot still. Today, pot stills are used for higher priced spirits known for their special rich flavors. These include Malt Scotches from Scotland, Cognac Brandy from France, Irish Whiskies and most dark rums. They may also be used for rectification in making Gin or other 'white' spirits.

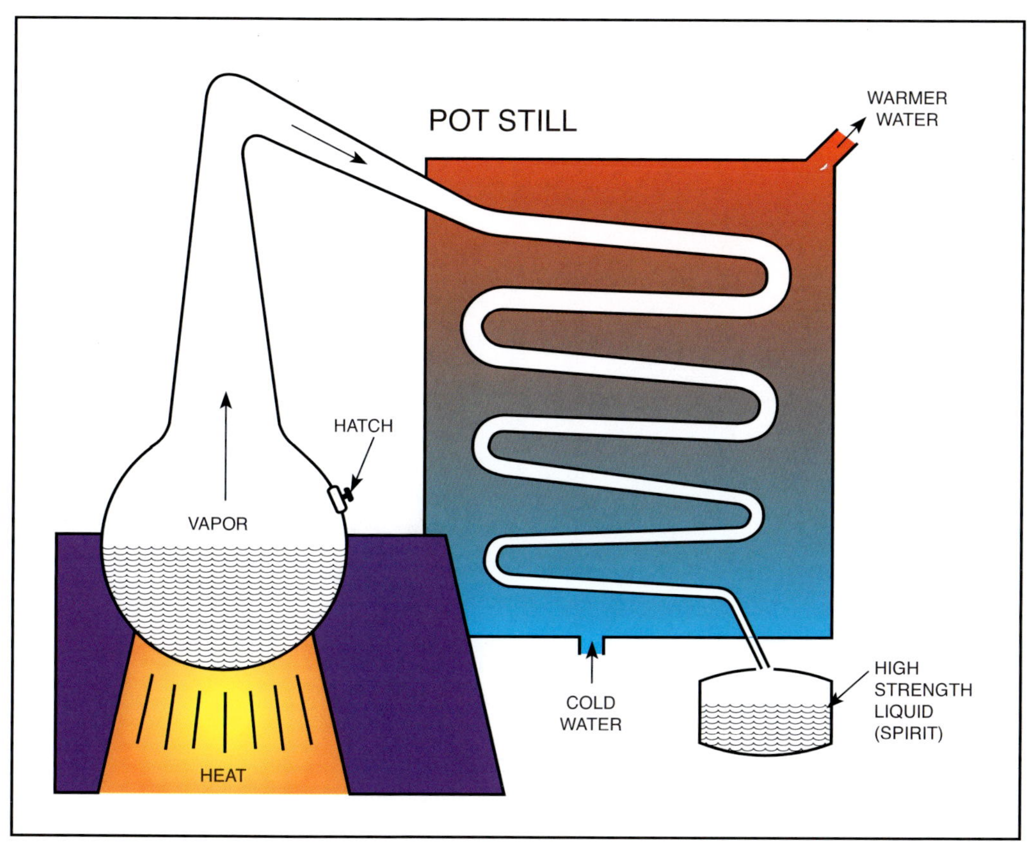

THE PATENT STILL

The PATENT STILL is also called the 'Continuous' or 'Coffey' still. It was invented in 1831 by A. Coffey, an Irishman.

It can be used almost continuously day and night, without the constant attention required by a pot still.

A steady stream of liquid enters the still at the top of a copper column where it is heated to steam and vaporized. The distillate then passes through condensing coils into another column where it is vaporized by steam and rectified. Specially designed plates inside the still ensure that the correct proportions of drinkable elements are collected.

The advantages of this system are many. Large quantities of spirits are produced at relatively low cost. In addition, the patent still is more successful at purifying alcohol than the pot still.

Depending on how often the spirit is passed through the still, the end product may taste neutral like Vodka, or have much flavor, like grain whiskies.

With the patent still, a famous brand of spirit may be made anywhere in the world. The product of the pot still depends on the local water and often specific operating conditions for its unique flavor.

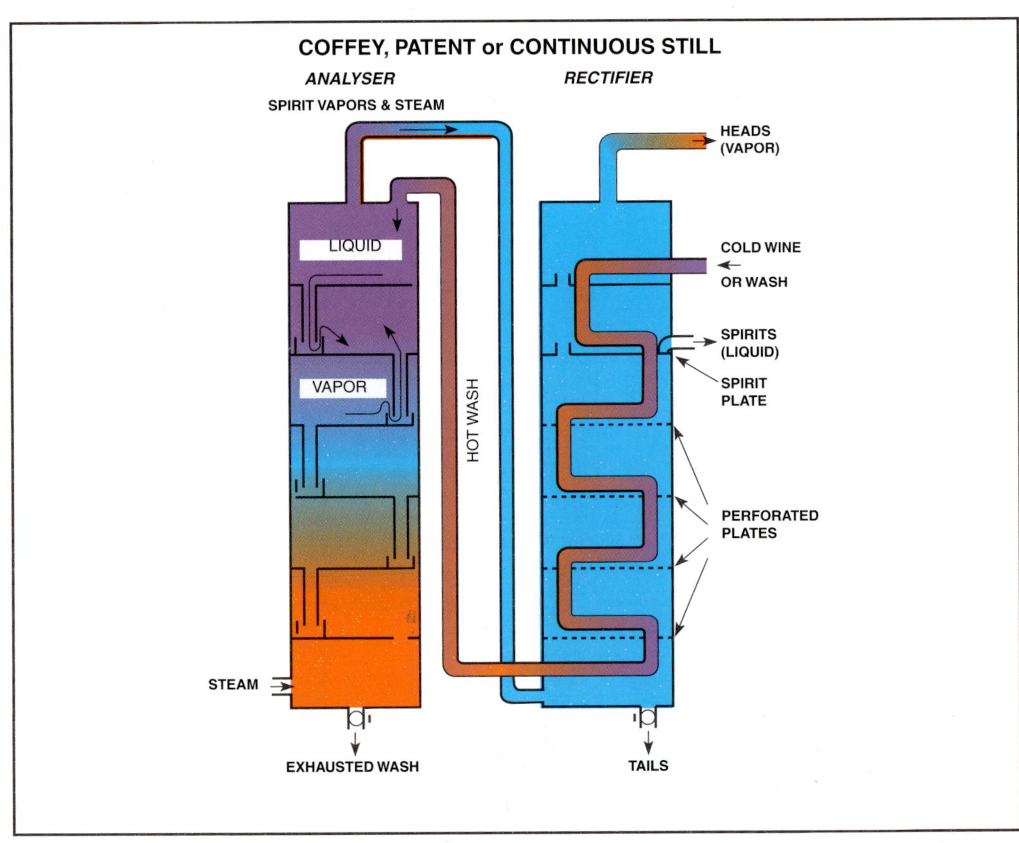

4. The Science of Cocktail Making

THE BASE

This is the fundamental and distinguishing ingredient of the cocktail and must always comprise more than 50% of the entire volume. Indeed, with a few rare exceptions, it should constitute 75% of total volume upwards. Strictly speaking, the base must always consist of a single spiritous liquor and this one liquor, being the predominant ingredient, determines the type of cocktail: Gin for Martinis, Whisky for Manhattans, Rum for Daiquiris. Within certain limits, however, it is possible to combine two (perhaps even more, but this is dangerous) liquors as a base. For example, Rye and Bourbon Whiskies, while differing decidedly in flavor, have the same essential characteristics and may be used pretty much either interchangeably or in combination as a base. Gin and White Cuban also blend very satisfactorily and may be used in combination. On the other hand, the indiscriminate mixture of three or five different liquors is practically certain to destroy the distinguishing flavor and aroma of all produce, a result about as palatable as a blend of castor oil and gasoline.

THE MODIFYING AGENT

It is this ingredient, in combination with the base of spiritous liquor, which characterises the cocktail. The flavor of the modifier itself should never predominate but should always remain submerged. The Gin Cocktail should still remain definitely and recognisably a Gin Cocktail. The Whisky Cocktail a Whisky Cocktail, but the modifier should add that elusive "je ne sais quoi" which makes the cocktail a smooth, fragrant, inspirational delight and not a mere drink of Gin or Whisky.
In general, modifying agents may be divided into three classes:
AROMATIC - including the aromatic wines, such as French and Italian Vermouth, Dubonnet, Byrrh, etc. and bitters of various types.
Fruit Juices - orange, lemon, lime, etc, with or without sugar.
Miscellaneous - "smoothing" agents - sugar, cream, eggs, etc.
All of these modifiers, particularly the aromatics and, above all, the bitters must be used with discretion. Just how far you should go with each agent you will learn by experience, relying both on your palate and on the comments of the customer. With a bitters, a safe rule, particularly if

bitters are used in conjunction with an aromatic wine, is no more than 2 or 3 dashes per drink. In using cream or eggs, remember that you are preparing a drink and not a meal.

A safe rule for these miscellaneous smoothing agents is an absolute maximum of half a whole egg. 1 tablespoon heavy cream or 1 teaspoon of sugar to each drink.

Cocktail Ingredients

Base	**Brandy, Gin, Rum, Whiskey, Tequila, Vodka**		
Modifying	**Aromatics**	**Wines**	Dry Vermouth Sweet Vermouth Dubonnet Sherry
		Bitters	Angostura Abbot's Aged Bronekamp Peychaud
		Citric Bitters	Orange Lime
		Miscellaneous	Amer Picon Campari Fernert Branca
	Fruit Juices		Apple Apricot Grapefruit Lemon Lime Orange Passion Fruit Pear Peach Pineapple Plum Raspberry Tomato

SPECIAL COLORING AND FLAVORING AGENTS

These include all the various cordials or liqueurs, as well as non-alcoholic fruit syrups. They should never dominate and overpower the flavor of the base. These special flavoring agents are to be measured by drops or dashes.

Modifying	**Miscellaneous**	Cream Egg Milk Milk (coconut) Milk (soya) Sugar
Color Flavoring	**Syrups, Cordials**	Grenadine Orgeat Mint Raspberry
	Liqueurs	Advocaat Anisette Amaretto Apricot Brandy Baileys Benedictine Chartreuse Cointreau Creme de Drambule Galliano

5. The Base Spirits

1. WHISKEYS

Scotch Whisky

The term scotch means that the whisky was distilled and matured in the country whose name it bears. Scotch is the most complex of whiskeys, with unusual combinations of sweetness and dryness. The sweetness coming from the primary grain, malted barley, which is the singular ingredient that is mostly associated with scotch. The dryness comes from the smoky qualities that are derived by drying the malted barley in kilns fired with peat from local bogs and the water which runs through the heather and peat moors.
Scotch is aged in a variety of barrels: used port, sherry, bourbon, etc. which add to the complexity and variety of scotches.
All of the largest selling scotches are blended, not only from malts but also from the lighter and more neutral tasting grain whiskeys made from unmalted barley or, more often, corn. The object of blending is to iron out the rough edges of individual whiskies and produce something that will appeal to (or be acceptable to) a broader taste. The blender usually has a wide variety of malts available from all four regions of scotch malts.
Like wines - and many other drinks - the single malts of Scotland are grouped by region. As with wines, these regions offer a guideline rather than a rule. Within Bordeaux, a particular Pomerol, for example, might have a richness more reminiscent of Burgundy; similar comparisons can be made in Scotland. The regions in Scotland have their origins in the regulation of licenses and duties, but they do also embrace certain characteristics.

The Lowlands

The Lowlands tend to produce whiskeys in which the softness of the malt itself is more evident, untempered by Highland peatiness or coastal brine and seaweed. The Lowlands is defined by a line following old country boundaries and running from the Clyde estuary to the river Tay. The line swings north of Glasgow and Dumbarton and runs to Dundee and Perth.

The Highlands

The Highlands is by far the bigger region, and inevitably embraces wide variations. The western part of the Highlands, at least on the mainland, has only a few, scattered distilleries, and it is difficult to generalize about their character. If they have anything in common, it is a rounded, firm, dry character, with some peatiness. The far north of the Highlands has several whiskies with a notably heathery, spicy character, probably deriving both from the soil and the coastal location of all distilleries. The more sheltered East Highlands and the Midlands of Scotland (sometimes described as the South Highlands) have a number of notably fruity whiskies.

None of these Highland areas are officially regarded as regions, but the area between them is known as Speyside, universally acknowledged as a heartland of malt distillation. This area, between the cities of Inverness and Aberdeen, sweeps from granite mountains down to fertile countryside, where barley is among the crops. It is the watershed of a system of rivers, the principal among which is the Spey. Although it is not precisely defined, Speyside is commonly agreed to extend at least from the river Findhorn to the Deveron.

The Speyside single malts are noted in general for their elegance and complexity, and often a refined smokiness. Beyond that, they have two extremes: the big, sherryish type and the lighter, more subtle style.

Within Speyside, the river Livet is so famous that its name is borrowed by some whiskies from far beyond its glen. Only one may call itself The Glenlivet; only two more are produced in the valley, and a further one in the parish. These are all delicate malts, and it could be more tentatively argued that other valleys have malts that share certain characteristics.

The Highland region includes a few good coastal and island malts, but one peninsula and just one island have been of such historical importance in the industry that they are each regarded as being regions in their own right.

Campbelltown

On the peninsula called the Mull of Kintyre, Campbeltown once had about 30 distilleries. Today, it has only three. One of these, Springbank, produces two different single malts. This apparent contradiction is achieved by the use of a lightly peated malt in one and a smokier kilning in the other. The Campbeltown single malts are very distinctive, with a briny character. Although there are only three of them, they are still considered to represent a region in their own right.

Islay

Pronounced "eye-luh", this is the greatest of whisky islands; much of it deep with peat, lashed by the wind, rain and sea in the inner Hebrides. It is only 25 miles long, but has no fewer than eight distilleries, although not all are working. Its single malts are noted for their seaweedy, iodine-like, phenolic character. A dash of Islay malt gives the unmistakable tang of Scotland to many blended whiskies.

Single Malts are the most natural of spirits formed, more than any other, by their environment. For that same reason, they are the most individualistic. No other Spirit offers such diversity of character nor epitomizes the distiller's art, more than Single Malts.

The term SINGLE has a very clear and precise meaning. It indicates that the whisky was made in only one distillery, and has not been blended with any from elsewhere.

The term MALT indicates the raw material: barley malt, and no other grain or fermentable material; infused with water, fermented with yeast and distilled in a pot.

The term SCOTCH means that the whisky was distilled and matured in the country whose name it bears. Outside Britain, there are two single malts (but no Scotch) made in Ireland. There are also three or four single malts (but no Scotch) made in Japan.

A SINGLE MALT SCOTCH must fulfill all three requirements. It must be the product of only one distillery; it must be made exclusively from barley malt; and it must be made in Scotland.

There has been the odd occasion when the product of one run of the still has been aged in identical casks, then bottled. This has been described as a "Single/Single". That is not the normal procedure. Although a single malt always comes from one distillery, whisky from half-a-dozen production batches over a two-year period, aged in different casks, might be married in wood for several weeks and then fed into one bottling run. The age on the bottle will represent the youngest whisky inside.

Some single malts are labeled as "Pure Malt." However, this term is also often used to indicate a vatting together of malt whiskies made in several distilleries. This type of whisky is technically known as vatted malt. It may also be labeled simply as a "Malt Whisky" or "Scotch Malt Whisky." Although such bottlings are perfectly legitimate and often excellent products, their labels usually identify only the brand-owner or blender, and not the distilleries.

A blended Scotch commonly contains about 40 percent malt; the odd one contains more than 60 percent.

The cheaper blends contain much less. The deluxe blends are likely to contain a good proportion of well-matured malt, which is why some carry an age statement. Once again the age statement reflects the age of the youngest whisky.

All single malts are individuals, in some cases as distinct from each other as they are from the blends they inhabit. But before looking at the variables that conspire to produce such a diverse family, a brief reminder of the processes used in the creation of all malts might be helpful.

MALTING: Barley has to be partially germinated before it can release its fermentable sugars. It is soaked in water until it begins to sprout, then this is arrested by drying the grains over heat. This steeping and drying process is called malting. Traditionally, the Scots dried their malt over a peat fire, which gives Scotch its characteristic smokiness. A proportion of peat is still burned during malting.

MASHING: To complete the conversion of starch into fermentable sugars, the malt (which has been milled after malting) is mixed with warm water in a vessel called a mashtum. The liquid drained off, is known as wort.

FERMENTATION: The sugars in the wort are now turned into alcohol during fermentation, which takes place with the addition of yeast, in a fermentation vessel.

DISTILLATON: This is the boiling of the fermented wort, in a pot-still. Because alcohol boils more rapidly than water, the spirit is separated as a vapor and collected as it condenses back to alcohol.

MATURATION: All malts are matured in oak barrels, for a legal minimum of three years, though usually much longer.

A single malt is distilled in traditional vessels that resemble a copper kettle or pot. These are known as pot-stills. Most other types of whisky are made predominantly from other grains, in a more modern system: a continuous still, shaped like a column.

Much of the flavor of the malt is retained in pot distillation because this Old Fashioned system is inherently inefficient. A column system can distill more thoroughly, but makes for a less flavorful spirit. Blended Scotch whiskeys contain a proportion of pot-still malt, leavened with continuous-still whisky made from cheaper, unmalted grains.

The pot-still is a vessel shaped by a coppersmith, and in no two distilleries is it identical. Some Scottish malt distilleries trace their history from the late 1700s, and many from the early and mid 1800s. Over the years, each distillery has been reluctant to change the shape of its stills. As they wear out, they are replaced by new ones of the same design. If the last still was dented, the distillery may get the same depression hammered into the new still.

The reason for this is that every variation in the shape of the still affects the character of the product. A small, squat still produces a heavy, oily, creamy spirit. In a large still, some of the vapors condense before they have left the vessel, fall back and are redistilled. This means that tall stills produce lighter, cleaner spirits.

Irish Whiskey

In the 6th Century AD, Irish monks journeyed to the Middle East and it is thought that it was there they observed how the alembic was used to distil perfume. On returning to Ireland they invented their own version - the 'Pot Still'. This they used to create a new spirit known as 'Uisce Beatha' - 'The Water of Life'

BARLEY - MALTED AND UNMALTED: Irish Whiskey is made either from malted barley or from a mixture of malted and unmalted barley and other cereals. In Ireland the malt is dried in closed Kilns unlike in Scotland, where malt is dried over open peat fires. This, the malting process used for Irish Whiskey, not only avoids a smoky taste but also ensures a smooth and natural flavor.

MILLING: Precise amounts of barley and other cereals are ground and then mixed with pure water in a large vessel called a 'mash run'.

PUREST WATER: From the underground springs, in bubbling streams and fast-flowing rivers Ireland is blessed with an abundance of clear, pure water.

FERMENTATION: The starches in the mash are converted into a sugary liquid 'wort'. This is separated from the residual grains and pumped into the 'wash backs' where yeast converts the sugars in the wort to low strength alcohol or 'wash'.

THREE SEQUENTIAL DISTILLATIONS: The art of distillation enables the creation of new whiskey for 'wash'. This is the heart of the process with the wash being heated in large copper pot stills of traditional design. In Ireland whiskey is obtained only after three separate distillations, each sequence resulting in a further process of purification.

At the first stage a distillate named 'low wines' is obtained. This full flavored product called 'feints' requires one further distillation which is carried out in a spirit still. Thus, through a repeated sequence of distillations, a final spirit of light and delicate character is obtained. It is this new whiskey which, after maturation, will become Irish Whiskey.

MATURING IN OAK CASKS: The maturing whiskey is stored for years in vast, dark, aromatic warehouses. Here it rests in fine oak casks, some of which have been used previously for sherry. While the whiskey matures, there is a complex interaction between the whiskey, natural wood extracts, and the air which 'breathes' through the wood of the cask, giving a superb, mellow bouquet to the whiskey.

American Whiskey

Blended American Whiskey is a broad category of spirits that is produced by the distillate of a fermented grain mash which is aged and then blended. There are whiskeys made in Pennsylvania, Tennessee, Virginia, Kentucky, etc., all in different manners and/or processes. The most famous American Whiskey, of course, are bourbon whiskies.

Bourbon is America's native spirit, with a history and tradition steeped in the cultures of the earliest settlers. This unique American product has continually evolved and been refined over the past 200 plus years.

Among the first settlers who brought their whiskey making traditions to this country were the Scotch-Irish of Western Pennsylvania. Although whiskey was produced throughout the colonies (George Washington was among the noted whiskey producers of the time), these settlers of Pennsylvania are where bourbon's roots began.

To help finance the revolution, the Continental Congress put a tax on whiskey production. So incensed were the settlers of Western Pennsylvania that they refused to pay. To restore order to the ensuing "Whiskey Rebellion" of 1791 to 1794, Washington was forced to send the Continental Army to quell the uprising. This turned out not to be as easy as Washington thought it might be. To save the government from a potentially embarrassing political situation and to avoid further troubles with the very tough and stubborn Scotch-Irish settlers, Washington made a settlement with them, giving incentives for those who would move to Kentucky (at that time part of Virginia). The significance of this is that the early whiskey was made primarily from rye, this was about to change with their move and "Bourbon" would be born.

The Governor of Virginia, Thomas Jefferson, offered pioneers sixty acres of land in Kentucky if they would build a permanent structure and raise "native corn." No family could eat sixty acres worth of corn a year and it was too perishable and bulky to transport for sale; if it were turned into whiskey, both problems evaporated.

This corn based whiskey, which was a clear distillate, would become "bourbon" only after two coincidentally related events happened. The French, having at that time their own territories in North America, assisted in the War of Independence against the British. In acknowledgment of this, French names were subsequently used for new settlements or counties.

In the Western part of Virginia, the then county of Kentucky, was subdivided in 1780 and again in 1786. One of these subdivisions was named Bourbon County, after the French Royal House. Kentucky became a state in 1792 and Bourbon one of its counties.

Being on the Ohio River, the town of Marysville became a primary shipping port. Bourbon County thus became associated with the shipping of Whiskey. The name of the spirit became synonymous because of this and one other event.

Although Evan Williams, in 1783, might have been the first commercial distiller in Louisville, Bourbon is sometimes considered to have begun with the Reverend Elijah Craig from Bourbon County. The legend goes that he was a might thrifty and used old barrels to transport his whiskey to market in New Orleans. He charred the barrels before filling them, thus after his whiskey made the long trip to market, it had "mellowed" and taken on a light caramel color from the oak. Being from Bourbon County he started calling the whiskey "Bourbon". Interestingly today, there is no whiskey produced in Bourbon County.

In 1964, a congressional resolution protected the term "Bourbon" and only since then has the product been defined. The basic elements of Bourbon are that it must be a minimum of two years old, at least 80° (proof) and be made from a mash of at least 51% corn. It must be aged in charred new oak barrels. 99% of Bourbon Whiskey comes from Kentucky, but it doesn't have to, the "law" does not stipulate origin. Most consider the unique limestone spring water found in Kentucky the only water with that "just right" combination of minerals suitable enough for the finest Bourbons.

The next stage for the Bourbon producers is how the elements of production, storage, aging and bottling are handled.
Bourbons vary in style, philosophy and approach to production. If the mix of small grains in the mash changes, or the yeast strain used is different, so is the product. Many distill and age their whiskey at a different proof. Some crack the corn, some roll it. There are those that pay detailed attention to every detail from the growing and preparation of the grain to the proper rack house barrel rotation. In all bourbons you can find a unique point of difference and it is these subtle differences in the end product that beg study and comparison.
It is also this great variety of possibilities that make Bourbon whiskey one of the most interesting classifications of distilled spirits to explore.

Canadian Whisky
Canadian whisky is often offered to the drinker who has ordered "a rye." Some Canadian whiskies are even designated as rye on the label. This is an accurate, but confusing description. Whatever their labels say, all Canadian whiskies are of the same style. The classic method of production is to blend rye and perhaps other whiskies, with relatively neutral spirit. These are, indeed rye whiskies - but as blends. They are quite different from the traditional straight rye of the United States. That is the original "rye."
The best Canadian whiskies have at least some of the spicy, bitter-sweet character of rye, lightened with the blending spirit. In some instances, this too is distilled from rye but the raw material hardly matters, since it is rectified close to neutrality. More often, the blending spirit is made from corn.
A further component of the palate is a dash of the vanilla sweetness to be found in Bourbon. This may result from a proportion of Bourbon-type whisky having been used in the blend, or it may derive from the wood used in aging. Such is the pungency of straight rye and Bourbon that their characteristics are powerfully evident in the palate of a good Canadian whisky, despite its being a very dilute blend.
There is as little as three percent of straight whisky in some Canadians, more often four or five, but not as much as ten. This dash of flavor is counterpointed with the lightness of body provided by the far greater proportion of the neutral spirit.

One characteristic of many Canadian whiskies is their use of rye that has been malted. This provides a characteristic smoothness and fullness of flavor. Unmalted ryes are also used. Most blends include more than one rye whisky, and for this purpose a single distillery may produce several. The character and weight of these will vary according to the mash bill and distillation methods.

The mash bill for a rye whisky being produced for blending may also include more than one rye whisky, and for this purpose a single distillery may produce several. The character and weight of these will vary according to the mash bill and distillation methods.

The mash bill for a rye whisky being produced for blending may also include a small portion of barley malt, or perhaps some corn. The proportion of these ingredients can be varied to produce ryes of differing characters.

Canadian distilleries also produce their own Bourbon-type whiskies for blending purposes. They also make corn whiskies, and even distill unmalted barley, again to produce components for their blends.

The biggest producers, Seagram's, have half a dozen distilleries in Canada, using several different yeasts, and making more than 50 different straight whiskies for blending.

A large number of these will go into some of the more complex blends, and general Canadian practice is to use perhaps 20 different whiskies. Even the least complex blend will probably contain 15 whiskies, built around six or seven basic types.

The changes are also rung in the extent to which the various whiskies for blending are aged. In the case of rye, aging tends not only to smoothen the whisky but also to make it heavier. This effect is more evident if the rye is aged as a straight - and that raises another variable.

The extent to which whisky is aged before or after blending is a matter on which there are different and passionate schools of thought in Canada.

2. BRANDY

Some historians credit the Chinese with discovering the art of turning fruit wine or grain-based mash into a higher alcohol, purer beverage. Others claim the Egyptians were the creators of distillation. It's possible that both cultures were experimenting with distillation in roughly the same period.

Whatever the case, we know for certain that the Moors first established distillation in Europe during their occupation of southern Spain from the 8th century to the late 15th century. The Spaniards of the period were skilled winemakers and started using the pot stills that were left behind by the Moors.

Within a century, brandies made from fermented grapes and other fruits spread across continental Europe.

"Brandy" is derived from brandywijn, a word of Dutch origin for "burnt". Created in a still to leave the water and remove the alcoholic vapor which then turns back into liquid form as it cools. In other languages too, it is the burning that is the essential feature.

In theory distillation is the simplest of physical processes. It is based on the fact that alcohol and water boil at different temperatures, water at 100°C, alcohol at 78.3°C. If a fermented liquid is heated, the vapor containing the alcoholic constituents is released first. It can then be trapped and cooled, then condensed to an alcoholic liquid.

The process was probably first observed by the Arabs, who carried the torch of science during the Dark Ages. We still use their words "al-ambiq" (alembic) for the still, "al-kuhl" (alcohol) for the distillate. Originally, the object was to produce medicinal properties, but it was soon discovered that the use of an appropriate raw material produced a drinkable liquid, a "water of life", aqua vitae. But the raw materials were generally so impure that the alcohol could only be consumed with safety if it had been repeatedly redistilled, which removed most of the essential characteristics of the original raw material as well.

The biggest breakthrough came in the 16th and early 17th centuries. It was found that distilling the sharp white wines that were produced on the slopes overlooking the little town of Cognac in western France, resulted in spirits that after as few as two passes through the stills, produced an eminently drinkable brandy, especially if aged for a few years in oak casks. It has proved to be an unbeatable formula.

The next essential in making fine brandy is the speed of distillation: the slower, the gentler, the more effectively the aromatic elements in the raw material are detached with the alcohol, the better. It is rather like stewing fruit: the lower the flame on the stove, the more intense the aromas released and the more thoroughly is the residue drained of them. Indeed, the Cognacais like to describe their method of distillation as (speeded-up) evaporation.

They are right: the vapors should contain as high a proportion as possible of the congeners, the hundreds of organic chemical compounds which are extracted with the alcohol. Some of these are undesirable, bringing with them rank and unpleasant aromas and have to be removed. This entails a close control over distillation process to remove the "heads", the first vapors emerging from the still, which contain the bulk of these undesirable elements, and then the "tails" which will simply be too feeble, without the requisite alcoholic concentration.

At the other extreme are the continuous stills, invented early in the 19th century by, and named after, an Irishman, Coffey. This still can concentrate wine 10 or more times up to the normal industrial maximum of 96.6%.

This fast, continuous process saves heat (pot-stills have to be reheated between each batch), is highly productive - and can be highly destructive of all the elements which make brandy interesting.

Newly distilled brandy tastes raw, oily and unappetizing. The key to its final quality is a more or less lengthy sojourn in oak casks. The choice of wood was originally accidental: oak happened to be the most easily available for making the casks required by the pioneering distillers. They were, of course, accustomed to using wood to mature and market their wines.

Because brandy, like wine, is a product of the grape, oak has proved suitable for maturing it. But there are many varieties of oak and as with so many aspects of brandy making, local practices differ so widely that only a few generalizations can be offered as applying to the whole range of brandies.

Most of the qualities which make oak so suitable are physical. For whatever the chemical qualities of the wood and the reactions they induce when in prolonged contact with the spirit, it is the porosity of the cask which allows the brandy to have steady, limited access to the air. The brandy gradually absorbs the oxygen required to oxidize and thus soften the raw spirit.

3. GIN

When we think of gin we think of England and her former colonies. The actual origins of gin can be traced to 17th century Holland. Dr. Franciscus de La Boie invented gin in 1650. He was a medical professor at the University of Leyden and was more widely known as Dr. Sylvius. As was with many other spirits, gin was originally intended to be used as a medicine. Dr. Sylvius was seeking an inexpensive, but effective diuretic to use in the treatment of kidney disorders. He mixed oil of juniper berries with grain alcohol, both of which have diuretic properties. He called his new medical concoction "genever", from the French word for juniper.

What made the recipe so revolutionary, was not the use of juniper, it had been used before in dozens of liqueur formulas, but the choice of grain alcohol. Until Dr. Sylvius, most beverage alcohol had been made from grapes or other fruit. In other words, brandies. While the Scotch and Irish were making whiskies from grain, they tempered them with years of aging in wooded casks. Unaged grain spirits, at least those produced with 17th century technology, were considered too harsh for human consumption. But genever tasted good and it was relatively inexpensive to produce.

At the same time, English soldiers, who were fighting on the continent, were introduced to what they termed "Dutch Courage." They returned to England with a preference for this new drink, and the population at large soon grew fond of this palatable yet inexpensive spirit, so much so that it eventually became identified as the national drink of England. It was the English, of course, that shortened the name to "Gin."

Gin was also quite popular with the English foreign service in the "colonies." It mixed naturally with quinine (tonic water) which was used as a profilacsis to nullify the effects of malaria. Even today it's easy to conjure up an image of the British colonial officers sitting on a wide veranda sipping a gin and tonic while surveying his vast dominion.

London Dry and other styles

The dry gin that London distillers eventually developed is very different from the Holland or geneva gin still made by the Dutch, which is heavy-bodied and strongly flavored with a pronounced malty taste and aroma.

London dry gin appeared soon after the continuous still was invented in 1831.

This new still made a purer spirit possible, encouraging English distillers to try an unsweetened or dry style. Sugars had been used to mask the rough and unpleasant flavors that could show up in older pot still production. Originally, the phrase "London dry gin" specified a geographic location; that the gin was made in or near London. Now, the term is considered to be generic and is used to describe a style of gin, (in fact, Beefeater is now the only gin distilled in London) and virtually every gin on the market uses the term "dry".

Gin is the distillate of a grain mash with various flavoring agents. It gets its primary flavor from juniper berries, but many other herbs and spices go into the make-up. The botanicals come from all over the world: cardamom from Sri Lanka, cassia bark from Vietnam, orange peel from Spain, coriander seed from the Czech Republic, angelica root from Germany. Most of the juniper berries themselves are imported from Italy. There are also dozens of other possible ingredients. Each distiller has his own secret formula and no two gin brands are exactly alike.

Production

The vast majority of this unaged spirit (federal regulations do not permit any age claims for gin, vodka and other neutral spirits) is either English dry gin or American dry gin. The English version uses 75% corn, 15% barley and 10% other grains for the mash. The fermentation process is similar to that of whiskey. Following fermentation the resulting liquid is distilled and rectified through a column still, producing a pure spirit of at least 90°. The liquid is then redistilled with the many flavoring agents. Methods vary from producer to producer.

Some combine the botanicals with the spirit and distil the mixture, while others suspend the botanicals above the spirit in the still and let the vapors pass through the many flavoring agents. The spirit that comes off is reduced to bottling strength, anywhere from 80° to 97°.

American gin is produced using one of two standard methods: distilling and compounding. Distilled gin is primarily made by adding the flavoring agents during a continuous process. There are two fairly similar methods of achieving this - direct distillation or redistillation.

In direct distillation the fermented grain mash is pumped into the still. Then it is heated and the spirit vapors pass through a "gin head", a sort of percolator basket filled with juniper, herbs and other natural ingredients. It picks up the delicate flavoring agents as it passes through and then condenses into a high proof gin. Water is added to bring the product down to its bottling strength, usually 80°.

The other method, redistillation, differs only in that the fermented mash is first distilled into a flavorless neutral spirit. Then it is placed in a second still, containing a "gin head", and is redistilled, with vapors absorbing the flavoring agents.

Compound gin, a less costly product, is simply the combination of neutral spirits with the oil and extracts of the botanicals. However, the dominant flavor must be from juniper berries.

4. TEQUILA

The Aztecs did not invent tequila. The one thing that held them back was the failure to discover the secret of distillation. The Aztecs did, however, drink an alcoholic beverage called “Pulque” by the Spaniards. “Pulque” was made by cutting off the flower stalk of the agave plant before it had a chance to bloom, then hollowing out the base of the plant and allowing the cavity to fill with sweet, milky plant sap. With no place to go, the juice would collect there and ferment in a sort of murky, foul-smelling wine.

The Spaniards tried bringing in grapes and grains to recreate alcoholic beverages popular in Europe, but they wouldn’t grow in the semi-arid areas where the agave plant thrived. The Spaniards didn’t like the taste of Pulque, so they tried distilling it. After experimenting with different types of agave, they finally produced a drinkable spirit, which they called “Mezcal.”

Tequila is not made from cactus. The confusion is common because various agave species are often confused with cacti. Agave leaves are succulent, rather than the stems, as in cactus.

About 125 years ago, several of the distillers around the town of Tequila, in the central Mexican state of Jalisco, began making a superior form of Mezcal. They used the whole heart of a specific variety of agave indigenous to the region: the Blue Agave. Today only spirits made within the confines of this region can bear the name Tequila, with one exception (Chinaco). If produced elsewhere, it must be called Mezcal.

Blue Agave is no longer a wild plant, but has become a carefully cultured species. On average, agave plants are about ten years old before they can be harvested for tequila production.

The juicy core of the plant, which resembles a large pineapple, is harvested. Called the "pina" (Spanish for pineapple), the core, which sometimes weighs upward of 100 pounds is trimmed, cut into chunks, then baked in huge steam ovens. A sweet juice (Aguamiel or honey juice) is extracted by steaming and compressing the pina.

The juice is fermented for several days and then distilled at a low proof. It is then double distilled to a powerful 110 proof.

Tequila is reduced to 80 proof with water before bottling.

Some tequila is aged in wood, Gold and "Anejo", and some is bottled clear, the White and Silver.

The Gold tequila rests in large oak vats for about nine months to one year, where it acquires a pale gold color.

By law, tequila, designated "Anejo", must be aged a minimum of one year in wood, however, it is usually aged in smaller oak barrels for at least three years and sometimes up to seven.

There are now premium mezcals made in the manner of tequila but produced outside of the Tequila region. Some mezcal is produced with an agave root worm in the bottle as a mark of authenticity.

5. RUM

Rum comes from sugarcane. It is the alcoholic distillate or a mixture of distillates from the fermented juice of sugarcane, sugarcane molasses, or other sugarcane by-products distilled at less than 190 proof (whether or not such proof is further reduced before bottling to not less than 80 proof).
The distillate must possess the taste, aroma and characteristics generally attributed to rum.
Rum is produced all over the world, wherever sugarcane grows and gets its name from the Latin "saccharum" which means sugar. Of all spirits, it retains the most of those natural taste factors which come to it from its product of origin.
The production of rum begins with harvesting the cane. The freshly cut cane is brought into the sugar mills, where it is passed through enormous, very heavy crushing rollers that express the juice. The juice is boiled to concentrate the sugar and evaporate the water. Then it is clarified. The result is a heavy, thick syrup. The sugar in the syrup is separated and removed. What remains is molasses. Sometimes this still retains up to 5% sugar. This molasses is then fermented and distilled into rum.

There are four main classifications of rum:
* Very dry, light bodied rums;
generally produced in the Spanish-speaking countries, of which Puerto Rico, Guatemala and Nicaragua are good examples.
* Medium-bodied rums; Barbados and Demerara being two examples.
* Rich, full-bodied, pungent rums; which are usually produced in the English-speaking islands and countries, such as Jamaica.
*Light-bodied but pungently aromatic; East Indian, Batavia, Arak rum as from Java.

All of these classifications of rum are not restricted to the examples used. Any country can produce more than one type, but some areas are more famous for one particular type more than others.

Full body and a distinctive richness of flavor used to be the qualities most appreciated in rum, but the last twenty-five years tastes have been gradually changing. Many people now prefer a lighter rum, subtler in favor and more delicate in aroma.

Rums are mainly produced in the region of the Caribbean Sea, including the West Indies and the surrounding countries of South and Central America. Like the wines of France, rums are labeled as to the areas of origin and by law cannot be classified by type. Also like wine, the subtle differences in rums can come from the growing area (weather, soil type, humidity, etc.) and the effects it has on the sugarcane plant.

The molasses carries the characteristics of the plants and concentrates them. Like most spirits and wines, rums are blended to achieve taste and quality consistency.

Other factors affecting the final product are the distillation process itself (Aguardientes, coming from the middle distillate), the aging process (how long, what type of barrel, charred or not, etc...) and as in special rums, the flavoring additives.

6. VODKA

Vodka is far and away the most popular spirit category in America, accounting for more than 20% of all distilled spirits consumption. It is defined by government regulations as a spirit without any distinctive character, aroma, taste or color. Vodka is essentially an unaged neutral spirit that can be distilled from just about anything fermentable. Although the legendary potato is used in the production of some vodkas, most brands today, including the imported ones, are made from grain...any grain, including rye, wheat and barley, but principally corn.

Vodka in most Slavic languages means "water." (Sometimes it's spelled "Woda", but the pronunciation is the same.) The word "vodka" translates literally as "dear little water", an affectionate diminutive for this clean, tasteless spirit that blends with virtually any beverage.

As with Whiskey, the historic origin of vodka remains in question. The Russians and the Poles are just two national groups that claim the distinction of discovering how to produce vodka. There are several others, and as the map of Eastern Europe continues to change, other national groups may lay claim to being the originator of vodka. One thing is certain, however: vodka originated somewhere in Northern and Eastern Europe and several sources note it's arrival in Russia as early as the 14th century.

Americans knew next to nothing about vodka before the 1930's and what they did know consisted mainly of impressions gleaned from Russian novels and old movies about Czarist Russia. Consumers weren't really aware of vodka until after World War II. Alcohol has always featured large in the lives of the Eastern Europeans. Its influence can be recorded as far back as 988! In that year the Grand Prince of

Kiev was told by his ambassadors that Islam forbade strong drink. Consequently the Prince became a Christian and was sent plentiful supplies of communion wine from Byzantium, which was the seat of orthodox Christianity.
Fermented drink was not enough to satisfy the Eastern Europeans for long. They discovered that the extremes of temperature in that part of the world enabled them to produce a beverage with a higher alcoholic strength.

In the 1540s the Russian tsar Ivan 'the Terrible' established his own network of distilling taverns and ensured that the profits went straight into the imperial treasury. He outlawed taverns that were outside his control and put a ban on distilling by potential rivals. He kept his options open, however! He was always in need of the support of the nobility, so he allowed them to continue distilling vodka.
Restrictions and threats of savage punishment didn't dampen the enthusiasm of people for vodka-making. Secret distilling survived through the next century. At the same time the tsar's taverns flourished and grew in number to such an extent that, by the late seventeenth century, a visitor to Russia remarked that they outnumbered bath-houses.
Successive rulers tightened their monopoly on vodka distilling but continued to curry favor with the nobility, gentry and government officials by granting them distilling rights. Thus, in addition to its social role, vodka had considerable political and economic significance in Russia.
From the beginning of the seventeenth century it had become customary for vodka to be served at Russian imperial banquets. All formal meals began with bread and vodka. Vodka was also drunk ceremoniously at religious festivals and in church ritual, and to refuse to partake could be considered impious.
Peter the Great, tsar of Russia from 1689 to 1721, was renowned for his hospitality and love of drinking. He served large quantities of vodka, his favorite drink, at his legendary banquets. On these occasions he would shock foreign guests by cutting open enormous pies out of which dwarfs would jump.

The Governor of Moscow trained a large bear to serve pepper vodka to his guests. If anyone showed reluctance in accepting the drink, the bear would remove the guest's clothes, an article at a time.

Making vodka was a lot easier in Poland, as fewer official restrictions were imposed. Indeed, in 1546, King Jan Olbrecht issued a decree allowing every citizen the right to make vodka.

As a result many families distilled their own spirit, and as early as the sixteenth century there were forty-nine commercial distilleries in the town of Poznan alone.

Vodka-making and drinking became established at all levels of society in Poland over the next few centuries. Poznan continues to be a major center for the production of vodka today.

The key to distillation is the separation of alcohol from the water content of fermented liquid. Because water freezes at a higher temperature than alcohol, the Eastern Europeans were able to separate the alcohol by freezing fermented liquid during the winter months. As a result they were left with a drink with a higher strength than that produced by fermentation alone. This was the earliest method of producing stronger spirit in Eastern Europe. The techniques of distillation didn't spread from the west until the fifteenth century. From that time to the mid nineteenth century all vodka was made in a pot-still using local natural resources such as wheat, barley, ryes, potatoes and rice.

A mash was created by heating the grain to release the starch for conversion into sugar. The sweet liquid was allowed to ferment naturally before distilling. Gradually vodka-making in Eastern Europe was refined. In the beginning vodka was the product of a single distillation to a relatively low proof, but distillers soon learned the benefits of two or more distillations on product quality.

Extra distillations mean the final spirit has a higher strength and greater purity. Next the Eastern Europeans introduced filtration to improve the purity of the spirit further. This was carried out initially with felt or river sand, but in the late eighteenth century charcoal began to be used. The filtration standards established at that time remain to this day.

With the invention of the continuous still in the last century, distillers were able to produce vodka to a very high proof in a continuous operation.
Most vodka has no color and carries only the clean aroma and character of pure spirit from the still. It has a characteristically light and very slightly oily texture. Different brands have their own characteristics and have been made over the centuries to a variety of styles.
There is a long heritage of making flavored vodkas in Eastern Europe. This goes back to the days of home distillation, when vodka was flavored with herbs, spices and fruit. Nowadays natural flavorings such as cherry, lime, lemon, orange, mint, etc., are added in the final distillation.

6. Techniques

METHODS OF MIXING COCKTAILS

The four methods below are the most common processes of mixing cocktails:

1. Shake 2. Stir
3. Build 4. Blend

Shake: To shake is to mix a cocktail by shaking it in a cocktail shaker by hand. First, fill the glass part of the shaker three quarters full with ice, then pour the ingredients on top of the ice. Less expensive ingredients are more frequently poured before the deluxe ingredients. Pour the contents of the glass into the metal part of the shaker and shake vigorously for ten to fifteen seconds. Remove the glass section and using a Hawthorn strainer, strain the contents into the cocktail glass. Shaking ingredients that do not mix easily with spirits is easy and practical (juices, egg whites, cream and sugar syrups). Most shakers have two or three parts. In a busy bar, the cap is often temporarily misplaced. If this happens, a coaster or the inside palm of your hand is quite effective. American shakers are best.
To sample the cocktail before serving to the customer, pour a small amount into the shaker cap and using a straw, check the taste.
Stir: To stir a cocktail is to mix the ingredients by stirring them with ice in a mixing glass and then straining them into a chilled cocktail glass. Short circular twirls are most preferred. (The glass part of the American shaker will do well for this.) Spirits, liqueurs and vermouths that blend easily together are mixed by this method.
Build: To build a cocktail is to mix the ingredients in the glass in which the cocktail is to be served, floating one on top of the other. Hi-Balls, long fruit juice and carbonated mixed cocktails are typically built using this technique. Where possible a swizzle stick should be put into the drink to mix the ingredients after being presented to the customer. Long straws are excellent substitutes when swizzle sticks are unavailable.
Blend: To blend a cocktail is to mix the ingredients using an electric blender/mixer. It is recommended to add the fruit (fresh or tinned) first. Slicing small pieces gives a smoother texture than if you add the whole fruit. Next, pour the alcohol. Ice should always be added last. This order ensures that the fruit is blended freely with the alcoholic ingredients, allowing the ice

to gradually mix into the food and beverage, chilling the flavor. Ideally, the blender should be on for at least 20 seconds. Following this procedure will prevent ice and fruit lumps that then need to be strained.
If the blender starts to rattle and hum, ice may be obstructing the blades from spinning. Always check that the blender is clean before you start. Angostura Bitter is ammonia based which is suitable for cleaning. Fill 4 to 5 shakes with hot water, rinse and then wipe clean.

TECHNIQUES OF MIXING COCKTAILS

Shake and Pour: After shaking the cocktail, pour the contents straight into the glass. When pouring into Hi-Ball glasses and sometimes Old Fashioned glasses the ice cubes are included. This eliminates straining.
Shake and Strain: Using a Hawthorn strainer (or knife) this technique prevents the ice going into the glass. Straining protects the cocktail ensuring melted ice won't dilute the flavor and mixture.
Float Ingredients: Hold the spoon right way up and rest it with the lip slightly above the level of the last layer. Fill spoon gently and the contents will flow smoothly from all around the rim. Use the back of the spoon's dish only if you are experienced.
Frosting (sugar and salt rims): This technique is used to coat the rim of the glass with either salt or sugar. First, rub lemon/orange slice juice all the way around only the glass rim. Next, holding the glass by the stem upside down, rest on a plate containing salt or sugar and turn slightly so that it adheres to the glass. Pressing the glass too deeply into the salt or sugar often results in chunks sticking to the glass. A lemon slice is used for salt and an orange slice is used for sugar.
To achieve color effects, put a small amount of Grenadine or colored liqueur in a plate and coat the rim of the glass, then gently place in the sugar. The Grenadine absorbs the sugar and turns it pink. This is much easier than mixing Grenadine with sugar and then trying to get it to stick to the glass.

HELPFUL HINTS

Cocktail mixing is an art which is expressed in the preparation and presentation of the cocktail.

How to make a Brandy Alexander Cross

Take two short straws and, with a sharp knife, slice one of the straws half way through in the middle and wedge the other uncut straw into the cut straw to create a cross.

Storing Fruit Juices

Take a 750mL/25fl oz bottle and soak it in hot water to remove the label and sterilize the alcohol. The glass has excellent appeal and you'll find it easier to pour the correct measurement with an attached nip pourer.

Sugar Syrup Recipe

Fill a cup or bowl (depending on how much you want to make) with white sugar, top it up with boiling water until the receptacle is just about full and keep stirring until the sugar is fully dissolved. Refrigerate when not in use. Putting a teaspoon of sugar into a cocktail is being lazy, it does not do the job properly as the sugar dissolves.

Juice Tips

Never leave juices, Coconut Cream or other ingredients in cans. Pour them into clean bottles, cap and refrigerate them. All recipes in this book have been tested with Berri fruit juices.

Ice

Ice is probably the most important part of cocktails. It is used in nearly all cocktails. Consequently ice must be clean and fresh at all times.

The small squared cubes and flat chips of ice are superior for chilling and mixing cocktails. Ice cubes with holes are inefficient. Wet ice, ice scraps and broken ice should only be used in blenders.

Crushed Ice

Take the required amount of ice and fold into a clean linen cloth. Although uncivilised, the most effective method is to smash it against the bar floor. Shattering with a bottle may break the bottle. Certain retailers sell portable ice crushers. Alternatively a blender may be used. Half fill with ice and then pour water into the blender until it reaches the level of the ice. Blend for about 30 seconds, strain out the water and you have perfectly crushed ice. Always try and use a metal scoop to collect the ice from the ice tray. Never pick up the ice with your hands. This is unhygienic.

Shovelling the glass into the ice tray to gather ice can also cause breakages and hence should be avoided where possible.
It is important that the ice tray is cleaned each day. As ice is colorless and odorless, many people assume wrongly it is always clean. Taking a cloth soaked in hot water, wipe the inside of the bucket warm. The blenders used for all of our bar requirements are Moulinex blenders with glass bowls. We have found these blenders to be of exceptional quality.

GLASSES

Cordial (Embassy):	30mL	Fancy Hi-Ball Glass:	220mL, 350mL, 470mL
Cordial (Lexington):	37mL	Hurricane Glass:	230mL, 440mL, 650mL
Tall Dutch Cordial:	45mL	Irish Coffee Glass:	250mL
Whisky Shot:	45mL	Margarita Glass:	260mL
Martini Glass:	90mL	Hi-Ball Glass:	270mL, 285mL, 330mL
Cocktail Glass:	90mL, 140mL	Footed Hi-Ball Glass:	270mL, 300mL
Champagne Saucer:	150mL	Salud Grande Glass:	290mL
Champagne Flute:	150mL, 190mL	Fiesta Grande Glass:	350mL, 490mL
Wine Goblet:	140mL, 190mL	Poco Grande Glass:	380mL
Brandy Balloon:	650mL	Fancy Cocktail:	210mL, 300mL
Old Fashioned Spirit:	185mL, 210mL, 290mL		

A proven method for cleaning glasses is to hold each glass individually over a bucket of boiling water until the glass becomes steamy and then with a clean linen cloth rub in a circular way to ensure the glass is polished for the next serve. Cocktails can be poured into any glass but the better the glass, the better the appearance of the cocktail. One basic rule should apply and that is: use no colored glasses as they spoil the appearance of cocktails. All glasses have been designed for a specific task, e.g.

1. Hi-Ball glasses for long, cool refreshing drinks.
2. Cocktail glasses for short, sharp, or stronger drinks.
3. Champagne saucers for creamy after-dinner style drinks, etc.

The stem of the glass has been designed so you may hold it whilst polishing, leaving the bowl free of marks and germs so that you may enjoy your drink. All cocktail glasses should be kept in a refrigerator or filled with ice while you are preparing the cocktails in order to chill the glass. An appealing affect on a 90mL cocktail glass can be achieved by running the glass under cold water and then placing it in the freezer.

GARNISHES AND JUICES

Banana
Celery
Cucumber
Lemons
Limes
Mint leaves
Olives
Celery salt
Chocolate flake
Cinnamon
Fresh eggs
Fresh single cream
Fresh milk
Apple
Carbonated waters
Coconut cream
Lemon – pure
Orange
Jelly Babies
Almonds
Apricot conserve
Vanilla ice cream
Onions
Oranges
Pineapple
Red Maraschino Cherries
Rockmelon
Strawberries
Canned fruit
Nutmeg
Pepper, Salt
Tomato
Sugar and sugar cubes
Tabasco sauce
Worcestershire sauce
Orange and Mango
Pineapple
Sugar syrup
Canned nectars
Canned pulps
Crushed pineapple
Blueberries
Red cocktail onions
Flowers (assorted)

Simplicity is the most important fact to keep in mind when garnishing cocktails. Do not overdo the garnish; make it striking, but if you can't get near the cocktail to drink it then you have failed. Most world champion cocktails just have a lemon slice, or a single red cherry.
Tall, refreshing Hi-Balls tend to have more garnish as the glass is larger. A swizzle stick should be served nearly always in long cocktails. Straws are always served for a lady, but optional for a man.
Plastic animals, umbrellas, fans and a whole variety of novelty goods are now available to garnish with, and they add a lot of fun to the drink.

ALCOHOL RECOMMENDED FOR A COCKTAIL BAR

Spirits

Ouzo	Scotch	Bourbon
Southern Comfort	Brandy	Tennessee Whiskey
Campari	Tequila	Canadian Club
Vandermint	Gin	Vodka
Malibu	Pernod	Rum

Liqueurs

Advocaat	Frangelico	Amaretto
Galliano	Baileys Irish Cream	Grand Marnier
Banana	Kahlúa	Benedictine
Kirsch	Blue Curaçao	Kirsch
Cassis	Mango	Chartreuse (both)
Melon	Cherry Advocaat	Orange
Cherry Brandy	Peach	Pimm's
Coconut	Sambucca – Clear	Sambucca – Black
Cointreau	Crème de cafe	Strawberry
Crème de Menthe Green	Triple Sec	Dark Crème de Cacao
Drambuie	Claytons Tonis (non-alcoholic)	

Vermouth

Cinzano Bianco Vermouth	Martini Bianco Vermouth
Cinzano Dry Vermouth	Martini Dry Vermouth
Cinzano Rosso Vermouth	Martini Rosso Vermouth

ESSENTIAL EQUIPMENT FOR A COCKTAIL BAR

Cocktail shaker	Waiter's friend corkscrew
Hawthorn strainer	Bottle openers
Mixing glass	Ice scoop
Spoon with muddler	Ice bucket
Moulinex Electric blender	Free pourers
Knife, cutting board	Swizzle sticks, straws
Measures (jiggers)	Hand cloths for cleaning glasses
Can opener	Scooper spoon (long teaspoon)
Coasters and napkins	

THE A-Z OF COCKTAILS

Scotland

Aberdeen Angus

Ingredients

Glass: 140mL/5fl oz Cocktail Glass
Mixers: 30mL/1fl oz scotch whisky
10mL/⅜fl oz Drambuie
1 tablespoon honey
10mL/⅜fl oz fresh lime juice

Method

Blend with ice and pour.
Garnish with two banana wheel slices wedged on rim of glass.

Abbey

United Kingdom

Ingredients

Glass: 140mL/5fl oz Cocktail Glass
Mixers: 60mL/2fl oz gin
1 dash sweet vermouth
30mL/1fl oz orange juice
1 dash Angostura Bitter

Method

Shake and strain into a glass and serve. Garnish with Maraschino cherry.

ABC

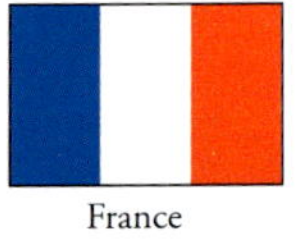
France

Ingredients

Glass: 185mL/6fl oz Wine Goblet
Mixers: 5 ice cubes
Champagne or sparkling white wine
20mL/⅜fl oz Armagnac
20mL/⅜fl oz Benedictine
1 dash Angostura Bitter

Method

Crack 2 ice cubes and place them into a shaker with Armagnac, Benedictine and Angostura Bitter and shake well. Crush remaining ice cubes and empty into a goblet. Drain contents of shaker of the crushed ice and top with champagne. Serve garnished with lemon slice, orange segments and cherries.

Sweden

Absolut Cosmopolitan

Ingredients

Glass: 90mL/3oz Martini Glass
Mixers: 45mL/1½fl oz Absolut Citron
20mL/⅝fl oz Triple Sec
20mL/⅝fl oz cranberry juice
juice of ½ fresh lime

Method

Shake with ice and strain into chilled martini glass.
Garnish with an orange twist.

Abortion

Australia

Ingredients

Glass: 90mL/3 oz Cocktail Glass
Mixers: 30 mL/1 oz vodka
30 mL/1 oz Sambucca
30 mL/1 oz Baileys Irish Cream
3 drops Grenadine

Method

Layer into cocktail glass and serve.

Absinth

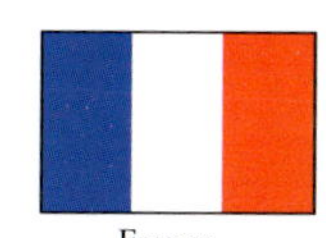
France

Ingredients

Glass: 90mL/3 oz Cocktail Glass
Mixers: 50mL/1¾fl oz Pernod
1 teaspoon anisette
2 tablespoon water
1 dash orange bitters

Method

Shake ingredients with ice and strain into a chilled cocktail glass.

Mexico

Acapulco

Ingredients

Glass: 150mL/5fl oz Old Fashioned Glass

Mixers: 30mL/1fl oz Bacardi
10mL/1fl oz Cointreau
1 egg white
15mL/⅜fl oz fresh lime juice
add sugar to taste

Method

Shake over ice and pour. Garnish with partially torn mint leaves.

Acapulco I

Mexico

Ingredients

Glass: 285mL/9½fl oz Cocktail Glass

Mixers: 30mL/1fl oz tequila
30mL/1fl oz dark rum
30mL/1fl oz Tia Maria
150mL/5fl oz coconut cream

Method

Shake ingredients and strain over ice into a cocktail glass and serve.

Admiral Cannon

U.S.A.

Ingredients

Glass: 140mL/5oz Cocktail Glass

Mixers: 45mL/1½fl oz bourbon
15mL/½fl oz lemon juice
30mL/1fl oz white rum
1 teaspoon maple syrup

Method

Shake and strain into cocktail glass over cracked ice and serve.

African Nipple

South Africa

Ingredients

Glass: 140mL/5oz Champagne Saucer
Mixers: 30 mL/1fl oz vodka
1 tsp Grenadine
30 mL/1fl oz Afrikoko
60 mL/2fl oz cream

Method
Shake and strain into a champagne saucer and serve.

After Eight

Australia

Ingredients

Glass: Tall Dutch Cordial
Mixers: 15mL/½fl oz Kahlúa
20 mL/¾fl oz Baileys Irish Cream
10 mL/⅜fl oz Crème de Menthe

Method
Layer ingredients in order into a tall Dutch cordial glass or shot glass and serve.

U.S.A.

Alabama Slammer

Ingredients
Glass: Whisky Shot
Mixers: 10 mL/⅜fl oz gin
10 mL/⅜fl oz Amaretto
10 mL/⅜fl oz orange juice
10 mL/½fl oz Southern Comfort

Method
Pour in order then shoot.
A real drink! From the heart of the Deep South, USA.

U.S.A.

Alaska

Ingredients

Glass: 130mL/4½oz Cocktail Glass

Mixers: 30mL/1fl oz gin
10mL/⅜fl oz Yellow Chartreuse
1-2 dashes of Orange Curaçao

Method

Shake over ice and strain. Garnish with orange twist.

Alexander

United Kingdom

Ingredients

Glass: 90mL/3 oz Cocktail Glass

Mixers: 45mL/1½fl oz gin
20mL/⅝ 2fl oz Crème de Cacao
nutmeg
15mL/½fl oz fresh cream

Method

Shake liquid ingredients and strain into cocktail glass. Cross two straws over glass, sprinkle nutmeg over the top. Remove straws and serve.

Alfonso

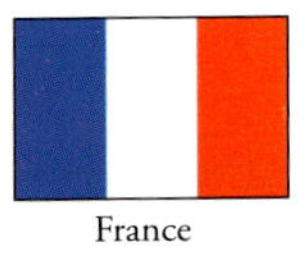

France

Ingredients

Glass: 90mL/3 oz Cocktail Glass

Mixers: 15mL/½fl oz dry gin
4 dashes sweet vermouth
15mL/½fl oz French vermouth
1 dash Angostura Bitter
30 mL/1 oz Grand Marnier
4 ice cubes

Method

Shake and strain into a 3 oz cocktail glass and serve.

Morocco

Alice in Wonderland

Ingredients

Glass: 170mL/6oz Champagne flute
Mixers: 100mL/3⅜fl oz grapefruit juice
30mL/1fl oz green tea
20mL/⅝fl oz lemon juice
15mL/½fl oz sugar syrup
top up with soda

Method

Build over ice and top up with soda. Garnish with white grapes.

Alice

Germany

Ingredients

Glass: 140mL/5oz Champagne flute
Mixers: 30mL/1 oz scotch whiskey
30mL/1 oz kümmel liqueur
30mL/1 oz sweet vermouth

Method

Half fill mixing glass with ice and add liquid ingredients. Stir and strain into 5 oz champagne glass. Garnish with lemon peel and serve.

All Night

Mexico

Ingredients

Glass: 90mL/3oz Cocktail Glass
Mixers: 30mL/1fl oz tequila
1 dash Grenadine
20mL/⅝fl oz lime juice
1 egg white

Method

Shake ingredients and strain into cocktail glass. Garnish with Maraschino cherry and serve.

Belgium

Almond Orange frost

Ingredients

Glass: 240mL/8oz Champagne Sherbert Glass

Mixers: 15mL/½fl oz Amaretto
15mL/½fl oz Frangelico
15mL/½fl oz Chambord
10mL/⅜fl oz fresh lime juice
10mL/⅜fl oz fresh lemon juice
1 teaspoon chopped almonds
2 scoops orange sherbert

Method

Blend with ice. Garnish with orange slice and chopped almonds.

Almond Joy

Ingredients

Italy

Glass: 300mL/10oz Tulip Glass

Mixers: 30mL/1fl oz Amaretto
90mL/3fl oz milk
1 dash Crème de Cacao
30mL/1fl oz coconut syrup
1 scoop ice cream

Method

Blend ingredients and pour into tulip glass, garnish with a pineapple wedge, straws and serve.

Altered States Shooter

Ingredients

U.S.A.

Glass: Whiskey shot

Mixers: banana
15mL/½fl oz Kahlúa
15mL/½fl oz peach liqueur
15mL/½fl oz Baileys Irish Cream

Method

Layer in a shot glass and serve.

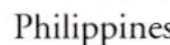

Philippines

Amaretto Choco Cream

Ingredients

Glass: 240mL/8oz Champagne Sherbert Glass

Mixers: 30mL/1fl oz Amaretto
30mL/1fl oz Kahlúa
30mL/1fl oz Chocolate Syrup
2 scoops of vanilla ice cream

Method

Blend without ice and pour over ice. Garnish with aerosol whipping cream. Comments: Filipinos love their ice cream and adopted this innovative recipe to include one of their favourite desserts.

Amaretto Sour

Italy

Ingredients

Glass: 140mL/5oz Wine Glass

Mixers: 45mL/1½fl oz Amaretto
½ lemon, squeezed
soda water

Method

Shake Amaretto, lemon juice and ice, pour into a wine glass and top with soda. Garnish with a strip of lemon peel and serve.

Amaretto Stinger

U.S.A.

Ingredients

Glass: 90mL/3oz Cocktail Glass

Mixers: 45mL/1½fl oz Amaretto
3 ice cubes
30mL/1fl oz white Crème de Menthe

Method

Shake well, strain into cocktail glass and serve.

Americano

Italy

Ingredients

Glass: 270mL/9oz Hi-Ball Glass
Mixers: 30mL/1fl oz campari
30mL/1fl oz Cinzano Rosso Vermouth
top up with soda

Method

Build over ice and top up with soda. Garnish with orange slice.
Comments: originated from European travellers visiting America desiring a taste of European aperitifs.

American Beauty

U.S.A.

Ingredients

Glass: 140mL/5oz Cocktail Glass
Mixers: 15mL/½fl oz brandy
15mL/½fl oz Grenadine
15mL/½fl oz dry vermouth
15mL/½fl oz orange juice
port wine
3 dashes white Crème de Menthe

Method

Shake all ingredients except port wine. Strain into a 5oz glass, top with port wine and serve.

Amsterdam

Netherlands

Ingredients

Glass: 90mL/3oz Cocktail Glass
Mixers: 30mL/1fl oz gin
4 dashes orange bitters
15mL/½fl oz orange juice
15mL/½fl oz Cointreau
cracked ice

Method

Shake ingredients and strain cocktail glass and serve.

Anabolic Steroid

Australia

Ingredients

Glass: Tall Dutch Cordial
Mixers: 15mL/½fl oz Midori
15mL/½fl oz Cointreau
15mL/½fl oz Blue Curaçao

Method
Layer in a shot glass and serve.

Angel Dew

Switzerland

Ingredients

Glass: Cordial (Embassy)
Mixers: 15mL/½fl oz Benedictine
15mL/½fl oz Baileys Irish Cream

Method
Layer in a shot glass and serve.

U.S.A.

Andy Williams

Ingredients
Glass: 290mL/10oz Old Fashioned Spirit Glass
Mixers: 60mL/2fl oz Clayton's Tonic
15mL/½fl oz lime juice
dash sugar syrup
top up with soda water

Method
Shake with ice and pour. Garnish with a thin lime slice floated in the drink.
Comments: a delightful predinner drink.

Angel's Kiss

Brazil

Ingredients

Glass: 290mL/9oz Poco Grande Glass

Mixers: scoop vanilla ice cream
1 tablespoon passionfruit pulp
150mL/5fl oz Apricot nectar

Method

Blend with ice and pour. Garnish with mint leaves.
A wonderful blend of passionfruit and apricots.

Angelique

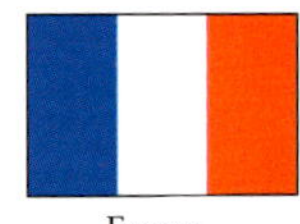
France

Ingredients

Glass: 140mL/5oz Champagne Saucer

Mixers: 30mL/1fl oz ouzo
30mL/1fl oz fresh cream
30mL/1fl oz Advocaat
30mL/1fl oz orange juice
30mL/1fl oz Strega

Method

Shake and strain into a champagne saucer. Garnish with Maraschino cherry and serve.

Angry Fijian

Fiji

Ingredients

Glass: 90mL/3oz Cocktail Glass

Mixers: 30mL/1fl oz banana liqueur
30mL/1fl oz Baileys Irish Cream
30mL/1fl oz Malibu

Method

Layer in a 3 oz cocktail glass and serve.

U.S.A.

Apple Buck

Ingredients

Glass: 270mL/9oz Footed Hi-Ball Glass

Mixers: 30mL/1fl oz apple brandy
10mL/$\frac{3}{8}$fl oz brandy
10mL/$\frac{3}{8}$fl oz lemon juice
2 slices of fresh ginger
top up with ginger ale

Method

Shake over ice and pour, then top with ginger ale. Garnish with apple peel.

Appease Me

Australia

Ingredients

Glass: 270mL/9oz Hi-Ball Glass

Mixers: 30mL/1fl oz mango liqueur
60mL/2fl oz orange juice
30mL/1fl oz Advocaat
30mL/1fl oz cream
30mL/1fl oz vodka
2 slices mango

Method

Blend ingredients with ice and pour into a 10oz hi-ball glass. Garnish with the pulp of half a passionfruit and serve with straws.

Apple Magic

U.S.A.

Ingredients

Glass: 270mL/9oz Hi-Ball Glass

Mixers: 30mL/1fl oz Midori
15mL/$\frac{1}{2}$fl oz orange juice
15mL/$\frac{1}{2}$fl oz Southern Comfort
90mL/3fl oz apple juice
15mL/$\frac{1}{2}$fl oz Grand Marnier
ice

Method

Blend and pour into a colada glass. Garnish with a slice of apple and strawberry and serve.

Apres Ski

Ingredients

Canada

Glass: 270mL/9oz Hi-Ball Glass

Mixers: 30mL/1fl oz Crème de Menthe
15mL/½fl oz Pernod
15mL/½fl oz vodka
lemonade

Method

Third fill a 10 oz hi-ball glass with ice and pour ingredients over ice. Top with lemonade and serve with straws.

Apricot Smoothie

U.S.A.

Ingredients

Glass: 390mL/12oz Poco Grande Glass

Mixers: 2 apricots
90mL/3fl oz milk
15mL/½fl oz lemon juice
30mL/1fl oz vanilla yoghurt

Method

Blend with ice and pour.
Garnish with apricot slice and straws.

Aqua Thunder

Cuba

Ingredients

Glass: 270mL/9oz Hi-Ball Glass

Mixers: 10mL/⅜fl oz Blue Curaçao
10mL/⅜fl oz banana liqueur
30mL/1fl oz melon liqueur
10mL/⅜fl oz freshly squeezed lemon
top-up with soda water

Method

Build over ice. Garnish with swizzle stick and slice of lemon.
Comments: watch in wonder as the soda waterfall splashes over the ice creating a thunderous aqua-colored spectacular.

Denmark

Aquavit fiz

Ingredients

Glass: 170mL/6oz Tulip Champagne Glass

Mixers: 45mL/1½fl oz Aquavit
30mL/1fl oz lemon juice
15mL/½fl oz Cherry Heering
10mL/⅜fl oz sugar syrup
1 egg white
top up with soda

Method

Shake over ice and strain then top up with soda. Garnish with a red cherry.

Argyle Tavern

Australia

Ingredients

Glass: 150mL/5oz Cocktail Glass

Mixers: 60mL/2fl oz brandy
15mL/½fl oz almond liqueur
15mL/½fl oz Galliano
30mL/1fl oz dry vermouth

Method

Half fill a mixing glass with cracked ice and add ingredients. Stir and strain into cocktail glass, garnish with Maraschino cherry and serve.

Aspiration

New Zealand

Ingredients

Glass: 150mL/5oz Cocktail Glass

Mixers: 30mL/1fl oz Midori
30mL/1fl oz pineapple juice
15mL/½fl oz Galliano
1 kiwifruit
10mL/⅜fl oz white curaçao
1 dash coconut cream

Method

Blend and pour into a colada glass. Garnish with a slice of kiwifruit and serve.

Atomic Bomb

China

Ingredients

Glass: Tall Dutch Cordial
Mixers: 20mL/⅝fl oz Tia Maria
15mL/½fl oz gin
10mL/⅜fl oz cream

Method

Layer in order, then float cream.

Astronaut

U.S.A.

Ingredients

Glass: 90mL/3oz Cocktail Glass
Mixers: 30mL/1fl oz dark rum
30mL/1fl oz vodka
15mL/½fl oz fresh lemon juice
6 drops of passionfruit pulp

Method

Shake over ice and strain. Garnish with ½ scoop of passionfruit.

Aussie Slinger

Australia

Ingredients

Glass: 270mL/9oz Hi-Ball Glass
Mixers: 45mL/1½fl oz any white spirit
lemonade
30mL/1fl oz Grenadine
1 dash Angostura Bitter
60mL/2fl oz lemon juice
1 cracked ice

Method

Half fill hi-ball glass with cracked ice, add ingredients and top with lemonade. Garnish with ½ orange slice, ½ lemon slice, 1 Maraschino cherry, swizzle stick, straws and serve.

Australia

Australian Gold

Ingredients

Glass: 90mL/3oz Cocktail Glass

Mixers: 30mL/1fl oz dark rum
30mL/1fl oz mango liqueur
30mL/1fl oz Galliano

Method

Build over ice.

Autumn Leaf

Sweden

Ingredients

Glass: 90mL/3oz Cocktail Glass

Mixers: 30mL/1fl oz Arrak
30mL/1fl oz Dazzinger goldwasser
30mL/1fl oz Crème de Cacao

Method

Mix in mixing glass with cracked ice, strain into cocktail glass and serve.

Avalanche

U.S.A.

Ingredients

Glass: 140mL/5oz Champagne Flute

Mixers: 30mL/1fl oz Cointreau
30mL/1fl oz orange juice
30mL/1fl oz Tia Maria
60mL/2fl oz cream

Method

Shake and strain into a champagne glass and serve.

Italy

B & B

Ingredients

Glass: Brandy Balloon
Mixers: 30mL/1fl oz Cognac
30mL/1fl oz Benedictine

Method

Build, no ice.
Tempt your pallet with this historical blend of choice liqueurs. Relaxing by the fire on winter nights, the genuine connoisseur will enjoy interesting conversation with friends. Ideal with coffee.

B & G

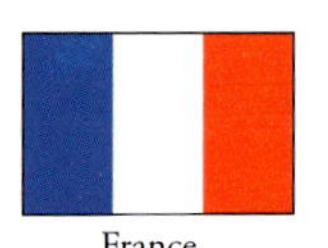
France

Ingredients

Glass: 180mL/6oz Old Fashioned Glass
Mixers: 30mL/1fl oz Benedictine
30mL/1fl oz Grand Mariner

Method

Pour over ice in an old fashioned glass.

B & P

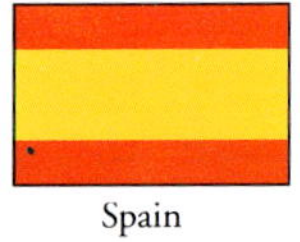
Spain

Ingredients

Glass: Brandy Balloon
Mixers: 30mL/1fl oz Benedictine
60mL/2fl oz port wine

Method

Pour over ice in a brandy balloon and serve.

Bacardi Blossom

Cuba

Ingredients

Glass: 90mL/3oz Cocktail Glass

Mixers: 45mL/1½fl oz Bacardi rum
10mL/⅜fl oz orange juice
10mL/⅜fl oz lemon juice
1 teaspoon sugar

Method

Shake and strain into cocktail glass and serve.

Bacardi No. 2

U.S.A.

Ingredients

Glass: 140mL/5oz Cocktail Glass

Mixers: 60mL/1fl oz Bacardi rum
1 egg white
dash of Grenadine
ice
20mL/⅝fl oz lemon or lime juice

Method

Shake and strain into cocktail glass and serve.

United Kingdom

Badminton

Ingredients

Glass: 250mL/8oz Red Wine Goblet

Mixers: 120mL/4fl oz red wine
1 teaspoon sugar
sprinkle of nutmeg
top up with soda

Method

Stir sugar in red wine and add nutmeg then top up with soda. Garnish with a cucumber slice.

Bahama Mama

Ingredients

The Bahamas

Glass: 285mL/9½oz Hi-Ball Glass
Mixers: 15mL/½fl oz Bacardi Gold Rum
15mL/½fl oz Malibu
15mL/½fl oz Banana Liqueur
15mL/½fl oz Grenadine
90mL/3fl oz orange juice
60mL/2fl oz pineapple juice

Method
Blend over ice. Garnish with a pineapple wedge and leaves.

Baileys Coconut Crean

Ingredients

Trinidad

Glass: 150mL/5oz Wine Glass
Mixers: 30mL/1fl oz Baileys Irish Cream
30mL/1fl oz cream
15mL/½fl oz Malibu
60mL/2fl oz orange juice

Method
Shake ingredients and pour over cracked ice in wine glass. Add a dash of Grenadine and serve with straws.

Ballet Russe

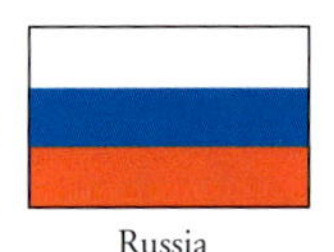

Russia

Ingredients
Glass: 150mL/5oz Old Fashioned Spirit Glass
Mixers: 30mL/1fl oz vodka
15mL/½fl oz Crême de Cassis
15mL/½fl oz fresh lime juice
15mL/½fl oz fresh lemon juice

Method
Shake with ice and strain. Garnish with an orange slice and a red cherry.

U.S.A.

Baltimore Zoo

Ingredients

Glass: 300mL/10oz Footed Pilsener Glass

Mixers: 15mL/½fl oz dark rum
15mL/½fl oz gin
15mL/½fl oz Cointreau
60mL/2fl oz cranberry juice
top with draft beer

Method

Shake with ice and strain then top with draft beer.

Bamboo

Spain

Ingredients

Glass: 150mL/5fl oz Cocktail Glass

Mixers: 30mL/1fl oz dry vermouth
30mL/1fl oz dry sherry
1 dash orange bitters
2 dashes Angostura Bitter

Method

Mix ingredients in a mixing glass, strain into cocktail glass. Garnish with Maraschino cherry and serve.

Banana Bender

Australia

Ingredients

Glass: 150mL/5oz Champagne Flute

Mixers: 30mL/1fl oz Cointreau
60mL/2fl oz cream
30mL/1fl oz banana liqueur
½ banana

Method

Blend ingredients until smooth, pour into champagne glass and serve.

Banana Bliss

Japan

Ingredients

Glass: 180mL/6oz Old Fashioned Glass
Mixers: 30mL/1fl oz cognac
crushed ice
30mL/1fl oz banana liqueur

Method

Fill a 6 oz old fashioned glass with crushed ice, build liquid ingredients and serve.

Banana-Choc Shake

U.S.A.

Ingredients

Glass: 440mL/14oz Hurricane Glass
Mixers: 1 ripe banana, sliced
2 scoops chocolate ice cream
210mL/7fl oz milk

Method

Blend with ice and pour.
Garnish with teaspoon of grated chocolate and straw.

Banana Colada

U.S.A.

Ingredients

Glass: 300mL/10oz Fancy Glass
Mixers: 30mL/1fl oz Bacardi
30mL/1fl oz sugar syrup
30mL/1fl oz coconut cream
30mL/1fl oz cream
120mL/4fl oz pineapple juice
½ banana

Method

Blend with ice and pour.
Garnish: slice of banana, pineapple spear and mint leaves. Serves with straws.

Cuba

Banana Daiquiri

Ingredients

Glass: 140mL/5oz Champagne Saucer

Mixers: 1 banana
15mL/½fl oz sugar syrup
30mL/1fl oz Bacardi
45mL/1½fl oz lemon juice
30mL/1fl oz banana liqueur

Method

Blend with ice and strain. Garnish with a round slice of banana and mint leaves.

Banana Jaffa

Portugal

Ingredients

Glass: 270mL/9oz Hi-Ball Glass

Mixers: 15mL/½fl oz Kahlúa
30mL/1fl oz cream
15mL/½fl oz brandy
½ banana
30mL/1fl oz orange juice

Method

Blend until smooth, pour into hi-ball glass. Garnish with an orange wheel. pineapple wedge, straws and serve.

Banana Margarita

Mexico

Ingredients

Glass: 150mL/5oz Margarita Glass

Mixers: 30mL/1fl oz tequila
30mL/1fl oz lemon juice
15mL/½fl oz Cointreau
½ small banana
15mL/½fl oz banana liqueur
cracked ice

Method

Blend until smooth, pour into a salt rimmed margarita glass and serve.

Bananarama

Australia

Ingredients

Glass: 140mL/5oz Cocktail Glass

Mixers: 30mL/1fl oz vodka
30mL/1fl oz Kahlúa
15mL/½fl oz Baileys Irish Cream
1 banana
60mL/2fl oz cream

Method

Blend with ice and pour.
Garnish with two banana wheel slices wedged on rim of glass.

Banger

U.S.A.

Ingredients

Glass: 300mL/10oz Hi-Ball Glass

Mixers: 30mL/1fl oz Bacardi rum
180mL/6fl oz orange juice
15mL/½fl oz Galliano
cracked ice

Method

Build over cracked ice in hi-ball glass. Garnish with orange wheel, straws and serve.

Bango

Barbados

Ingredients

Glass: 170mL/6oz Tulip Champagne Glass

Mixers: 45mL/1½fl oz mango liqueur
slice of pineapple
15mL/½fl oz Malibu
60mL/2fl oz pineapple juice

Method

Blend until smooth, pour into a flute glass and serve.

Banshee

Antigua

Ingredients

Glass: Brandy Balloon
Mixers: 30mL/1fl oz rum
60mL/2fl oz cream
20mL/$\frac{5}{8}$fl oz Crème de Cacao
1 banana
15mL/$\frac{1}{2}$fl oz banana liqueur

Method
Blend until smooth, pour into a brandy balloon and serve.

Banshee No. 2

Antigua

Ingredients

Glass: 150mL/5oz Cocktail Glass
Mixers: 30mL/1fl oz banana liqueur
60mL/2fl oz cream
30mL/1fl oz white Crème de Cacao
ice

Method
Shake and strain into cocktail glass. Garnish with a cherry and serve.

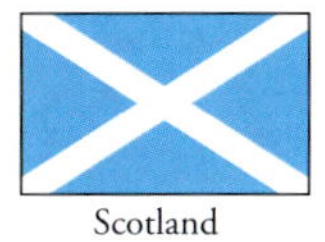
Scotland

Barley Punch

Ingredients
Glass: 210mL/7oz Fancy Hi-Ball Glass
Mixers: 60mL/2oz ground barley
30mL/1oz sugar
top up with boiling water
peel of 1 lime

Method
Build and top up with boiling water. Refrigerate until ready to serve. Garnish with lime peel.

Bee Sting

United Arab Emirates

Ingredients

Glass: Cordial (Lexington)
Mixers: 20mL/⅝fl oz tequila
10mL/⅜fl oz yellow Chartreuse

Method
Layer in order in a shot glass, ignite and serve.

Bellini

Italy

Ingredients

Glass: 140mL/5oz Champagne Flute
Mixers: 45mL/1½fl oz peach juice
Champagne (chilled)

Method
Place peach juice in a tulip flute, top with champagne and serve.

Bellini (frozen)

Italy

Ingredients
Glass: 140mL/5oz Champagne Flute
Mixers: 60mL/2fl oz peach slices with syrup
30mL/1fl oz vodka
30mL/1fl oz peach liqueur
1 teaspoon sugar
top up with Champagne

Method
Blend with ice, strain and top up with champagne.

Saudi Arabia

Belly Dancer

Ingredients

Glass: 90mL/3oz Cocktail Glass - Frosted

Mixers: 30mL/1fl oz cream
15mL/½fl oz lime juice
60mL/2fl oz coconut cream
15mL/½fl oz Grenadine

Method

Shake over ice and strain. Garnish with grated coconut.

Ben's Play Lunch

U.S.A.

Ingredients

Glass: 330mL/12oz Hi-Ball Glass

Mixers: 1 ripe banana
3 tablespoons crushed pineapple
60mL/2fl oz coconut cream
60mL/2fl oz tropical fruit juice
15mL/½fl oz lemon juice

Method

Blend with ice and pour.
Garnish with desiccated coconut.

Berlin

Germany

Ingredients

Glass: 150mL/5oz Cocktail Glass

Mixers: 20mL/⅝fl oz gin
20mL/⅝fl oz orange juice
20mL/⅝fl oz Madeira
1 dash Angostura Bitter

Method

Crush ice and shake with other ingredients. Pour into cocktail glass and serve with straws.

Bermuda

Bermuda Rose

Ingredients

Glass: 90mL/3oz Cocktail Glass

Mixers: 30mL/1fl oz gin
10mL/$\frac{3}{8}$fl oz lime juice
5mL/$\frac{1}{8}$fl oz Grenadine
4-5 drops of Apricot Brandy

Method

Shake over ice and strain. Garnish with a slice of lime.

Berlin Binge

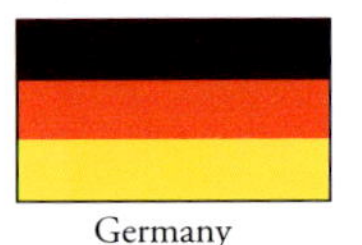

Germany

Ingredients

Glass: 120mL/4oz Cocktail Glass

Mixers: 30mL/1fl oz bourbon
30mL/1fl oz vodka
30mL/1fl oz gin
30mL/1fl oz cognac

Method

Mix ingredients over ice, garnish with olive and serve.

Bessie & Jessie

Ireland

Ingredients

Glass: 300mL/10oz Hi-Ball Glass

Mixers: 60mL/2fl oz blended whiskey
180mL/6fl oz milk
30mL/1fl oz Advocaat

Method

Shake ice, whiskey and milk. Pour into hi-ball glass, float Advocaat and serve with straws.

U.S.A.

Between the Sheets

Ingredients

Glass: 140mL/5oz Champagne Saucer

Mixers: 30mL/1fl oz brandy
30mL/1fl oz Bacardi
30mL/1fl oz Cointreau
15mL/½fl oz lemon juice

Method

Shake with ice and strain.
Garnish with lemon slice and twist.
A predinner cocktail. A fine blend of traditional spirits for the mature pallet. It may be served with a lemon twist.

Bikini

Norway

Ingredients

Glass: 150mL/5oz Cocktail Glass

Mixers: 90mL/3fl oz vodka
30mL/1 oz milk
15 mL/½ oz lemon juice

Method

Shake and strain into cocktail glass and serve.

Bill Bailey

U.S.A.

Ingredients

Glass: 270mL/9oz Hi-Ball Glass

Mixers: 60mL/2fl oz Baileys Irish Cream
soda water
30mL/1fl oz vodka

Method

Pour ingredients over ice in a colada glass and serve.

B-52

U.S.A.

Ingredients

Glass: 140mL/5oz Old Fashioned Glass

Mixers: 30mL/1fl oz Kahlúa
30mL/1fl oz Baileys Irish Cream
30mL/1fl oz Cointreau

Method

Build over ice.

Black Dream

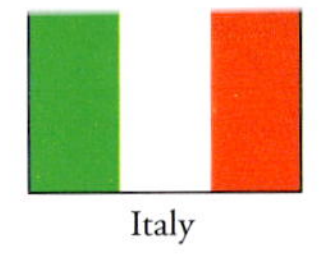

Italy

Ingredients

Glass: Cordial (Lexington)

Mixers: 20mL/⅝fl oz black Sambucca
10mL/⅜fl oz Baileys Irish Cream

Method

Layer in a shot glass and serve.

Black Forrest

Germany

Ingredients

Glass: 300mL/10oz Hi-Ball Glass

Mixers: 30mL/1fl oz vodka
90mL/3fl oz apple juice
30mL/1fl oz Cointreau
1 tablespoon raspberries
15mL/½fl oz blackberry liqueur

Method

Blend until smooth, pour over ice in hi-ball glass. Serve with straws.

Blackjack

U.S.A.

Ingredients

Glass: 120mL/4oz Cocktail Glass
Mixers: 30mL/1fl oz Kirsch
45mL/1½fl oz ice coffee
10mL/⅜fl oz brandy

Method
Stir with ice and pour into a 130mL Cocktail Glass. Garnish with coffee granules.

Black on White

Italy

Ingredients

Glass: Cordial (Embassy)
Mixers: 15mL/½fl oz black Sambucca
15mL/½fl oz Sambucca

Method
Layer in a shot glass and serve.

Black Opal

Australia

Ingredients
Glass: 90mL/3oz Cocktail Glass
Mixers: 15mL/½fl oz black Sambucca
15mL/½fl oz Cointreau
15mL/½fl oz Baileys Irish Cream
15mL/½fl oz cream

Method
Build black Sambucca and Cointreau then light. Next, pour Baileys and cream over flaming ingredients.
A novel demonstration of lifestyle cocktails - the heat of the flame illuminates the Black Opal.

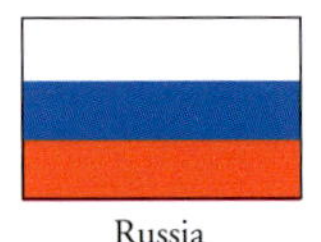
Russia

Black Russian

Ingredients

Glass: 210mL/7oz Old Fashioned Glass

Mixers: 30mL/1fl oz Vodka
30mL/1fl oz Kahlúa

Method

Build over ice.
Superb after dinner as vodka lubricates the way for the scrumptious chocolate Kahlúa. You may add cola in a hi-ball glass to stretch the drink, and even a dollop of cream on top of the cola is an inviting garnish.
Tia Maria or Dark Crème de Cacao may be substituted for Crème de Café, making the drink a "Black Pearl."

Black Velvet

Ireland

Ingredients

Glass: 140mL/5oz Champagne Flute

Mixers: Champagne
stout

Method

Half fill a champagne flute with chilled stout. Top with chilled champagne and serve.

Black Widow

U.S.A.

Ingredients

Glass: Whiskey Shot

Mixers: 15mL/½fl oz black Sambucca
15mL/½fl oz cream
15mL/½fl oz strawberry liqueur

Method

Layer in a shot glass and serve.

Blood and Sand

Austria

Ingredients

Glass: 140mL/5oz Champagne Saucer

Mixers: 30mL/1fl oz Scotch whiskey
30mL/1fl oz orange juice
30mL/1fl oz cherry brandy
30mL/1fl oz sweet vermouth

Method

Half fill mixing glass with cracked ice, add liquid ingredients and stir. Strain into champagne saucer, garnish with orange peel and serve.

Blood Bath

U.S.A.

Ingredients

Glass: Whiskey Shot

Mixers: 10mL/⅜fl oz rosso vermouth
15mL/½fl oz strawberry liqueur
20mL/⅝fl oz tequila

Method

Pour in order then layer the tequila. Cheery grins and rosey cheeks characterise the after effects of this blood thirsty experience. Only issued after midnight and before dawn!

United Kingdom

Bloody Mary

Ingredients

Glass: 300mL/10oz Hi-Ball Glass

Mixers: 30mL/1fl oz Vodka
Worchestershire sauce to taste
120mL/4fl oz tomato juice
Tabasco sauce to taste
salt and pepper to taste
celery salt, optional

Method

Build or shake over ice and strain
Garnish with a stick of celery, slice of lemon.
Remember to add the spices first, then vodka and followed by tomato juice.
Lemon juice and slices are optional ingredients. The celery stick is not part of the garnish, so feel free to nibble as you drink. The glass may also be salt-rimmed.

Blossom

Cuba

Ingredients

Glass: 140mL/5oz Champagne Saucer

Mixers: 30mL/1fl oz Bacardi rum
30mL/1fl oz orange juice
30mL/1fl oz apple juice
15mL/½fl oz sugar syrup

Method

Half fill shaker with cracked ice, add ingredients, shake and strain into a 5 oz champagne saucer and serve.

Blow Up

U.S.A.

Ingredients

Glass: 150mL/5oz Cocktail Glass

Mixers: 30mL/1fl oz Bacardi rum
5 drops green Crème de Menthe
30mL/1fl oz Chartreuse
5 drops Grenadine
30mL/1fl oz Parfait Amour
cracked ice

Method

Half fill a mixing glass with cracked ice and add Bacardi rum, Chartreuse and Parfait Amour. Stir and strain into cocktail glass, add other ingredients and serve.

Blow Job

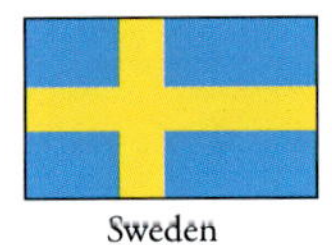

Sweden

Ingredients

Glass: Tall Dutch Cordial

Mixers: 30mL/1fl oz Kahlúa
15mL/½fl oz Baileys Irish Cream

Method

Layer in order and shoot.

Australia

Blueberry Delight

Ingredients

Glass: 140mL/5oz Cocktail Glass

Mixers: 30mL/1fl oz black Sambucca
20mL/⅝fl oz coconut liqueur
10mL/⅜fl oz strawberry liqueur
60mL/2fl oz cream

Method

Shake with ice and strain.
Garnish with strawberry on side of glass with blueberries on a toothpick.

Blueberry Delight No. 2

Italy

Ingredients

Glass: 300mL/10oz Hi-Ball Glass

Mixers: 15mL/½fl oz Galleon Liverno
15mL/½fl oz Blue Curaçao
15mL/½fl oz dry vermouth

Method

Shake ingredients except lemonade and strain into hi-ball glass. Top with lemonade, garnish with an lemon wheel, mint leaves, straws and serve.

Blue Blazer

Scotland

Ingredients

Glass: 140mL Champagne Saucer

Mixers: 60mL/1fl oz Scotch whiskey
60mL/1fl oz boiling water
2 Mugs (silver or copper)
sugar

Method

Pour whiskey into one mug and water into the other. Ignite whiskey and pour into water mug. Pour ingredients from one mug to the other a few times. Add sugar to taste, garnish with lemon peel and serve.

Blue Day

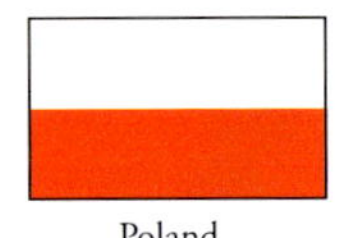
Poland

Ingredients

Glass: 90mL/3oz Cocktail Glass
Mixers: 45mL/1½fl oz vodka
20mL/⅝fl oz Blue Curaçao
peel ½ lemon

Method
Crack ice and place in shaker with liquid ingredients, shake and strain into cocktail glass. Squeeze ½ lemon peel over the top, garnish with the lemon slice and serve.

Blue Dove

U.S.A.

Ingredients

Glass: 300mL/10oz Hi-Ball Glass
Mixers: 30mL/1fl oz Blue Curaçao
lemonade
20mL/⅝fl oz vodka
whipped cream

Method
Pour Blue Curaçao and vodka over ice in hi-ball glass. Top with lemonade, add whipped cream to top and serve.

Blue French

France

Ingredients
Glass: 285mL/10oz Hi-Ball Glass
Mixers: 30mL/1fl oz Pernod
5mL/⅛fl oz Blue Curaçao
liqueur
5mL/⅛fl oz lemon juice
top-up with bitter lemon

Method
Build over ice and stir.
Garnish with lemon slice on side of glass, swizzle stick and straws.
A great thirst quencher. Ideal when relaxing by the pool.

U.S.A.

Blue Hawaii

Ingredients

Glass: 300mL/10oz Hi-Ball Glass

Mixers: 30mL/1fl oz Bacardi
30mL/1fl oz Blue Curaçao liqueur
60mL/2fl oz pineapple juice
30mL/1fl oz lemon juice
30mL/1fl oz sugar syrup

Method

Build over ice and pour.
Garnish with pineapple wedge, mint and cherry. Serve with straws.
A favourite Hawaiian drink. The mixing of pineapple juice and Blue Curaçao tends to turn the cocktail aqua-green in color.

Blue Haze

Italy

Ingredients

Glass: 150mL/5oz Champagne Saucer

Mixers: 30mL/1fl oz Bacardi rum
15mL/½fl oz Cointreau
15mL/½fl oz sweet vermouth
15mL/½fl oz Rossi vermouth
4 drops Blue Curaçao
15mL/½fl oz Parfait Amour

Method

Add all ingredients except Blue Curaçao in mixing glass. Strain into a champagne saucer, add Blue Curaçao and serve.

Blue Heaven

U.S.A.

Ingredients

Glass: 300mL/10oz Hi-Ball Glass

Mixers: 60mL/2fl oz vodka
150mL/5fl oz lemonade
30mL/1fl oz Blue Curaçao

Method

Shake vodka and Blue Curaçao. Pour over ice in hi-ball glass. Top with lemonade and serve with straws.

Blue Lady

United Kingdom

Ingredients

Glass: 90mL/3oz Cocktail Glass
Mixers: 30mL/1fl oz gin
15mL/½fl oz Blue Curaçao
3 ice cubes
15mL/½fl oz lemon juice

Method
Shake and strain into cocktail glass. Garnish with Maraschino cherry and serve.

Blue Lagoon No. 2

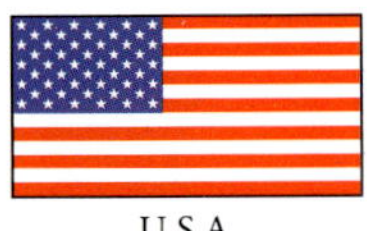
U.S.A.

Ingredients

Glass: 90mL/3oz Cocktail Glass
Mixers: 30mL/1fl oz vodka
15mL/½fl oz lemon juice
5mL/⅛fl oz Blue Curaçao

Method
Shake and strain into cocktail glass and serve.

Blue Lagoon

U.S.A.

Ingredients
Glass: Brandy Balloon
Mixers: 30mL/1fl oz Gilbey's Gin
10mL/⅜fl oz Blue Curaçao
top up with lemonade

Method
Build over ice and top up with lemonade. Garnish with a lemon wheel.
Named after the movie which bears this cocktail's name.

Blue Train

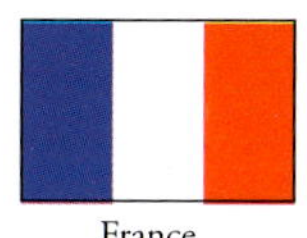

France

Ingredients

Glass: 210mL/7oz Wine Goblet
Mixers: 45mL/1½fl oz brandy
45mL/1½fl oz pineapple juice
30mL/1fl oz Blue Curaçao
Champagne
cracked ice

Method

Layer brandy, curaçao and pineapple juice over cracked ice. Top with champagne, garnish with Maraschino cherry and serve.

Blushing Berry

Australia

Ingredients

Glass: 260mL/8oz Margarita Glass
Mixers: 150mL/5fl oz milk
60mL/2fl oz raspberry cordial
60mL/2fl oz cream
15mL/½fl oz coconut milk
frozen raspberries

Method

Blend with ice, raspberry cordial, coconut milk, milk and whipped cream. Garnish: place frozen raspberries around rim.

U.S.A.

Blunt Screwdriver

Ingredients

Glass: 300mL/10oz 10oz Hi-Ball Glass
Mixers: 120mL/4fl oz ginger ale
120mL/4fl oz orange juice

Method

Build over ice. Garnish with an orange slice and a red cherry.
This cousin of the well known alcoholic Screwdriver which substitutes the vodka for ginger ale. Add 15mL/½fl oz Grenadine for a Roy Rogers.

Bobby Dazzler

Australia

Ingredients

Glass: 290mL/10oz Poco Grande Glass
Mixers: 60mL/2fl oz Grenadine
200mL/7fl oz cola
whipped cream
hundreds and thousands

Method

Blend Grenadine with ice and pour into glass. Top with cola then whipped cream and sprinkle with hundreds and thousands. Place strawberry on side and serve with swizzle stick and straw.

Bobby Burns

United Kingdom

Ingredients

Glass: 90mL/3oz Cocktail Glass
Mixers: 15mL/½fl oz Scotch whiskey
1 dash Benedictine
10mL/⅜fl oz sweet vermouth
10mL/⅜fl oz dry vermouth

Method

Stir ingredients in a mixing glass, strain into cocktail glass. Garnish with lemon peel and serve.

Body Heat

Jamaica

Ingredients

Glass: 300mL/10oz Hi-Ball Glass
Mixers: 30mL/1fl oz Malibu
30mL/1fl oz pineapple juice
30mL/1fl oz banana liqueur
30mL/1fl oz orange juice
1 dash Grenadine
10mL/⅜fl oz lemon juice

Method

Blend all ingredients with ice until smooth, pour into hi-ball glass. Add Grenadine and serve with straws.

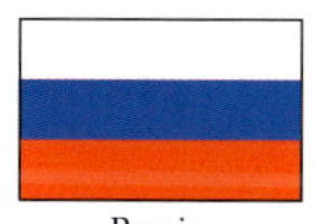
Russia

Bolshoi Punch

Ingredients

Glass: 285mL/9½oz Footed Hi-Ball Glass

Mixers: 30mL/1fl oz vodka
10mL/⅜fl oz dark rum
10mL/⅜fl oz Crème de Cassis
15mL/½fl oz lime juice
15mL/½fl oz lemon juice
top up with bitter lemon

Method

Blend with ice and strain then top up with bitter lemon. Garnish with an orange slice and red cherry.

Boilermaker

United Kingdom

Ingredients

Glass: Whiskey shot

Mixers: Serve 30-60mL/1-2fl oz Scotch whiskey with a beer chaser.

Bombay

India

Ingredients

Glass: 90mL/3oz Cocktail Glass

Mixers: 60 mL/2 oz brandy
3 dashes Crème de Cacao
10mL/⅜fl oz dry vermouth
ice
10mL/⅜fl oz sweet vermouth

Method

Shake and strain into cocktail glass and serve.

India

Bombay Punch

Ingredients

Glass: 285mL/9½oz Footed Hi-Ball Glass

Mixers: 30mL/1fl oz Cognac
10mL/⅜fl oz dry sherry
10mL/⅜fl oz Cointreau
10mL/⅜fl oz Maraschino cherry
20mL/⅝fl oz lemon juice
top up with soda and Champagne

Method

Blend with ice and strain then top up with soda and champagne. Garnish with a red cherry.

Bondi Blue

Ingredients

Australia

Glass: 300mL/10oz Hi-Ball Glass

Mixers: 45mL/1½fl oz Bacardi rum
½ egg white
30mL/1fl oz Blue Curaçao
cracked ice
30mL/1fl oz banana liqueur
lemonade

Method

Shake all ingredients except lemonade, strain over ice in hi-ball glass. Top with lemonade, add straws and serve.

Born to be Alive

Ingredients

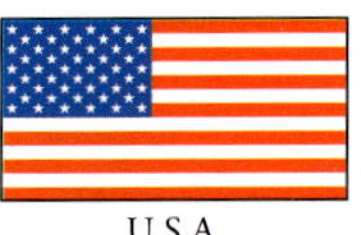

U.S.A.

Glass: 150mL/5oz Cocktail Glass

Mixers: 30mL/1fl oz Bacardi rum
15mL/½fl oz Peter Herring
15mL/½fl oz Advocaat
15mL/½fl oz Blue Curaçao
15mL/½fl oz green Chartreuse
5mL/⅛fl oz Galliano Liverno
15mL/½fl oz yellow Chartreuse

Method

Gently layer ingredients in cocktail glass with Advocaat in the centre. Serve.

United Kingdom

Bosom Caresser

Ingredients

Glass: 140mL/5oz Champagne Saucer

Mixers: 30mL/1fl oz brandy
15mL/½fl oz orange liqueur
5mL/⅛fl oz Grenadine cordial
1 egg yolk

Method

Shake with ice and strain.
Garnish with two red cherries, slit on side of glass.
Close to every lady's heart! Egg yolk allows the cocktail to breathe supporting the brandy's body and bounce. Fine on any occasion.

Bosom Caresser No. 2

United Kingdom

Ingredients

Glass: 90mL/3oz Cocktail Glass

Mixers: 45mL/1½fl oz brandy
1 egg yolk
15mL/½fl oz Blue Curaçao
1 teaspoon Grenadine

Method

Shake and strain into cocktail glass and serve.

Bossa Nova

Brazil

Ingredients

Glass: 285mL/9½oz Footed Hi-Ball Glass

Mixers: 30mL/1 oz Galleon Liverno
60mL/1 oz pineapple juice
30mL/1 oz light dark rum
10mL/⅜fl oz lemon juice
10mL/⅜fl oz apricot brandy
15mL/½fl oz egg white

Method

Shake and pour over ice in a hi-ball glass. Garnish with fruit and serve.

Boston Cream

U.S.A.

Ingredients

Glass: 120mL/4oz Cocktail Glass, Frosted

Mixers: 30mL/1fl oz cream
15mL/½fl oz lime juice
30mL/1fl oz coconut cream
15mL/½fl oz Grenadine

Method

Shake over ice and strain. Garnish with a chocolate cross.

Boston Cocktail

U.S.A.

Ingredients

Glass: 90mL/3oz Cocktail Glass

Mixers: 30mL/1fl oz gin
30mL/1fl oz apricot brandy
5mL/⅛fl oz lemon juice
5mL/⅛fl oz Grenadine

Method

Shake over ice and strain then add Grenadine. Garnish with a red cherry.

Bourbon Banana

U.S.A.

Ingredients

Glass: Brandy Balloon

Mixers: 30mL/1fl bourbon
30mL/1fl orange juice
30mL/1fl Kahlúa
30mL/1fl cream
1 banana

Method

Blend ingredients with ice and serve in a brandy balloon.

Brain Dead

U.S.A.

Ingredients

Glass:	Whiskey Shot
Mixers:	10mL/⅜fl oz Southern Comfort 10mL/⅜fl oz tequila 10mL/⅜fl oz Galliano 10mL/⅜fl oz Tia Maria 10mL/⅜fl oz Blue Curaçao

Method

Layer in a test tube or shot glass and serve.

Brandy Boss

Netherlands

Ingredients

Glass:	140mL/5oz Champagne Saucer
Mixers:	30mL/1fl oz brandy 15mL/½fl oz Tia Maria 15mL/½fl oz Vandermint 60mL/2fl oz cream

Method

Shake and strain into a champagne saucer and serve.

United Kingdom

Brandy Alexander

Ingredients

Glass:	140mL/5oz Champagne Saucer
Mixers:	30mL/1fl oz Brandy 30mL/1fl oz Dark Crème de Cacao Liqueur 5mL/⅛fl oz Grenadine cordial 30mL/1fl oz cream

Method

Shake with ice and strain.

Garnish with a sprinkle of nutmeg and a cherry.

An after-dinner cocktail. An "Alexander" replaces the cacao with green Crème de Menthe. Cognac may be substituted for brandy to deliver an exceptional after taste.

Brandy Daisy

France

Ingredients

Glass: 285mL/9⅛oz Wine Goblet
Mixers: 60 mL/2fl oz brandy
6 dashes Grenadine
30mL/1fl oz lemon juice
soda water
cracked ice

Method

Fill a goblet with cracked ice, shake brandy, lemon juice and Grenadine. Strain into goblet, top soda. Garnish with mint leaves and orange slice.

Brandy Egg Nog

U.S.A.

Ingredients

Glass: 300mL/10oz Hi-Ball Glass
Mixers: 30mL/1fl oz brandy
1 egg yolk
5mL/⅛fl oz sugar syrup
milk

Method

Shake all ingredients except milk, strain into hi-ball glass. Top with milk, sprinkle with nutmeg, add straws and serve.

Brandy Ice

Portugal

Ingredients

Glass: 285mL/9⅛oz Tall Wine Glass
Mixers: 30mL/1fl oz brandy
15mL/½fl oz vanilla extract
2 scoops vanilla ice cream
15mL/½fl oz lemon juice
top up with bitter lemon

Method

Blend with ice and strain then top up with bitter lemon. Garnish with an orange slice and a cherry.

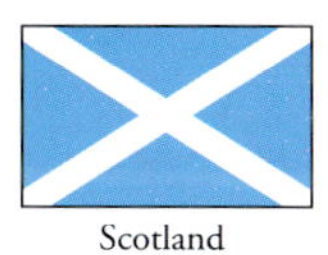
Scotland

Brandy Snaps

Ingredients

Glass: Cordial (Embassy)

Mixers: 10mL/⅜fl oz brandy
10mL/⅜fl oz peach schnapps
10mL/⅜fl oz apple juice

Method

Layer brandy onto peach schnapps, then pour apple juice. Garnish with floated cream (optional).

Brandy Riviera

France

Ingredients

Glass: 140mL/5oz Champagne Saucer

Mixers: 30mL/1fl oz brandy
30mL/1fl oz Vandermint
30mL/1fl oz banana liqueur

Method

Pour ingredients over ice in a champagne saucer and serve.

Brandy Toddy

Wales

Ingredients

Glass: 140mL/3oz Cocktail Glass

Mixers: 60mL/2fl oz brandy
1 teaspoon sugar
water
cracked ice

Method

Dissolve sugar in a little water in the cocktail glass. Add ice, brandy and serve.

Brazil

Brazilian Monk

Ingredients

Glass:	285mL/9⅛oz Tulip Wine Glass
Mixers:	30mL/1fl oz Kahlúa 15mL/½fl oz Frangelico 15mL/½fl oz dark Crème de Cacao 2 scoops vanilla ice cream

Method

Blend with ice. Garnish with a wild flower or flower petals.
Very popular in the South American countries and the United States.
Frangelico is imported from Italy and made from wild flowers infused into hazelnuts.

Brazilian Breakdance

Brazil

Ingredients

Glass:	390mL/12oz Poco Grande Glass
Mixers:	2 teaspoons instant coffee scoop vanilla ice cream 125mL/4fl oz Milk

Method

Blend with ice and pour.
Garnish with a teaspoon chocolate flakes.
A luscious, thick glass of iced coffee flavor, with just a hint of sweetness.

Break Shooter

Australia

Ingredients

Glass:	Cordial (Lexington)
Mixers:	10 mL Kahlúa 10mL/⅜fl oz ouzo 10mL/⅜fl oz banana liqueur

Method

Layer in order in a shot glass and serve.

France

Brittany

Ingredients

Glass:	150mL/5oz Old Fashioned Spirit Glass
Mixers:	30mL/1fl oz gin
	15mL/½fl oz Amer Picon
	10mL/⅜fl oz orange juice
	10mL/⅜fl oz lemon juice

Method

Blend with ice and pour.
Garnish with two banana wheel slices wedged on rim of glass.

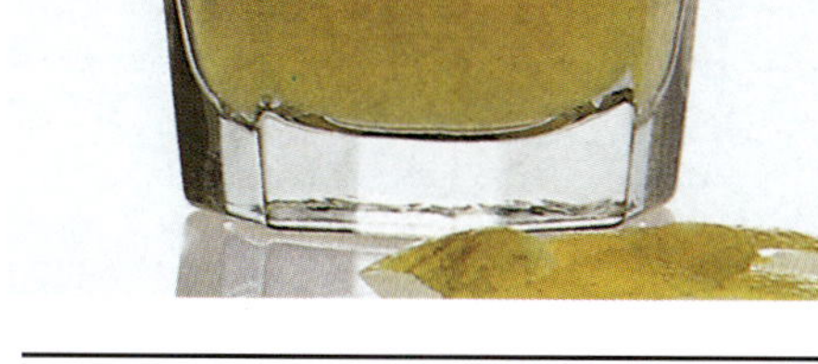

Bronx

U.S.A.

Ingredients

Glass:	90mL/3oz Cocktail Glass
Mixers:	30mL/1fl oz gin
	15mL/½fl oz orange juice
	1 dash French vermouth
	cracked ice
	1 dash Italian vermouth

Method

Shake and strain into 3 oz cocktail glass and serve.

Brown Betty

United Kingdom

Ingredients

Glass:	Brandy Balloon
Mixers:	60mL/2fl oz beer or ale
	1 tablespoon brown sugar
	15mL/½fl oz brandy
	1 pinch cinnamon
	30mL/1fl oz water
	nutmeg
	pinch ground cloves
	½ slice toasted bread
	½ fresh ginger root

Method

Dissolve sugar in water and allow to stand for 15 minutes. Add cloves, brandy and beer or ale and stir well. Pour into brandy balloon, break toasted bread into it. Sprinkle with nutmeg and grate ginger root over top and serve.

Café Nero

Italy

Ingredients

Glass: 140mL/5oz Champagne Saucer

Mixers: 30mL/1fl oz Galliano
black coffee
fresh cream
sugar

Method

Firstly, sprinkle white sugar inside the glass after coating with Galliano. Set Galliano alight and twirl the glass so that flames burn brightly. Pour black coffee gently into glass then layer cream on top of the burning coffee. Sprinkle grated chocolate over the coffee.

Café Paris

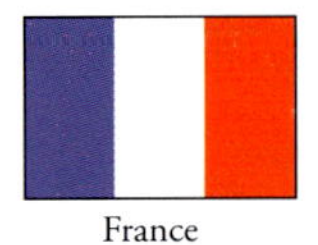

France

Ingredients

Glass: 140mL/5oz Cocktail Glass

Mixers: 60 mL/2fl oz gin
10mL/⅜fl oz double cream
5mL/⅛fl oz Pernod
1 egg white

Method

Shake over ice and strain. Garnish with half a slice of lemon.

Café Royal

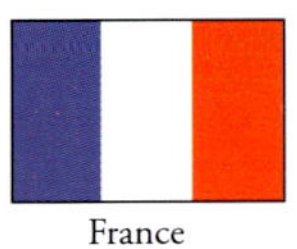

France

Ingredients

Glass: Irish Coffee Glass

Mixers: black coffee
1 lump sugar
30mL/1fl oz brandy

Method

Place sugar in spoon and hold over coffee, fill spoon with brandy and ignite. When flame starts to fade place spoon in coffee and serve.

Cameron Cannon

U.S.A.

Ingredients

Glass: 150mL/5oz Cocktail Glass
Mixers: 30mL/1fl oz Kahlúa
30mL/1fl oz Baileys Irish Cream
90mL/3fl oz vodka
dash Crème de Menthe
3 drops green Chartreuse

Method
Shake and strain into cocktail glass and serve.

Campino

Italy

Ingredients

Glass: 210mL/7oz Old Fashioned
Mixers: 15mL/½fl oz Campari
2 dashes Crème de Cassis
15mL/½fl oz sweet vermouth
15mL/½fl oz dry vermouth
soda water
15mL/½fl oz gin

Method
Mix all ingredients except soda water and peel in mixing glass. Pour into tumbler and top with soda. Garnish with orange peel and serve.

Canadian Daisy

Canada

Ingredients
Glass: 285mL/9½oz Hi-Ball Glass
Mixers: 30mL/1fl oz Canadian Club Whisky
10mL/⅜fl oz brandy
10mL/⅜fl oz lemon juice
5mL/⅛fl oz raspberry syrup
top up with soda

Method
Shake over ice and strain then top up with soda. Garnish with assorted colorful cherries.

Czech Republic

Candy Cane

Ingredients

Glass: 285mL/9½oz Tall Wine Glass

Mixers: dash Grenadine
30mL/1fl oz white Crème de Cacao
30mL/1fl oz peppermint liqueur
30mL/1fl oz sweet 'n' sour
2 scoops vanilla ice cream

Method

Blend all ingredients with ice and strain. Sprinkle with peppermint chocolate. Comment: sweet 'n' sour is made from an equal mix of lemon juice and lime juice.

Cape Kennedy

U.S.A.

Ingredients

Glass: 90mL/3oz Cocktail glass

Mixers: 5mL/⅛fl oz dark rum
30mL/1fl oz lemon juice
5mL/⅛fl oz Scotch whiskey
30mL/1fl oz orange juice
5mL/⅛fl oz Benedictine
2-3 ice cubes
5mL/⅛fl oz sugar syrup

Method

Shake and strain into 3 oz cocktail glass and serve.

Caper's Caper

U.S.A.

Ingredients

Glass: 300mL/10oz Colada Glass

Mixers: 30mL/1fl oz Advocaat
¼ Avocado
30mL/1fl oz Frangelico
1 scoop ice cream
4-5 strawberries

Method

Blend ingredients with ice and pour into colada glass. Float coffee bean and serve with straws.

Careless Whisper

Switzerland

Ingredients

Glass: 90mL/3oz Cocktail Glass

Mixers: 30mL/1fl oz strawberry liqueur
10mL/⅜fl oz cream
10mL/⅜fl oz Cheri-Suisse
20mL/⅝fl oz Amanda

Method

Shake and strain into cocktail glass, garnish with grated chocolate, cherry and serve.

Carlton

Canada

Ingredients

Glass: 90mL/3oz Cocktail Glass

Mixers: 30mL/1fl oz Canadian whiskey
10mL/⅜fl oz orange juice
15mL/½fl oz Cointreau
cracked ice

Method

Shake and strain into cocktail glass and serve.

Caribbean Champagne

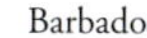

Barbados

Ingredients

Glass: 140mL/5oz Champagne Saucer

Mixers: 100mL/3½fl oz Champagne
10mL/⅜fl oz Bacardi
10mL/⅜fl oz banana liqueur
5mL/⅛fl oz orange bitters

Method

Stir without ice and strain. Garnish with a slice of banana.

France

Champagne Cocktail

Ingredients

Glass: 140mL/5oz Champagne Flute
Mixers: 1 sugar cube
6 drops of Angostura Bitter
15mL/½fl oz cognac or brandy
top up with Champagne

Method

Soak sugar cube in Angostura Bitter in flute, before adding brandy, then top with Champagne. Garnish with a red cherry (optional).

Cha Cha

Italy

Ingredients

Glass: 90mL/3oz Cocktail Glass
Mixers: 30mL/1fl oz Frangelico
15mL/½fl oz cream
30mL/1fl oz Crème de Cacao

Method

Float ingredients in cocktail glass and serve.

Champagne Cocktail No.

United Kingdom

Ingredients

Glass: 140mL Champagne Saucer
Mixers: 15mL/½fl oz brandy
1 sugar cube
chilled Champagne
1 dash Angostura Bitter
1 dash orange curaçao

Method

Place sugar cube in a champagne saucer, add Angostura Bitter and curaçao. Fill almost to top with champagne, float brandy on top. Garnish with orange peel and serve.

Switzerland

Champagne St Moritz

Ingredients

Glass: 140mL/5oz Champagne Saucer

Mixers: 10mL/$\frac{3}{8}$fl oz gin
10mL/$\frac{3}{8}$fl oz Apricot Brandy
10mL/$\frac{3}{8}$fl oz orange juice
top up with Champagne

Method

Shake over ice and strain then top up with champagne. Garnish with a slice of orange.

Champagne Pick-Me-Up

U.S.A.

Ingredients

Glass: 140mL/3oz Champagne Flute

Mixers: 30mL/1fl oz brandy
30mL/1fl oz orange juice
chilled Champagne
5mL/$\frac{1}{8}$fl oz Grenadine

Method

Shake ingredients with ice except champagne and strain into a flute glass. Top with champagne and serve.

Champagne Tory

France

Ingredients

Glass: 140mL/5oz Champagne Saucer

Mixers: 15mL/$\frac{1}{2}$fl oz Midori
15mL/$\frac{1}{2}$fl oz Rubis
15mL/$\frac{1}{2}$fl oz banana liqueur
chilled Champagne

Method

Pour ingredients into a champagne saucer, top with champagne and serve.

Chastity Belt

Morocco

Ingredients

Glass: Tall Dutch Cordial

Mixers: 20mL/⅝fl oz Tia Maria
10mL/⅜fl oz Frangelico
10mL/⅜fl oz Baileys Irish Cream
5mL/⅛fl oz cream

Method

Layer in order, then float the cream. Morality implores you not to succumb to the super-sweet delicacies of drinking's perversity.

Channel 64

Australia

Ingredients

Glass: Cordial (Lexington)

Mixers: 10mL/⅜fl oz Advocaat
10mL/⅜fl oz Baileys Irish Cream
10mL/⅜fl oz banana liqueur

Method

Layer in order in a shot glass and serve.

Chee Chee

U.S.A.

Ingredients

Glass: 140mL/5oz Champagne Saucer

Mixers: 30mL/1fl oz vodka
60mL/2fl oz pineapple juice
30mL/1fl oz coconut milk

Method

Shake and strain into a champagne saucer, garnish with pineapple wedge and serve.

Brazil

Cheeky Girl

Ingredients

Glass:	285mL/9oz Hurricane Glass
Mixers:	30mL/1fl oz Kahlúa
	30mL/1fl oz banana liqueur
	15mL/½fl oz brandy
	15mL/½fl oz Malibu
	½ a banana
	60mL/2fl oz cream

Method
Blend with ice. Garnish with a round slice of banana and straws.

Cheer

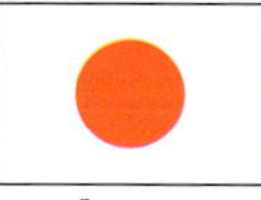
Japan

Ingredients

Glass:	300mL/10oz Hi-Ball Glass
Mixers:	30mL/1fl oz Midori
	30mL/1fl oz gin
	30mL/1fl oz lime cordial
	lemonade

Method
Blend Midori, gin and lime cordial with some ice. Pour into hi-ball glass and top with lemonade.

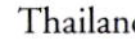

Thailand

Cherries Jubilee

Ingredients

Glass: 140mL/5oz Cocktail Glass

Mixers: 30mL/1fl oz cherry Advocaat
30mL/1fl oz white Crème de Cacao
15mL/½fl oz Malibu
45mL/1½fl oz cream
15mL/½fl oz milk

Method

Shake with ice and strain.
Grated chocolate and cherry and coconut rind on side of glass.

Cherry

Israel

Ingredients

Glass: 300mL/10oz Hi-Ball Glass

Mixers: 15mL/½fl oz cherry brandy
15mL/½fl oz double cream
1 teaspoon white rum
90mL/3fl oz sparkling white wine

Method

Stir all ingredients except wine in hi-ball glass. Top with wine, garnish with mint, straws and serve.

Cherry Alexander

United Kingdom

Ingredients

Glass: 150mL/5oz Cocktail Glass

Mixers: 30mL/1fl oz cherry brandy
60mL/2fl oz cream
30mL/1fl oz Crème de Cacao

Method

Shake and strain into cocktail glass and serve.

China

Cherry Bomb

Ingredients

Glass: 270mL/9oz Margarita Glass, sugar rimmed

Mixers: 30mL/1fl oz vodka
15mL/½fl oz cherry brandy
5mL/⅛fl oz Grenadine
top up with lemonade

Method

Color sugar with Grenadine and prepare glass by sugar coating rim. Blend over ice and pour then top up with lemonade. Garnish with an orchid.
Comments: watch as the magical color fizzes up like a Cherry Bomb. Red is the historical color of cultural China.

Cheryl

U.S.A.

Ingredients

Glass: 150mL/5oz Cocktail Glass

Mixers: 30mL/1fl oz vodka
1 scoop vanilla ice cream
30mL/1fl oz Galleon Liverno

Method

Shake and strain into cocktail glass, garnish with Maraschino cherry and serve.

Chi Chi

U.S.A.

Ingredients

Glass: 210mL/7oz Fancy Cocktail Glass

Mixers: 45mL/1½fl oz vodka
20mL/⅝fl oz coconut cream
20mL/⅝fl oz Malibu
15mL/½fl oz lime cordial
15mL/½fl oz lemon cordial
1 slice pineapple
60mL/2fl oz pineapple juice
1 dash cream

Method

Blend until smooth and pour into cocktail glass and serve.

Chiquita

Chile

Ingredients

Glass: 285mL/9½oz Footed Hi-Ball Glass

Mixers: 45mL/1½fl oz vodka
10mL/⅜fl oz banana liqueur
10mL/⅜fl oz lime juice
half a sliced banana
pinch of sugar

Method

Blend with ice and pour. Garnish with banana slices.

Chicago

U.S.A.

Ingredients

Glass: 140mL/5oz Champagne Saucer

Mixers: 45mL/1½fl oz brandy
1 dash Angostura Bitter
1 teaspoon Cointreau
2 ice cubes
sparkling white wine

Method

Place ingredients in a champagne saucer, top with white wine and serve.

Choc Mint

U.S.A.

Ingredients

Glass: 140mL/5oz Champagne Saucer

Mixers: 30mL/1fl oz white Crème de Cacao
15mL/½fl oz white Crème de Menthe
60mL/2fl oz cream

Method

Shake with ice and serve in champagne saucer.

Norway

Chocolate Chip Mint

Ingredients

Glass: 285mL/9½oz Footed Hi-Ball Glass

Mixers: 30mL/1fl oz white Crème de Cacao
30mL/1fl oz green Crème de Menthe
2 scoops vanilla ice cream
15mL/½fl ozl lemon juice
2 chocolate chips
top up with lemonade

Method

Blend with ice and strain then top up with lemonade. Serve with chocolate chip cookies on a side plate.

Chocolate Baby

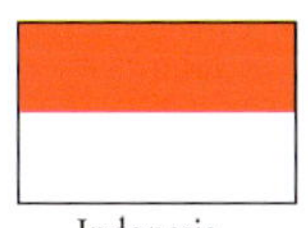
Indonesia

Ingredients

Glass: 300mL/10oz Hi-Ball Glass

Mixers: 45mL/1½fl oz Crème de Cacao
cola

Method

Half fill hi-ball glass with ice, add Crème de Cacao. Top with Coca-Cola and serve with straws.

Chocolate Chip

Netherlands

Ingredients

Glass: Tall Dutch Cordial

Mixers: 15mL/½fl oz Vandermint
15mL/½fl oz Baileys Irish Cream
15mL/½fl oz Crème de Menthe

Method

Layer in a shot glass and serve.

Cointreau Caipirinha

Brazil

Ingredients

Glass: 175mL/6oz Prism Rocks Glass
Mixers: 30mL/1fl oz Cointreau
¼ fresh lime or lemon
crushed ice

Method

Cut lime into pieces and place in glass. Extract juice by using the Cointreau Pestle, fill glass with crushed ice and add Cointreau and mini pestle. Stir.
The pestle is a new Cointreau product which assists in the initial extraction of the lime or lemon juice.

Canada

Columbia Skin

Ingredients

Glass: 300mL/10oz Beer Mug
Mixers: ½ lemon, thinly peeled
30mL/1fl oz Scotch whisky
240mL/8fl oz of boiling water

Method

Pour in order. Garnish with a slice of lemon.

Columbus

U.S.A.

Ingredients

Glass: 90mL/3oz Cocktail Glass

Mixers: 20mL/⅝fl oz rum
20mL/⅝fl oz lemon juice
20mL/⅝fl oz apricot brandy

Method

Shake with ice. Strain into cocktail glass then serve.

Comfort Baby

U.S.A.

Ingredients

Glass: 140mL Champagne Saucer

Mixers: 45mL/1½fl oz Southern Comfort
1 cube sugar
45mL/1½fl oz fresh milk
2-3 ice cubes
nutmeg

Method

Place sugar cube in an old fashioned glass and add liquid ingredients. Stir gently until sugar is dissolved, sprinkle with nutmeg and serve.

Denmark

Copenhagen Special

Ingredients

Glass: 150mL/5oz Tulip Champagne Glass

Mixers: 30mL/1fl oz Aquavit
30mL/1fl oz Arrack
15mL/½fl oz lemon juice

Method

Shake over ice and strain. Garnish with a slice of lemon.

Daiquiri

Cuba

Ingredients

Glass:	140mL/5oz Champagne Saucer
Mixers:	45mL/1½fl oz white rum 30mL/1fl oz pure lemon juice 15mL/½fl oz sugar syrup ½ egg white, optional

Method

Shake with ice and strain.
Garnish: lemon slice or lemon spiral.

Daiquiri - American

U.S.A.

Ingredients

Glass:	150mL/5oz Cocktail Glass
Mixers:	30mL/1fl oz white rum 1 teaspoon sugar 1 teaspoon Cointreau 15mL/½fl oz lime juice

Method

Shake and strain over crushed ice in a 5 oz cocktail glass. Garnish with a slice of lime on glass and a Maraschino cherry dropped into the drink.

Daiquiri - Kings

United Kingdom

Ingredients

Glass: 140mL/5oz Champagne Saucer

Mixers: 45mL/1½fl oz white rum
15mL/½fl oz lemon juice
15mL/½fl oz Parfait Amour
¼ teaspoon sugar
1 dash egg white

Method

Blend with ice until smooth, pour into a champagne saucer and serve.

Daiquiri - Kiwifruit

New Zealand

Ingredients

Glass: 140mL/5oz Champagne Saucer

Mixers: 30mL/1fl oz Bacardi light rum
30mL/1fl oz lemon juice
30mL/1fl oz Cointreau
15mL/½fl oz sugar syrup
30mL/1fl oz Midori
½ kiwifruit

Method

Blend ingredients until smooth, pour into a champagne saucer and serve.

Daiquiri - Mango

Cuba

Ingredients

Glass: 210mL/7oz Fancy Cocktail Glass

Mixers: 45mL/1½fl oz Bacardi rum
20mL/⅝fl oz lemon juice
30mL/1fl oz Cointreau
15mL/½fl oz sugar syrup
30mL/1fl oz mango liqueur
½ mango

Method

Blend until smooth and pour into cocktail glass and serve.

Daiquiri - Strawberry

Cuba

Ingredients

Glass: 210mL/7oz Fancy Cocktail Glass

Mixers: 45mL/1½fl oz Bacardi rum
20mL/⅝fl oz lemon juice
30mL/1fl oz Cointreau
15mL/½fl oz sugar syrup
30mL/1fl oz strawberry liqueur
10 strawberries

Method

Blend until smooth and pour into cocktail glass and serve. Garnish with half a strawberry on side of glass.

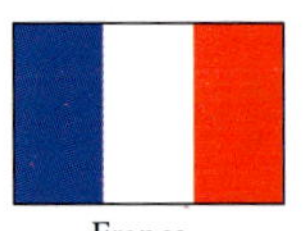

France

Death in the Afternoon

Ingredients

Glass: 140mL/5oz Champagne Flute
Mixers: 15mL/½fl oz Pernod
Champagne

Method

Build, no ice.
Ernest Hemingway's favorite cocktail. A bubbly occasion deserves this fully imported French aphrodisiac mixer.

Death by Chocolate

U.S.A.

Ingredients

Glass: 210mL/7oz Old Fashioned
Mixers: 30mL/1fl oz Baileys Irish Cream
30mL/1fl oz Crème de Cacao
30mL/1fl oz Kahlúa
90mL/3fl oz thickened cream
30mL/1fl oz Tia Maria

Method

Shake and strain into a champagne saucer, garnish with grated chocolate and serve.

Deep Throat

U.S.A.

Ingredients

Glass: Whiskey Shot
Mixers: 20mL/⅝fl oz Kahlúa
20mL/⅝fl oz Grand Marnier
10mL/⅜fl oz cream

Method

Layer in order in a shot glass and serve.

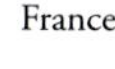
France

Depth Charge

Ingredients

Glass: 375mL/12½oz Beer Glass
Mixers: 330mL/11fl oz beer
30mL/1fl oz Cointreau

Method

Pour beer into glass, fill a 1 oz shot glass with Cointreau. Drop shot glass into beer.

De Rigueur

Australia

Ingredients

Glass: 175mL/6oz Prism Rocks
Mixers: 30mL/1oz Scotch whiskey
10mL/⅜fl oz grapefruit juice
10mL/⅜fl oz honey

Method

Shake over ice and pour. Garnish with a swizzle stick.

Deshler

Canada

Ingredients

Glass: 90mL/3oz Cocktail Glass
Mixers: 30 mL/1 oz Canadian whiskey
1 dash Angostura Bitter
15mL/½ oz Dubonnet
1 dash Cointreau

Method

Shake and strain into cocktail glass, garnish with lemon and orange peel and serve.

Devil's Handbrake

Thailand

Ingredients

Glass: Tall Dutch Cordial

Mixers: 15mL/½fl oz Banana Liqueur
15mL/½fl oz Mango Liqueur
15mL/½fl oz Cherry Brandy

Method

Layer in order.

Diplomat

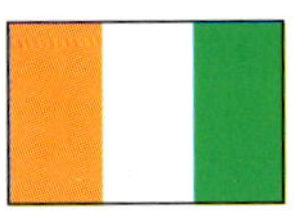

Ivory Coast

Ingredients

Glass: 240mL/8oz Hi-Ball Glass

Mixers: 45mL/1½fl oz vodka
90mL/3fl oz pineapple juice
45mL/1½fl oz Midori
5mL/⅛fl oz lemon juice

Method

Shake and strain into a hi-ball glass and serve with straws.

Dirty Mother

Mexico

Ingredients

Glass: 300mL/10oz Hi-Ball Glass

Mixers: 30mL/1fl oz tequila
milk
30mL/1fl oz Tia Maria

Method

Shake and strain over ice in a hi-ball glass, top with milk and serve.

Switzerland

Dizzy Blonde

Ingredients

Glass: 285mL/9½oz Hi-Ball Glass

Mixers: 60mL/2fl oz Advocaat
30mL/1fl oz Pernod
top up with lemonade

Method

Shake over ice and pour then top up with lemonade. Garnish with an orange slice and cherry.

Dizzy Whistle

Austria

Ingredients

Glass: 90mL/3oz Martini Glass

Mixers: 15mL/½fl oz Frangelico
10mL/⅜fl oz pineapple juice
10mL/⅜fl oz green Crème de Menthe
10mL/⅜fl oz cream

Method

Layer pineapple juice onto Frangelico then shake green Crème de Menthe with cream and layer.

Doctor Dangerous

Puerto Rico

Ingredients

Glass: 210mL/7oz Old Fashioned

Mixers: 45mL/1½fl oz brandy
60mL/1fl oz milk
45mL/1½fl oz Baileys Irish Cream

Method

Shake and strain into an old fashioned glass and serve.

Dog's Special

Malaysia

Ingredients

Glass: 120mL/4oz Cocktail Glass
Mixers: 30mL/1fl oz Midori
30mL/1fl oz pineapple juice
30mL/1fl oz vodka
15mL/½fl oz cream

Method
Float ingredients in order in a 4 oz cocktail glass and serve.

Double Blazer

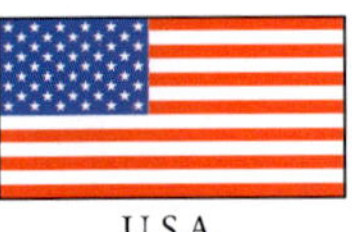

U.S.A.

Ingredients

Glass: 150mL/5oz Wine Glass
Mixers: 30mL/1fl oz white Crème de Menthe
30mL/1fl oz Southern Comfort

Method
Pour Crème de Menthe into a white wine glass. Slowly add Southern Comfort and ignite. Serve and extinguish flame in front of customer.

Dolomint

Morocco

Ingredients
Glass: 250mL/8oz Gibraltar Cooler Glass
Mixers: 30mL/1fl oz gin
30mL/1fl oz Galliano
30mL/1fl oz lime juice
top up with soda
fresh mint leaves

Method
Pour over ice and top up with soda. Coat rim of glass with sprig of mint and add 2 fresh mint leaves.

Italy

Double Jeopardy

Ingredients

Glass: 285mL/9½oz Hi-Ball Glass

Mixers: 45mL/1½fl oz Frangelico
45mL/1½fl oz black Sambucca
scoop of vanilla ice cream
top-up with milk

Method

Blend with ice and stir. Scooper spoon (long teaspoon) and straws.

Dragon's Fire

U.S.A.

Ingredients

Glass: Whiskey Shot

Mixers: 10mL/⅓fl oz cherry Advocaat
10mL/⅓fl oz Galleon Liverno
10mL/⅓fl oz orange curaçao
10mL/⅓fl oz Southern Comfort
10mL/⅓fl oz Blue Curaçao
10mL/⅓fl oz Advocaat

Method

Layer in order in a shot glass and serve.

Drambuie High

Maldives

Ingredients

Glass: 300mL/10oz Hi-Ball Glass

Mixers: 30mL/1fl oz Drambuie
20mL/⅝fl oz coconut cream
30mL/1fl oz golden rum
30mL/1fl oz pineapple juice
30mL/1fl oz cream
½ banana
1 scoop crushed ice

Method

Blend until smooth, pour into hi-ball glass. Garnish with pineapple leaves and serve.

Dubonnet Cocktail

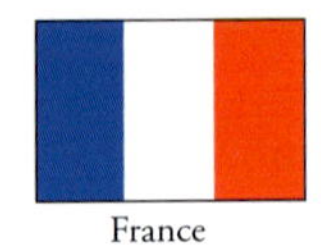
France

Ingredients

Glass: 120mL/4oz Cocktail Glass, chilled
Mixers: 30mL/1fl oz Dubonnet
15mL/½fl oz gin
1 dash orange bitters

Method
Build over ice. Garnish with a lemon twist.

France

Dubonnet Fizz

Ingredients
Glass: 285mL/9½oz Hi-Ball Glass
Mixers: 30mL/1fl oz Dubonnet
30mL/1fl oz cherry liqueur
30mL/1fl oz orange juice
15mL/½fl oz lemon juice
top up with soda

Method
Shake over ice and pour then top up with soda. Garnish with lemon rind and a red cherry.

United Kingdom

Duke of Marlborough

Ingredients

Glass: 120mL/4oz Cocktail Glass
Mixers: 30mL/1fl oz Sherry
30mL/1fl oz rosso vermouth
30mL/1fl oz lime juice
2 dashes raspberry cordial

Method

Shake and pour over ice. Garnish with a red cherry and a swizzle stick.

Dunk

New Zealand

Ingredients

Glass: 90mL/3oz Cocktail Glass
Mixers: 30mL/1fl oz dry vermouth
5mL/⅛fl oz curaçao
30mL/1fl oz gin
15mL/½fl oz Galliano Liverno

Method

Stir and strain into cocktail glass, garnish with Maraschino cherry and serve.

Dust Settler

Egypt

Ingredients

Glass: 285mL/10oz poco Grande Glass
Mixers: 90mL/3oz crushed pineapple
90mL/3fl oz apple juice
top-up with lemonade

Method

Blend with ice and pour.
Garnish with apple slice.

Dyevtchka

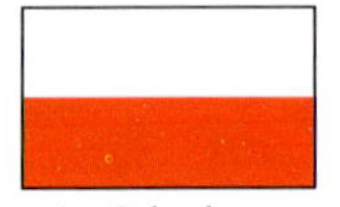
Poland

Ingredients

Glass: 285mL/9½oz Hi-Ball Glass
Mixers: 30mL/1fl oz vodka
30mL/1fl oz Cointreau
20mL/⅝fl oz fresh lime juice
20mL/⅝fl oz fresh lemon juice
15mL/½fl oz pineapple juice

Method
Shake with ice and pour. Garnish with a pineapple wedge & cherry.

U.S.A.

El Burro

Ingredients
Glass: 285mL/10oz Fancy Cocktail Glass
Mixers: 15mL/½fl oz oz Kahlúa
15mL/½fl oz oz rum
30mL/1fl oz coconut cream
30mL/1fl oz cream
½ banana

Method
Blend with ice and strain. Garnish with banana and mint leaves.

Mexico

El Diablo

Ingredients

Glass: 285mL/9½oz Hi-Ball Glass

Mixers: 30mL/1fl oz tequila
15mL/½fl oz Crème de Cassis
10mL/⅜fl oz lime juice
top up with ginger ale

Method

Build over ice and top up with ginger ale. Garnish with puréed lime.

Eldorado

U.S.A.

Ingredients

Glass: 120mL/4oz Cocktail Glass

Mixers: 30mL/1fl oz white rum
30mL/1fl oz Advocaat
30mL/1fl oz Crème de Cacao

Method

Shake and strain into cocktail glass and serve. Garnish with grated coconut.

Electric Blue

Iceland

Ingredients

Glass: 300mL/10oz Hi-Ball Glass

Mixers: 15mL/½fl oz vodka
30mL/1fl oz dry vermouth
15mL/½fl oz Blue Curaçao
lemonade

Method

Pour vodka, vermouth and curaçao over ice in hi-ball glass. Top with lemonade and serve.

Esme's Peril

Cuba

Ingredients

Glass: Tankard
Mixers: 90mL/3fl oz Bacardi rum
60mL/2fl oz lemon juice
30mL/1fl oz dark rum
30mL/1fl oz orange juice
2 tablespoons banana liqueur
3 tablespoons cream
½ banana
2 teaspoon sugar
4 strawberries

Method
Blend all ingredients until smooth, pour into a tankard and serve.

Eton Blazer

United Kingdom

Ingredients

Glass: 300mL/10oz Hi-Ball Glass
Mixers: 30mL/1fl oz gin
15mL/½fl oz lemon juice
30mL/1fl oz kirsch
soda water
2 teaspoons sugar syrup
2 Maraschino cherries

Method
Place ingredients except soda and Cherries in hi-ball glass, top with soda, garnish with Maraschino cherries and serve.

Ireland

Evergreen

Ingredients
Glass: 90mL/3oz Cocktail Glas
Mixers: 15mL/½fl oz dry vermouth
30mL/1fl oz gin
15mL/½fl oz Midori
10mL/⅜fl oz Blue Curaçao

Method
Stir over ice and strain.
Garnish with red cherry on lip of glass.
Stir the first three ingredients of this pre dinner cocktail over ice and strain into cocktail glass. Then drop the Blue Curaçao creating a visible layer. A poignant tasting cocktail consumed in summer.

Fair Lady

United Kingdom

Ingredients

Glass: 150mL/5oz Cocktail Glass
Mixers: 60mL/1fl oz gin
270mL/9fl oz grapefruit juice
1 dash Cointreau
powdered sugar
1 egg white

Method
Rim two cocktail glass with egg white and sugar. Shake remaining ingredients and strain into glasses and serve.

Falcon's Delight

U.S.A.

Ingredients

Glass: Whiskey Shot
Mixers: 15mL/½fl oz Sambucca
15mL/½fl oz tequila
15mL/½fl oz Crème de Cacao

Method
Layer in shot glass and serve.

Fallen Angel

Australia

Ingredients
Glass: 300mL/10oz Hi-Ball Glass
Mixers: 20mL/⅝fl oz Advocaat
20mL/⅝fl oz cherry brandy
top-up with lemonade

Method
Build over ice and stir.
Garnish with a red cherry or strawberry.
Serve with straws.
Although requiring individual taste bud approval, ensure Advocaat and cherry brandy is mixed thoroughly before topping up with lemonade.
A "Ruptured Rooster" doesn't require the ingredients to be mixed.

Firemans Sour

U.S.A.

Ingredients

Glass: 210mL/7oz Old Fashioned
Mixers: 90mL/3fl oz white rum
1 teaspoon Grenadine
6 small lemon triangles
3 Maraschino cherries
15mL/½fl oz lemon juice
soda water

Method
Shake ice, rum, lemon juice and Grenadine. Strain into a tumble glass and add lemon triangles. Top with soda and serve.

Fizz

Cuba

Ingredients

Glass: 300mL/10oz Hi-Ball Glass
Mixers: 60mL/2fl oz Bacardi rum
soda water
60mL/2fl oz lemon juice
cracked ice

Method
Shake all ingredients except soda water and strain over ice in hi-ball glass. Top with soda water, add straws and serve.

Norway

Fjord

Ingredients
Glass: 120mL/4oz Cocktail Glass
Mixers: 30mL/1fl oz brandy
10mL/⅜fl oz Aquavit
10mL/⅜fl oz orange juice
10mL/⅜fl oz lime juice
5mL/⅛fl oz Grenadine

Method
Shake over ice and strain then add Grenadine. Garnish with an orange slice.

Italy

Flaming Sambucca

Ingredients

Glass: Cordial (Embassy)
Mixers: 30mL/1fl oz Sambucca
3 coffee beans

Method

Pour Sambucca, float coffee beans and light. Shoot after flame extinguished. Provides relief from the cold winter. The other way we do it is to pour Sambucca into a wine glass then light. Cup your hand entirely over the rim while it flames, creating suction. Shake the glass, place under your nose, take your hand from the glass to inhale the fumes, then shoot!

Flirt with Dirt

Monaco

Ingredients

Glass: 90mL/3oz Cocktail Glass
Mixers: 30mL/1fl oz Kahlúa
30mL/1fl oz Malibu
15mL/½fl oz Vandermint
1 float cream

Method

Shake Kahlúa, Vandermint and Malibu and strain into a 3 oz cocktail glass. Float cream and serve.

Flower

U.S.A.

Ingredients

Glass: 285mL/9½oz Hi-Ball Glass
Mixers: 30mL/1fl oz tequila
15mL/½fl oz mango liqueur
15mL/½fl oz white curaçao
75mL/2½fl oz orange juice

Method

Blend for two seconds, pour into a hi-ball glass over ice and serve.

Fluffy Duck No. 1

U.S.A.

Ingredients

Glass: 300mL/10oz Hi-Ball Glass
Mixers: 30mL/1fl oz rum
30mL/1fl oz Advocaat
top-up with lemonade
cream, floated

Method
Build over ice. Garnish with an orange slice and a red cherry. Serve with straws.
Most cocktail bars shake ingredients with cream before topping up with lemonade.
When using a post mix gun, squirt the lemonade directly into the middle of the liquid surface instead of spraying against the back of the glass. This gives a billowing cloud effect.

U.S.A.

Fluffy Duck No. 2

Ingredients
Glass: 140mL/5oz Champagne Saucer
Mixers: 30mL/1fl oz rum
30mL/1fl oz Advocaat
30mL/1fl oz orange juice
30mL/1fl oz cream

Method
Shake with ice and strain.
Garnish with an orange slice and a red cherry.
An after-dinner variation of the popular Fluffy Duck cocktail. A smoother and shorter drink.

Flying Carpet

Saudi Arabia

Ingredients

Glass: 90mL/3oz Cocktail Glass
Mixers: 30mL/1fl oz vodka
15mL/½fl oz banana liqueur
15mL/½fl oz Advocaat
30mL/1fl oz cream

Method

Shake and strain into cocktail glass and serve.

Flying High

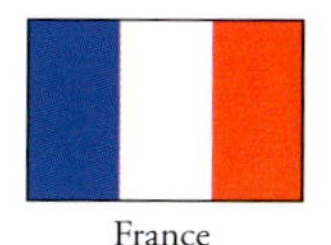

France

Ingredients

Glass: 90mL/3oz Cocktail Glass
Mixers: 30mL/1fl oz Baileys Irish Cream
15mL/½fl oz Drambuie
30mL/1fl oz Cointreau

Method

Shake and strain into cocktail glass and serve.

Netherlands

Flying Dutchman

Ingredients

Glass: 180mL/6oz Old Fashioned Spirit Glass
Mixers: 10mL/⅜fl oz Cointreau
30mL/1fl oz Gilbey's Gin

Method

Coat glass with Cointreau then pour Gilbey's Gin over ice. Garnish with a lemon twist.

Austria

Fog Cutter

Ingredients

Glass: 285mL/9½fl oz Hi-Ball Glass
Mixers: 15mL/½fl oz dark rum
10mL/⅜fl oz brandy
15mL/½fl oz Orgeat
30mL/1fl oz lemon juice
150mL/5fl oz orange juice

Method

Shake over ice and pour. Garnish with a strawberry.
Orgeat is an almond-flavored non-alcoholic syrup. Amaretto may be used as a substitute.

Forty Winks

New Zealand

Ingredients

Glass: Whiskey Prism Shot Glass
Mixers: 1 teaspoon honey
15mL/½fl oz peach liqueur
15mL/½fl oz orange curaçao
4-5 drops Grenadine

Method

Pour peach liqueur onto honey, layer orange curaçao, then drop Grenadine.

Forth of July

U.S.A.

Ingredients

Glass: 285mL/9½fl oz Hi-Ball Glass
Mixers: 30mL/1fl oz bourbon
orange juice
30mL/1fl oz Kahlúa
cream
Galleon Liverno

Method

Place bourbon and Kahlúa in hi-ball glass. Fill to 2.5cm/1 inch from top with orange juice and add cream. Float Galleon Liverno on top and serve.

401 Fraise Année

Luxembourg

Ingredients

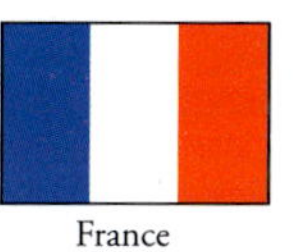

France

Glass: 120mL/4oz Cocktail Glass
Mixers: 30mL/1fl oz strawberry liqueur
45mL/1½fl oz cream
30mL/1fl oz white Crèam de Cacao
15mL/½fl oz brandy

Method

Blend ingredients and pour into a colada glass. Garnish with a strawberry and serve.

Ingredients

Glass: Cordial (Lexington)
Mixers: 10mL/⅜fl oz Kahlúa
5mL/⅛fl oz Baileys Irish Cream
10mL/⅜fl oz banana liqeur
5mL/⅛fl oz Cointreau

Method

Layer in order in shot glass and serve.

Franjelico Luau

Italy

Ingredients

Glass: 285mL/9½fl oz Hi-Ball Glass
Mixers: 45mL/1½fl oz Frangelico
210mL/7fl oz pineapple juice
dash of Grenadine

Method

Blend with ice and pour. Garnish with a pineapple slice and leaves.

Frappe

U.S.A.

Ingredients

Glass: 90mL/3oz Cocktail Glass
Mixers: quantity of preferred liqueur (e.g. green Crème de Menthe liqueur)

Method

Build over crushed ice. Two short straws.
Spoon the required quantity of crushed ice into the glass. Create spectacular rainbow effects with small quantities of liqueurs. Green Crème de Menthe is highly recommended because it acts as a breath freshener after dessert.

Frappe Byrrh

U.S.A.

Ingredients

Glass: 90mL/3oz Cocktail Glass
Mixers: 60mL/1fl oz Byrrh

Method

Fill cocktail glass with crushed ice and pour Byrrh over ice. Garnish with lemon twist and serve.

Crème de Menthe Frappe

U.S.A.

Ingredients

Glass: 90mL/3oz Cocktail Glass
Mixers: 60mL/1fl oz Crème de Menthe

Method
Fill cocktail glass with ice and pour Crème de Menthe over ice. Garnish with lemon and serve.

Grand Marnier Frappe

U.S.A.

Ingredients

Glass: 90mL/3oz Cocktail Glass
Mixers: 60mL/1fl oz Grand Marnier
grated chocolate

Method
Fill cocktail glass with cracked ice and pour Grand Marnier over top. Garnish with grated chocolate and serve.

Midori & Cointreau Frappe

U.S.A.

Ingredients

Glass: 150mL/5oz Cocktail Glass
Mixers: 15mL/½fl oz Midori
15mL/½fl oz Cointreau

Method
Fill cocktail glass with crushed ice. Build ingredients over ice, garnish with cherry, 2 short straws and serve.

Southern Peach Frappe

U.S.A.

Ingredients

Glass: 150mL/5oz Cocktail Glass
Mixers: 30mL/1fl oz strawberry liqueur
30mL/1fl oz Southern Comfort

Method
Build ingredients over crushed ice in cocktail glass and serve.

Freddy Fud Pucker

U.S.A.

Ingredients

Glass: 285mL/9½fl oz Hi-Ball Glass
Mixers: 30mL/1fl oz tequila
120mL/4fl oz orange juice
15mL/½fl oz Galliano, floated

Method

Build over ice. Garnish with an orange slice and a cherry. Serve with straws.

French 69

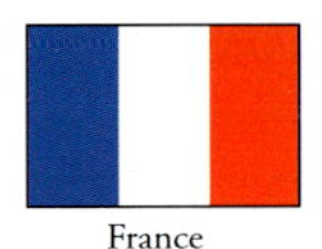
France

Ingredients

Glass: 140mL/5oz Champagne Flute
Mixers: 15mL/½fl oz gin
5mL/⅙fl oz lemon juice
10mL/⅜fl oz Pernod
5mL/⅙fl oz sugar syrup
Champagne

Method

Pour ingredients into champagne glass, top with champagne and serve.

French 75

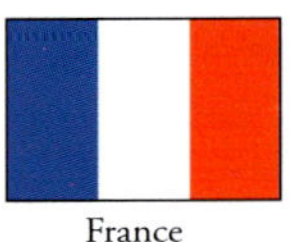
France

Ingredients

Glass: 300mL/10oz Hi-Ball Glass
Mixers: 45mL/1½fl oz gin
juice ½ lemon
90mL/3fl oz Champagne
1 teaspoon powered sugar

Method

Combine gin, sugar, lemon juice and ice in a mixing glass. Strain into a hi-ball glass and fill with champagne. Garnish with lemon peel and serve.

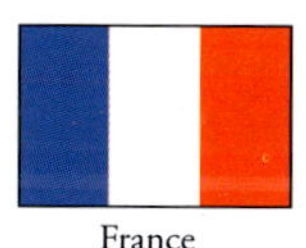

France

French Connection

Ingredients

Glass: Brandy Balloon

Mixers: 30mL/1fl oz cognac
30mL/1fl oz Amaretto

Method

Pour over ice.

French Fantasy

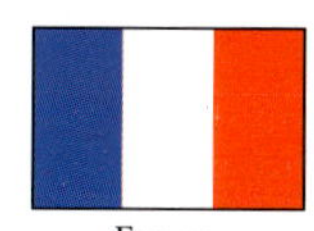

France

Ingredients

Glass: 150mL/5oz Cocktail Glass

Mixers: 30mL/1fl oz vodka
30mL/1fl oz Crème de Grand Marnier
15mL/½fl oz Tia Maria
30mL/1fl oz orange juice
30mL/1fl oz pineapple juice

Method

Blend and pour into cocktail glass, garnish with a slice of banana and a Maraschino cherry and serve.

French Greenery

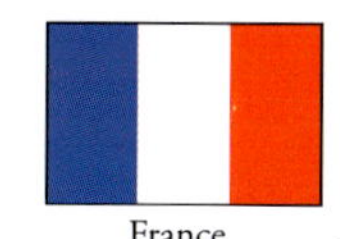

France

Ingredients

Glass: 210mL/7oz Old Fashioned Glass

Mixers: 30mL/1fl oz Pernod
30mL/1fl oz Crème de Menthe

Method

Pour ingredients over ice in an old fashioned glass. Garnish with the sprig of mint and serve.

French Safari

France

Ingredients

Glass: 90mL/3oz Cocktail Glass
Mixers: 30mL/1fl oz Rubis
15mL/½fl oz Afrikoko
15mL/½fl oz Cointreau
30mL/1fl oz cream

Method
Shake and strain into cocktail glass and serve.

Froth & Bubble

Australia

Ingredients

Glass: 150mL/5oz Cocktail Glass
Mixers: 60mL/2fl oz vodka
15mL/½fl oz orange juice
15mL/½fl oz Blue Curaçao
½ egg white
15mL/½fl oz Galleon Liverno

Method
Shake and strain into cocktail glass, garnish with Maraschino cherry and serve.

Frisco Sour

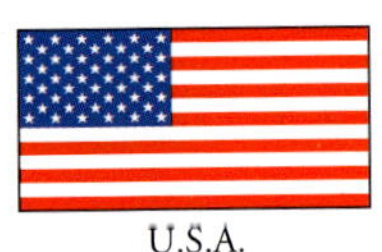
U.S.A.

Ingredients
Glass: 140mL/5oz Champane Saucer
Mixers: 60mL/2fl oz Scotch whisky
10mL/⅜fl oz lemon juice
10mL/⅜fl oz lime juice
10mL/⅜fl oz Grenadine
top up with soda

Method
Shake with ice and pour, then top up with soda. Garnish with a lime slice.

Norway

Frozen Aquavit

Ingredients

Glass: 140mL/5oz Cocktail Glass

Mixers: 45mL/1½fl oz Aquavit
10mL/⅜fl oz Kirsch
10mL/⅜fl oz lime juice
10mL/⅜fl oz sugar syrup
10mL/⅜fl oz egg white

Method

Blend over ice and pour. Garnish with one cocktail onion.

Frozen Guava Daiquiri

Fiji

Ingredients

Glass: 140mL/5oz Champagne Saucer

Mixers: 30mL/1fl oz Bacardi
30mL/1fl oz guava nectar
15mL/½fl oz lime juice
10mL/⅜fl oz banana liqueur
10mL/⅜fl oz sugar syrup

Method

Blend with ice and pour. Garnish with a red cherry.

Frozen Leango

Singapore

Ingredients

Glass: 360mL/12oz Tulip Glass

Mixers: 30mL/1fl oz gin
60mL/2fl oz orange juice
30mL/1fl oz banana liqueur
2 scoops ice
30mL/1fl oz mango liqueur

Method

Blend and pour into tulip glass and serve with straws.

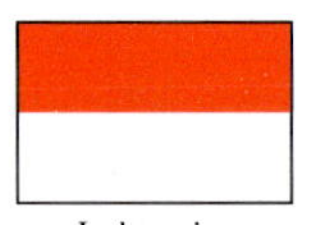
Indonesia

Frozen Mudslide

Ingredients

Glass: 290mL/10oz Poco Grande Glass

Mixers: 30mL/1fl oz vodka
20mL/⅝fl oz Baileys Irish Cream
20mL/⅝fl oz Kahlúa
top up with milk
whipped cream
hundreds and thousands
thickened chocolate

Method

Blend with ice, pour into glass. Top up with milk then add whipped cream in a swirling motion. With a teaspoon slide the thickened chocolate, thereby creating a Mud Slide. Place strawberry on side of glass with hundreds and thousands.

Fruit Passion

U.S.A.

Ingredients

Glass: 300mL/10oz Hi-Ball Glass

Mixers: 30mL/1fl oz vodka
15mL/½fl oz passionfruit pulp
30mL/1fl oz rum
pineapple juice

Method

One third fill hi-ball glass with cracked ice, add vodka, rum and passionfruit pulp. Stir and top with pineapple juice, garnish with a pineapple wedge, straws and serve.

Fruit Salad

Spain

Ingredients

Glass: Cordial (Lexington)

Mixers: 10mL/⅓fl oz banana liqueur
10mL/⅓fl oz strawberry liqueur
10mL/⅓fl oz Malibu
½ teaspoon vanilla ice-cream

Method

Layer in order, then float vanilla ice cream.

Galliano Hot Shot

Italy

Ingredients

Glass: Whiskey Shot
Mixers: 15mL/½fl oz Galleon Liverno
5mL/⅛fl oz cream (float)
25mL/⅞fl oz hot black coffee

Method
Top Galliano with black coffee in shot glass. Float cream and serve.

Garden City

India

Ingredients

Glass: 150mL/5oz Cocktail Glass
Mixers: 60mL/2fl oz brandy
30mL/1fl oz orange juice
30mL/1fl oz sweet vermouth
15mL/½fl oz Pernod

Method
Shake and strain into cocktail glass, garnish with Maraschino cherry and serve.

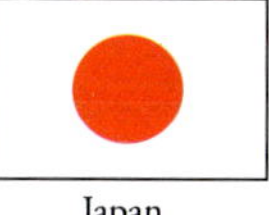
Japan

Geisha

Ingredients
Glass: 135mL/4½oz Tulip Champagne Glass
Mixers: 30mL/1fl oz Bourbon
30mL/1fl oz sake
10mL/⅜fl oz lemon juice
10mL/⅜fl oz sugar syrup

Method
Shake over ice and strain. Garnish with a red cherry.

Geisha Delight

Ingredients

Japan

Glass: 140mL/5oz Tulip Champagne Glass

Mixers: 30mL/1fl oz Midori
5mL/⅛fl oz coconut rum
15mL/½fl oz Galliano
60mL/2fl oz pineapple juice
15mL/½fl oz Cointreau

Method

Shake over ice and strain. Garnish with a red cherry.

Genoa

Ingredients

Italy

Glass: 200mL/7oz Gilbraltar Hi-Ball Glass

Mixers: 30mL/1fl oz sugar syrup
30mL/1fl oz Bacardi
30mL/1fl oz lemon juice

Method

Shake over ice and strain then add ice. Garnish with olives.

Georgia Peach

U.S.A.

Ingredients

Glass: 285mL/9½oz Hi-Ball Glass

Mixers: 30mL/1fl oz Bacardi
30mL/1fl oz peach liqueur
90mL/3fl oz cranberry juice

Method

Build over ice and pour. Garnish with a peach slice.

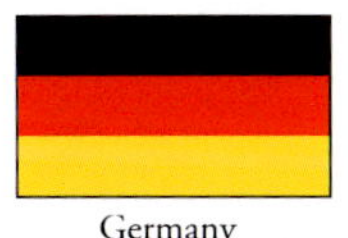

Germany

German Chocolate Cake

Ingredients

Glass: 285mL/9½oz Hurricane Glass

Mixers: 30mL/1fl oz Kahlúa
30mL/1fl oz Malibu
30mL/1fl oz chocolate syrup
2 chopped pecan nuts
2 scoops vanilla ice cream

Method

Blend without ice and pour over crushed ice. Garnish with shredded pecans. More like a meal than a cocktail! From a country where eating and drinking are national pastimes, the Germans have created this delicious multi gastronomic after dinner delight.

Get Going

United Kingdom

Ingredients

Glass: 285mL/9½fl oz Hi-Ball Glass

Mixers: 45mL/1½fl oz gin
30mL/1fl oz lemon juice
1 dash sugar syrup
1 dash Grenadine
lemonade

Method

Half fill hi-ball glass with cracked ice. Add ingredients, top with lemonade, add straws and serve.

Ghetto Blaster

U.S.A.

Ingredients

Glass: Tall Dutch Cordial

Mixers: 10mL/⅜fl oz Kahlúa
10mL/⅜fl oz rye whiskey
25mL/⅞fl oz tequila

Method

Layer in a shot glass and serve.

Gibson

United Kingdom

Ingredients

Glass: 120mL/4oz Cocktail Glass
Mixers: 60mL/2fl oz gin
10mL/⅜fl oz dry vermouth

Method

Shake over ice and strain. Garnish with one cocktail onion.

Gigolo's Delight

United Kingdom

Ingredients

Glass: 210mL/7oz Old Fashioned
Mixers: 30mL/1fl oz gin
60mL/2fl oz sweet vermouth
30mL/1fl oz orange juice

Method

Shake and strain over ice in a rocks glass. Garnish with 2 strips orange peel, Maraschino cherry and serve.

Gilroy

Switzerland

Ingredients

Glass: 90mL/3oz Cocktail Glass
Mixers: 15mL/½fl oz cherry brandy
10mL/⅜fl oz lemon juice
15mL/½fl oz gin
1 dash orange bitters
10mL/⅜fl oz sweet vermouth

Method

Shake and strain into cocktail glass and serve.

United Kingdom

Gimlet

Ingredients

Glass: 175mL/6oz Prism Rocks Glass

Mixers: 60mL/2fl oz gin
30mL/1fl oz lime juice

Method

Shake over ice and pour then add cubed ice. Garnish with two cocktail onions on toothpicks sunk in glass.

Gin and It

United Kingdom

Ingredients

Glass: 90mL/3oz Cocktail Glass

Mixers: 30mL/1fl oz sweet vermouth
45mL/1½fl oz gin

Method

Shake and strain into cocktail glass and serve.

Gin and Sin

U.S.A.

Ingredients

Glass: 210mL/7oz Old Fashioned Glass

Mixers: 60mL/2fl oz gin
soda water
30mL/1fl oz lime juice

Method

Shake ingredients except soda water and strain into an old fashioned glass. Top with soda water and serve.

Gin Twist

France

Ingredients

Glass: 140mL/5oz Cocktail Glass
Mixers: 30mL/1fl oz gin
1 dash orange bitters
30mL/1fl oz Dubonnet
10mL/⅜fl oz Pernod

Method
Shake and strain into cocktail glass.
Garnish with slice of orange and serve.

Ginger Sin

Lebanon

Ingredients

Glass: 300mL/10oz Hi-Ball Glass
Mixers: 30mL/1fl oz gin
30mL/1fl oz lime juice
ginger beer

Method
Stir ingredients and strain into a hi-ball glass. Top with ginger beer and serve.

Australia

Ginger Mick

Ingredients
Glass: 285mL/9½oz Footed Hi-Ball Glass
Mixers: 120mL/4fl oz dry ginger ale
15mL/½fl oz lime juice
30mL/1fl oz Claytons Tonic
30mL/1fl oz lemon juice
60mL/2fl oz apple juice

Method
Blend with ice and pour.
Garnish with two banana wheel slices wedged on rim of glass.

Girl Talk

U.S.A.

Ingredients

Glass: 140mL/5oz Cocktail Glass
Mixers: 45mL/1½fl oz white rum
1 dash Angostura bitter
15mL/½fl oz sweet vermouth
15mL/½fl oz orange juice
15mL/½fl oz dry vermouth

Method

Half fill mixing glass with cracked ice. Add ingredients and stir. Strain into a cocktail glass. Garnish with cherry and serve.

Globe Gladness

Austria

Ingredients

Glass: 300mL/10oz Hi-Ball Glass
Mixers: 30mL/1fl oz Grand Marnier
1 dash Galleon Liverno
15mL/½fl oz schnapps
lemonade
15mL/½fl oz Tia Maria

Method

Shake Grand Marnier, Tia Maria and schnapps. Strain into a hi-ball glass. Top with lemonade. Float Galleon Liverno and serve.

Glasgow

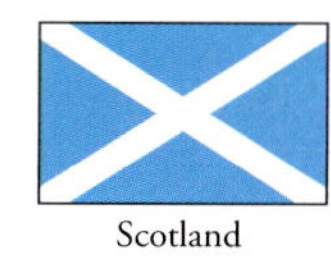
Scotland

Ingredients

Glass: 150mL/5oz Old Fashioned Spirit Glass
Mixers: 30mL/1fl oz Scotch whisky
10mL lemon juice
5mL/⅛fl oz dry vermouth
5mL/⅛fl oz almond extract

Method

Shake over ice and pour then add cubed ice. Garnish with shredded almonds and a dried flower.

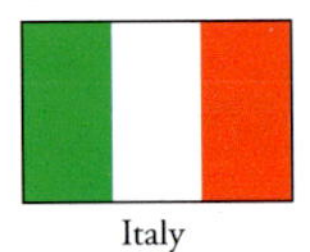

Italy

Godfather

Ingredients

Glass:	185mL/6oz Old Fashioned Spirit Glass
Mixers:	30mL/1fl oz Scotch whisky 30mL/1fl oz Amaretto

Method

Build over ice. To be drunk as either a pre dinner drink or a night-cap. The guiding hand of Amaretto tempers the boldness of the Scotch.

Goddaughter

Italy

Ingredients

Glass:	140mL/5oz Champagne Saucer
Mixers:	30mL/1fl oz Sambucca 30mL/1fl oz cream 30mL/1fl oz Amaretto 5mL/⅛fl oz Grenadine

Method

Shake ingredients and strain into a champagne saucer. Garnish with chocolate, strawberry and a sprig of mint.

Godmother

Italy

Ingredients

Glass:	185mL/6oz Old Fashioned Glass
Mixers:	45mL/1½fl oz vodka 20mL/⅝fl oz Amaretto

Method

Build into a old fashioned glass filled with ice and serve.

Gold Passion

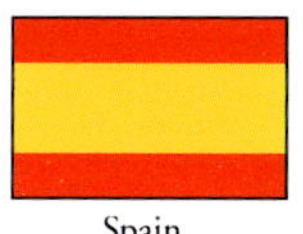
Spain

Ingredients

Glass: 185mL/6oz Old Fashioned
Mixers: 30mL/1fl oz Bacardi rum
chilled pineapple juice
30mL/1fl oz vodka
30mL/1fl oz passionfruit

Method
Pour ingredients over ice in an old fashioned glass and top with pineapple juice. Garnish with a slice of pineapple, pineapple leaves, cherry and serve.

Golden

Cuba

Ingredients

Glass: 300mL/10oz Hi-Ball Glass
Mixers: 60mL/2fl oz Bacardi rum
1 egg yolk
1 teaspoon sugar
60mL/2fl oz lemon juice
soda water

Method
Shake ingredients except soda water and strain over ice in hi-ball glass. Top with soda water, add straws and serve.

U.S.A.

Golden Cadillac

Ingredients
Glass: 140mL/5oz Cocktail Glass
Mixers: 30mL/1fl oz Galliano
30mL/1fl oz white Crème de Cacao
30mL/1fl oz cream

Method
Shake with ice and strain.
Garnish with red cherry or strawberry.

Golden Dream

U.S.A.

Ingredients

Glass: 140mL/5oz Cocktail Glass
Mixers: 20mL/⅝fl oz Galliano
20mL/⅝fl oz Cointreau
20mL/⅝fl oz orange juice
20mL/⅝fl oz cream

Method

Shake with ice and strain.
Garnish with a red cherry on a toothpick on side of glass.
Chilled orange juice tarts the Galliano and freezes the Cointreau leaving a creamy, tangy lining from your throat to your toes. Cointreau may be replaced with triple sec.

Golden Dream No. 2

U.S.A.

Ingredients

Glass: 150mL/5fl oz Cocktail Glass
Mixers: 30mL/1fl oz brandy
15mL/½fl oz lemon juice
30mL/1fl oz Grand Marnier
60mL/2fl oz orange juice

Method

Shake and strain into cocktail glass and serve.

Golden Dragon

China

Ingredients

Glass: 90mL/3fl oz Cocktail Glass
Mixers: 30mL/1fl oz Galliano
20mL/⅝fl oz white curaçao
20mL/⅝fl oz cream
1 dash egg white

Method

Shake and strain into a cocktail glass and serve.

Golden Orchid

Ingredients

China

Glass: 150mL/5fl oz Cocktail Glass
Mixers: 30mL/1fl oz Scotch whiskey
15mL/½fl oz Maraschino
30mL/1fl oz Advocaat

Method
Shake and strain into cocktail glass and serve.

Golden Shot

Ingredients

Chile

Glass: 185mL/6oz Old Fashioned
Mixers: 30mL/1fl oz Scotch whiskey
90mL/3fl oz orange juice
1 egg yolk

Method
Blend and pour into a rocks glass and serve.

Golden Slipper

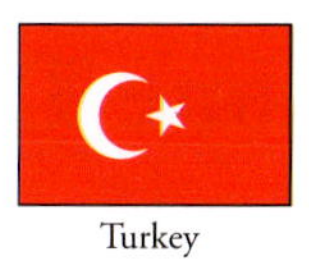

Turkey

Ingredients
Glass: 90mL/3oz Cocktail Glass
Mixers: 30mL/1fl oz yellow Chartreuse
10mL/⅜fl oz apricot brandy
1 egg yolk

Method
Shake over ice and strain.

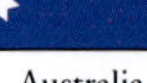
Australia

Gomango

Ingredients

Glass: 440mL/14oz Hurricane Glass
Mixers: 15mL/½fl oz triple sec
15mL/½fl oz white Crème de Cacao
15mL/½fl oz cherry Advocaat
15mL/½fl oz orange juice
15mL/½fl oz cream
1 cheek of fresh mango

Method

Blend with ice.
Butterfly strawberry on side of glass for garnish.

Gone Troppo

Ingredients

Samoa

Glass: 180mL/6oz Tulip Glass
Mixers: 45mL/1½fl oz peach liqueur
3 strawberries
30mL/1fl oz banana liqueur
1 scoop ice
30mL/1fl oz pineapple juice
2 pineapple leaves

Method

Blend ingredients except pineapple juice and pour into tulip glass. Float pineapple juice on top. Garnish with a pineapple wedge, cherry and two pineapple leaves and serve.

Grand Baileys

Ingredients

United Kingdom

Glass: Cordial (Embassy)
Mixers: 20mL/⅝fl oz Baileys Irish Cream
10mL/⅜fl oz Grand Marnier

Method

Layer in a shot glass and serve.

U.S.A.

Grasshopper

Ingredients

Glass: 140mL/5oz Champagne Saucer

Mixers: 30mL/1fl oz Crème de Menthe
30mL/1fl oz white Crème de Cacao
30mL/1fl oz cream

Method

Shake with ice and strain.
Garnish with 2 red cherries slit on the side of the glass.
Jump right into this very popular after dinner cocktails. Some people prefer dark Crème de Cacao instead of white Crème de Cacao. Shake until smooth.

Gravedigger

France

Ingredients

Glass: 150mL/5oz Champagne Saucer

Mixers: 45mL/1½fl oz dry vermouth
1 dash Angostura bitter
20mL/⅝fl oz brandy
45mL/1½fl oz orange juice
20mL/⅝fl oz Cointreau

Method

Shake and strain into a cocktail glass and serve.

Great White North

Philippines

Ingredients

Glass: Tall Dutch Cordial

Mixers: 15mL/½fl oz Kahlúa
15mL/½fl oz ouzo
15mL/½fl oz Baileys Irish Cream

Method

Layer in order in a shot glass and serve.

Greek Buck

Greece

Ingredients

Glass: 285mL/9½oz Tall Wine Glass
Mixers: 30mL/1fl oz brandy
10mL/⅜fl oz lemon juice
top up with ginger ale
10mL/⅜fl oz ouzo

Method
Shake brandy with lemon juice and top up with ginger ale then float ouzo. Garnish with a lemon slice.

Greece

Greek God

Ingredients
Glass: Whisky Shot
Mixers: 15mL/½fl oz ouzo
15mL/½fl oz Pernod

Method
Pour in order then shoot.

U.S.A.

Green Back

Ingredients

Glass: 90mL/3oz Cocktail Glass
Mixers: 30mL/1fl oz gin
10mL/⅜fl oz lime juice
10mL/⅜fl oz green Crème de Menthe

Method

Stir over ice and pour. Garnish with a lime slice (optional).

Green

Saudi Arabia

Ingredients

Glass: 300mL/10oz High-Ball Glass
Mixers: 15mL/½fl oz Crème de Menthe
30mL/1fl oz lemon juice
60mL/2fl oz gin
1 egg white
10mL/⅜fl oz sugar syrup
soda water

Method

Shake all ingredients except soda water and strain over ice in hi-ball glass. Top with soda water, add straws and serve.

Green Devil

Germany

Ingredients

Glass: 120mL/4oz Cocktail Glass
Mixers: 45mL/1½fl oz vodka
45mL/1½fl oz Crème de Menthe
30mL/1fl oz lemon juice

Method

Mix and strain into a cocktail glass, garnish with lemon peel and serve.

Green Eyes

Maldives

Ingredients

Glass: 300mL/10oz Hi-Ball Glass
Mixers: 30mL/1fl oz Midori
15mL/½fl oz coconut milk
30mL/1fl oz dark rum
15mL/½fl oz lime juice
45mL/1½fl oz pineapple juice

Method

Blend ingredients and pour into a hi-ball glass. Garnish with pineapple wedge, straws and serve.

Green Paradise

Bermuda

Ingredients

Glass: 150mL/5oz Cocktail Glass
Mixers: 45mL/1½fl oz Midori
15mL/½fl oz orange juice
20mL/⅝fl oz Cointreau
15mL/½fl oz pineapple juice
10mL/⅜fl oz lemon juice
1 scoop crushed ice
Grenadine

Method

Blend all ingredients except Grenadine until frozen. Place a dash of Grenadine in the bottom of cocktail glass. Pour in frozen ingredients and serve.

Green Slime

Greenland

Ingredients

Glass: Whiskey Shot
Mixers: 20mL/⅝fl oz melon liqueur
15mL/½fl oz vodka
5mL/⅛fl oz egg white

Method

Pour in order, then stir.
Add more egg white for greater slime.
Melon will keep the taste buds occupied, vodka dilutes the egg white.

Zimbabwe

Green With Envy

Ingredients

Glass: 210mL/7oz Hurricane Glass
Mixers: 30mL/1fl oz ouzo
30mL/1fl oz Blue Curaçao
120mL/4fl oz pineapple juice

Method

Shake with ice and pour.
Garnish with pineapple spear with leaves and cherry. Serve with straws.
An afternoon cocktail. The aniseed in ouzo chills the pungent pineapple juice. As they say... "Jealousy's a curse, Envy is worse."

Green Slammer

Canada

Ingredients

Ingredients

Glass: 150mL/5oz Cocktail Glass
Mixers: 45mL/1½fl oz vodka
30mL/1fl oz lemon juice
30mL/1fl oz Midori
15mL/½fl oz Galliano

Method

Shake and strain into cocktail glass, garnish with a lemon wheel and serve.

Greenhorn

South Africa

Ingredients

Glass: 300mL/10oz Hi-Ball Glass
Mixers: 60mL/1 oz Crème de Menthe
soda water
20mL/⅝fl oz lemon juice

Method

Shake all ingredients except soda water over ice into hi-ball glass. Top with soda water, add straws and serve.

Greenpeace Sorbet

New Zealand

Ingredients

Glass:	150mL/5oz Cocktail Glass
Mixers:	30mL/1fl oz Cointreau 1 kiwifruit (peeled) 60mL/2fl oz white wine 2 scoops crushed ice

Method
Blend until smooth and pour into a 5 oz cocktail glass and serve.

Gringo

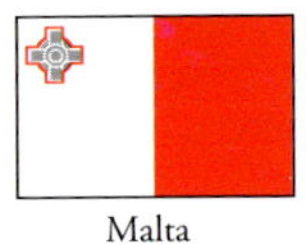
Malta

Ingredients

Glass:	150mL/5oz Cocktail Glass
Mixers:	30mL/1fl oz tequila 30mL/1fl oz vodka 30mL/1fl oz Midori 10mL/⅜fl oz lemon juice

Method
Shake and strain into cocktail glass and serve.

India

Gypsy King

Ingredients

Glass:	Cordial (Lexington)
Mixers:	5mL/⅛fl oz lime cordial 10mL/⅜fl oz Parfait Amour 10mL/⅜fl oz green Crème de Menthe 10mL/⅜fl oz yellow Chartreuse

Method
Pour in order, then layer yellow Chartreuse.

Hair of the Dog

Scotland

Ingredients

Glass: 185mL/6oz Old Fashioned
Mixers: 30mL/1fl oz Scotch whiskey
30mL/1fl oz honey
60mL/2fl oz cream
ice

Method
Fill an old fashioned glass with ice, shake other ingredients and strain over ice and serve.

Hairless Duck

United Kingdom

Ingredients

Glass: 300mL/10oz Hi-Ball Glass
Mixers: 30mL/1fl oz Advocaat
15mL/½fl oz Bacardi rum
30mL/1fl oz vodka
orange juice

Method
Shake Advocaat, vodka and rum together and strain over ice in a hi-ball glass. Top with orange juice, add straws and serve.

United Kingdom

Half Nelson

Ingredients
Glass: Whiskey Shot
Mixers: 15mL/½fl oz Crème de Menthe
10mL/⅜fl oz strawberry liqueur
20mL/⅝fl oz Grand Marnier

Method
Layer in order, shoot.

Halo

Switzerland

Ingredients

Glass: 150mL/5oz Tumbler
Mixers: 30mL/1fl oz Sambucca
lemonade
30mL/1fl oz gin

Method
Place Sambucca and gin in tumbler. Slowly top with lemonade and serve.

Harbour Mist

Singapore

Ingredients

Glass: 150mL/5oz Cocktail Glass
Mixers: 30mL/1fl oz banana liqueur
15mL/½fl oz Blue Curaçao
20mL/⅝fl oz Grand Marnier
30mL/1fl oz cream

Method
Shake and strain into cocktail glass and serve.

Harbour Lights

U.S.A.

Ingredients
Glass: Cordial (Lexington)
Mixers: 10mL/⅜fl oz Kahlúa
10mL/⅜fl oz Sambucca
10mL/⅜fl oz green Chartreuse

Method
Layer in order.

Australia

Hard On

Ingredients

Glass: Cordial (Lexington)
Mixers: 20mL/⅝fl oz Crème de Cafe
15mL/½fl oz banana liqueur
10mL/⅜fl oz cream

Method

Layer in order, shoot.

Hard On (Bloody)

Australia

Ingredients

Glass: 90mL/3oz Cocktail Glass
Mixers: 30mL/1fl oz Kahlua
30mL/1fl oz strawberry liqueur
30mL/1fl oz Baileys Irish Cream

Method

Layer ingredients in cocktail glass then serve.

Hard On (Black)

Australia

Ingredients

Glass: 90mL/3oz Cocktail Glass
Mixers: 30mL/1fl oz black Sambucca
30mL/1fl oz banana liqueur
30mL/1fl oz Baileys Irish Cream

Method

Layer ingredients in cocktail glass then serve.

U.S.A.

Harvey Wallbanger

Ingredients

Glass: 285mL/9oz Hi-Ball Glass
Mixers: 40mL/1⅜fl oz vodka
125mL/4fl oz Orange juice
15mL/½fl oz Galliano, floated

Method

Build over ice. Garnish with orange slice and cherry.
The local Hawaiian bartenders will tell you a visiting Irishman called Harvey pin-balled down the corridor to hotel room after a night out. Hence, he was known a "Harvey Wallbanger."

Harlequin

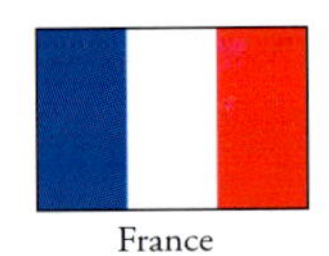
France

Ingredients

Glass: 150mL/5oz Cocktail Glass
Mixers: 30mL/1fl oz cognac
15mL/½fl oz Grand Marnier

Method

Frost the cocktail glass with harlequin frosting - coffee and sugar combined. Stir and strain liquid ingredients into glass and serve.

Havana Club

Cuba

Ingredients

Glass: 90mL/3oz Cocktail Glass
Mixers: 40mL/1⅜fl oz Bacardi rum
20mL/⅝fl oz sweet vermouth

Method

Shake and strain into a 3 oz cocktail glass and serve. Garnish with a Maraschino cherry.

U.S.A.

Hawaiian Punch

Ingredients

Glass: 285mL/9½oz Hi-Ball Glass

Mixers: 20mL/⅝fl oz Southern Comfort
20mL/⅝fl oz Amaretto
15mL/½fl oz vodka
40mL/1⅜fl oz pineapple juice
40mL/1⅜fl oz orange juice
20mL/⅝fl oz lime juice
20mL/⅝fl oz Grenadine

Method

Shake over ice and pour then add Grenadine. Garnish with orange slice and a red cherry.

Hazy Cuban

Cuba

Ingredients

Glass: 210mL/7oz Old Fashioned

Mixers: 30mL/1fl oz Bacardi rum
30mL/1fl oz coconut cream
30mL/1fl oz milk
60mL/2fl oz pineapple juice

Method

Blend and pour into an old fashioned glass and serve. Garnish with 1 slice pineapple

Head Stud

Zimbabwe

Ingredients

Glass: 150mL/5oz Cocktail Glass

Mixers: 30mL/1fl oz Galliano
30mL/1fl oz Afrikoko
60mL/2fl oz cream

Method

Layer in cocktail glass and serve.

Health Farm

Morocco

Ingredients

Glass: 270mL/9oz Hi-Ball Glass
Mixers: 90mL/3fl oz pineapple juice
2 slices cantaloupe melon
90mL/3fl oz orange juice
2 teaspoons honey
½ ripe banana

Method

Blend with ice and pour.
Garnish with cantaloupe wedge and swizzle stick.
A great drink for the health conscious.

Heartbraker

Ingredients

Canada

Glass: 24mL/8oz Colada Glass
Mixers: 30mL/1fl oz strawberry liqueur
60mL/2fl oz cream
15mL/½fl oz Tia Maria
4 strawberries
15mL/½fl oz Cointreau

Method

Blend until smooth and pour into a colada glass and serve.

Helen's Hangover

Ingredients

Ireland

Glass: 140mL Champagne Saucer
Mixers: 30mL/1fl oz Advocaat
pineapple juice
30mL/1fl oz Galliano

Method

Pour Advocaat and Galliano over ice in hi-ball glass. Top with orange juice, add straws and serve.

Egypt

Hellraiser

Ingredients

Glass: Whisky Shot

Mixers: 15mL/½fl oz melon liqueur
15mL/½fl oz strawberry liqueur
15mL/½fl oz black Sambucca

Method

Layer in order, shoot.

Hemmingway

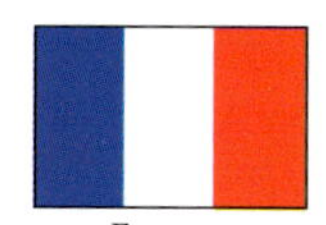

France

Ingredients

Glass: 150mL/5oz Champagne Saucer

Mixers: 40mL/1⅜fl oz Cointreau
40mL/1⅜fl oz grapefruit juice
40mL/1⅜fl oz Bacardi rum
sparkling white wine

Method

Shake all ingredients except white wine, strain into a champagne saucer. Top with sparkling white wine and serve.

Highland Flying

Scotland

Ingredients

Glass: 300mL/10oz Hi-Ball Glass

Mixers: 30mL/1fl oz Scotch whiskey
30mL/1fl oz orange juice
30mL/1fl oz Kahlúa
30mL/1fl oz cream

Method

Blend until smooth, pour over ice in hi-ball glass. Add straws and serve.

Honey Bee

France

Ingredients

Glass: 150mL/5oz Cocktail Glass
Mixers: 30mL/1fl oz brandy
15mL/½fl oz honey
15mL/½fl oz Galliano
60mL/2fl oz cream
15mL/½fl oz Grenadine

Method
Shake and strain into cocktail glass and serve.

Honeyed Nuts

Australia

Ingredients

Glass: Brandy Balloon
Mixers: 30mL/1fl oz Frangelico
30mL/1fl oz honey
15mL/½fl oz Kahlúa
120mL/4fl oz cream
15mL/½fl oz Advocaat

Method
Blend ingredients and pour into a brandy balloon rimmed with crushed hazelnuts and honey and serve.

Honey Tea

Scotland

Ingredients
Glass: 250mL/8oz Irish Coffee Mug, preheated
Mixers: 1 orange spice tea bag
30mL/1fl oz Drambuie
top up with hot water

Method
Pour in order then top up with hot water. Garnish with a lemon twist.

Horangi

South Korea

Ingredients

Glass: 140mL/5oz Champagne Saucer
Mixers: 45mL/1½fl oz vodka
30mL/1fl oz passionfruit juice
30mL/1fl oz Advocaat

Method

Shake and strain into a champagne saucer and serve.

Horse Guards

United Kingdom

Ingredients

Glass: 180mL/6oz Tumbler
Mixers: 20mL/⅝fl oz rum
1 egg yolk
20mL/⅝fl oz Cointreau
sparkling white wine

Method

Shake ingredients except wine and lemon peel. Strain into tumbler glass, top with wine and garnish with lemon peel and serve.

Hot Buttered Rum

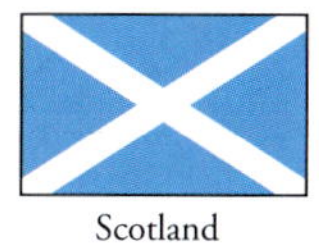

Scotland

Ingredients

Glass: 250mL/8oz Irish Coffee Mug, preheated
Mixers: 60mL/2fl oz rum
1 lemon slice
1 cinnamon stick
1 clove
top up with warm apple cider

Method

Build and top up with warm apple cider. Garnish with a teaspoon of sweet butter and nutmeg.

Hot Danish Cider

Denmark

Ingredients

Glass: 250mL/8oz Irish Coffee Mug, preheated

Mixers: 180mL/6fl oz apple cider, heated
15mL/½fl oz Orgeat

Method

Build. Garnish with a cinnamon stick. Orgeat is an almond-flavored non-alcoholic syrup. Amaretto may be used as a substitute.

Greenland

Hot Milk Punch

Ingredients

Glass: 250mL/8oz Irish Coffee Mug, preheated

Mixers: 30mL/1fl oz Bacardi
30mL/1fl oz brandy
sugar to taste
top up with hot milk

Method

Build and top up with hot milk. Garnish with sprinkle of cinnamon stick.

Hot Whiskey Toddy

Ingredients

Glass:	250mL/8oz Irish Coffee Mug, preheated
Mixers:	30mL/1fl oz Irish Whiskey sugar to taste top up with boiling water

Method
Build and top up with boiling water then stir. Garnish with a lemon slice studded with cloves and nutmeg.

Hurricane

U.S.A.

Glass:	210mL/7oz Hurricane Glass
Mixers:	30mL/1fl oz Bacardi 30mL/1fl oz Passoa 15mL/½fl oz lime cordial 45mL/1½fl oz lemon juice 45mL/1½fl oz sugar syrup top with 15mL/½fl oz Bacardi Gold

Method
Shake with ice and pour.
Garnish with orange slice and cherry.
Serve with straws.

I Love You

Iceland

Ingredients

Glass: 90mL/3oz Cocktail Glass
Mixers: 30mL/1fl oz Kahlúa
30mL/1fl oz Galliano
30mL/1fl oz Baileys Irish Cream

Method
Float ingredients in cocktail glass and serve.

Ice Wings

U.S.A.

Ingredients

Glass: 120mL/4oz Cocktail Glass
Mixers: 75mL/2½ vodka
30mL/1fl oz white Crème de Menthe

Method
Shake and strain into a cocktail glass and serve.

Ice Kachany

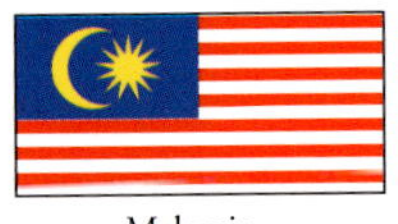

Malaysia

Ingredients
Glass: 350mL/12oz Gilbraltar Cooler Glass
Mixers: 30mL/1fl oz vodka
15mL/½fl oz peach liqueur
30mL/1fl oz cranberry juice
30mL/1fl oz orange juice
top up with lemonade
diced fruit pieces

Method
Mix ingredients and pour over crushed ice. Serve with two straws and a long spoon. Known as a dessert delight from the old Portuguese trading port of Malacca, East Malaysia, this cocktail will add another dimension to how you can consume alcohol.

Ichigo

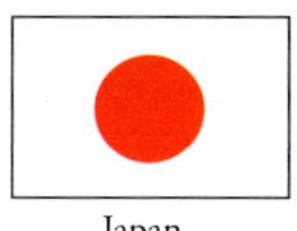

Japan

Ingredients

Glass: 90mL/3oz Cocktail Glass

Mixers: 30mL/1fl oz strawberry liqueur
20mL/⅝fl oz pineapple juice
15mL/½fl oz Galliano
20mL/⅝fl oz orange juice

Method

Shake and strain into a cocktail glass and serve.

Illusion

Australia

Ingredients

Glass: 150mL/5oz Cocktail Glass

Mixers: 45mL/1½fl oz vodka
90mL/3fl oz lemon juice
15mL/½fl oz Cointreau
splash lime cordial

Method

Shake and strain into a cocktail glass and serve.

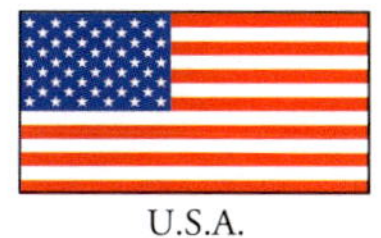

U.S.A.

Independence Day Punch

Ingredients

Glass: 285mL/9½oz Hi-Ball Glass

Mixers: 30mL/1fl oz Bourbon
100mL/3⅜fl oz pineapple juice
15mL/½fl oz lime juice
top up with soda

Method

Stir over ice and pour then top up with soda. Garnish with a pineapple slice and American 'Independence Day' Flag.

Indo Shiner

Ingredients

Indonesia

Glass:	285mL/9½oz Hi-Ball Glass
Mixers:	1 teaspoon of sugar 120mL/4fl oz pineapple juice 30mL/1fl oz lemon juice 15mL/½fl oz lime juice 1 dash Angostura Bitter 5mL/⅛fl oz blue vegetable coloring

Method
Blend over ice and pour. Garnish with a lemon and lime slice.

Ink Street

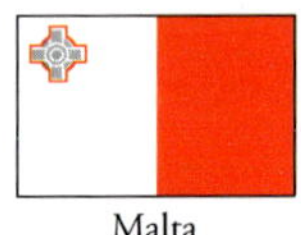

Ingredients

Malta

Glass:	140mL/5oz Champagne Flute
Mixers:	30mL/1fl oz Scotch whiskey 30mL/1fl oz lemon juice 30mL/1fl oz orange juice cracked ice

Method
Shake and strain into a champagne glass, garnish with a twist of orange peel and serve.

Inkahlúarable

Jamaica

Ingredients

Glass:	Cordial (Embassy)
Mixers:	10mL/⅜fl oz Kahlúa 10mL/⅜fl oz triple sec 10mL/⅜fl oz Grand Marnier

Method
Layer in order.

Intimate

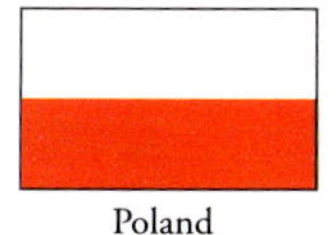
Poland

Ingredients

Glass: 90mL/3oz Cocktail Glass
Mixers: 20mL/⅝fl oz vodka
20mL/⅝fl oz apricot brandy
1 twist lemon peel
20mL/⅝fl oz dry vermouth
2 dashes orange bitters

Method
Mix liquid ingredients and strain into a cocktail glass. Garnish with olive, lemon peel and serve.

Irish Eyes

Ireland

Ingredients

Glass: 150mL/5oz Cocktail Glass
Mixers: 45mL/1½fl oz Irish whiskey
60mL/2fl oz cream
60mL/2fl oz Crème de Menthe

Method
Shake and strain into cocktail glass. Garnish with Maraschino cherry.

Irish Coffee

Ireland

Ingredients
Glass: 250mL/8oz Irish Coffee Glass
Mixers: 30mL/1fl oz Baileys Irish Cream
1 teaspoon brown sugar
top-up with hot black coffee
float fresh Cream

Method
Build (no ice).
Garnish: Chocolate flake optional.
The most widely drunk liqueur coffee which verifies its approval amongst coffee lovers. Other liqueur coffees are: French - brandy, English - gin, Russian - vodka, American - bourbon, Calypso - dark rum, Jamaican - Tia Maria, Parisienne - Grand Marnier, Mexican - Kahlúa, Monks - Benedictine, Scottish - Scotch, Canadian - rye.

Ireland

Irish Flag

Ingredients

Glass: Cordial (Lexington)

Mixers: 10mL/⅜fl oz green Crème de Menthe
10mL/⅜fl oz Baileys Irish Cream
10mL/⅜fl oz brandy

Method

Layer in order.
A stroll through verdant pastures. Brandy may be replaced with an Irish Whisky.

Iron Lady

United Kingdom

Ingredients

Glass: 120mL/4oz Cocktail Glass

Mixers: 15mL/½fl oz Malibu
45mL/1½fl oz cream
20mL/⅝fl oz Rubis
5mL/⅛fl oz vanilla essence
15mL/½fl oz white Crème de Cacao
1 scoop ice cream

Method

Blend until smooth, pour into a cocktail glass serve.

Island Cooler

Maldives

Ingredients

Glass: 150mL/5oz Champagne Saucer

Mixers: 15mL/½fl oz vodka
2 scoops crushed ice
30mL/1fl oz orange juice
2 drops Grenadine
30mL/1fl oz Midori
¼ kiwifruit
10mL/⅜fl oz lemon juice

Method

Blend vodka, orange juice and ice until frozen and place in a champagne saucer, add Grenadine. Blend Midori, kiwifruit and lemon juice and add to glass, serve.

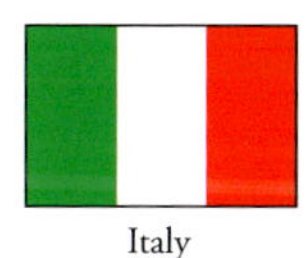

Italy

Italian Cocktail

Ingredients

Glass: 120mL/4oz Cocktail Glass
Mixers: 30mL/1fl oz rosso vermouth
20mL/⅝fl oz Fernet-Branca
20mL/⅝fl oz Pernod
2 dashes of sugar syrup

Method

Stir over ice and strain.
Fernet-Branca is a very bitter herbal Italian aperitif. 5mL/⅛fl oz Angostura Bitter may be used as a substitute.

Italian Streaker

Italy

Ingredients

Glass: 120mL/4oz Cocktail Glass
Mixers: 15mL/½fl oz Galliano
30mL/1fl oz Anisette
45mL/1½fl oz cream

Method

Shake over ice and pour. Garnish with an orange slice.

Jack in the Box

Australia

Ingredients

Glass: 150mL/5oz Cocktail Glass
Mixers: 60mL/2fl oz brandy
1 dash Angostura Bitter
60mL/2fl oz pineapple juice

Method
Shake and strain into cocktail glass and serve.

Jack Rose

U.S.A.

Ingredients

Glass: 90mL/3oz Cocktail Glass
Mixers: 45mL/1½fl oz brandy
½ lemon, squeezed
1 teaspoon Grenadine

Method
Shake and strain into cocktail glass and serve.

Belgium

Jaffa

Ingredients
Glass: 180mL/6oz Old Fashioned Glass
Mixers: scoop chocolate ice cream
90mL/3fl oz orange juice

Method
Blend with ice and pour.
Garnish with 1 teaspoon grated chocolate on top.

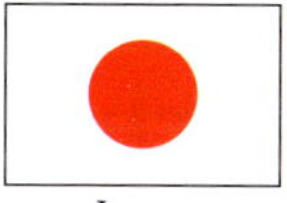

Japanese Slipper

Ingredients

Glass: 90mL/3oz Cocktail Glass
Mixers: 30mL/1fl oz Melon Liqueur
30mL/1fl oz Cointreau
30mL/1fl oz Lemon juice

Method

Shake with ice and strain
Garnish with slice of lemon on side of glass.
Comments: simple to prepare and the habit preferences of consumers has ensured this cocktail will remain one most often requested. Pouring 5mL Grenadine upon completion of the cocktail gives a marvellous visual effect and sweetens the sour element.

Japanese Sunrise

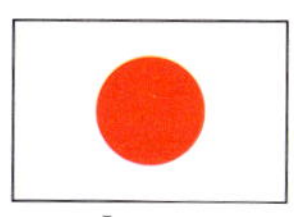

Japan

Ingredients

Glass: 90mL/3oz Cocktail Glass
Mixers: 30mL/1fl oz Midori
30mL/1fl oz lemon juice
10mL/⅜fl oz Galliano
3-4 strawberries
10mL/⅜fl oz orange curaçao

Method

Blend and pour into cocktail glass, garnish with a slice of rockmelon, ½ strawberry and serve.

Jaw Breaker

India

Ingredients

Glass: 120mL/4oz Cocktail Glass
Mixers: 30mL/1fl oz Kahlúa
30mL/1fl oz Sambucca
30mL/1fl oz banana liqueur

Method

Float ingredients over ice in cocktail glass and serve.

Jealous June

PNG

Ingredients

Glass: 300mL/10oz Hi-Ball Glass
Mixers: 30mL/1fl oz Midori
15mL/½fl oz Cointreau
20mL/⅝fl oz white rum
90mL/3fl oz pineapple juice

Method

Shake and strain into a hi-ball glass and serve.

Jellybean (Garbos)

Greece

Ingredients

Glass: 300mL/10oz Hi-Ball Glass
Mixers: 45mL/1½fl oz ouzo
1 dash Grenadine
15mL/½fl oz gin
lemonade
15mL/½fl oz vodka

Method

Place ice in a 10 oz hi-ball glass, add ingredients. Top with lemonade and serve.

Jellybean

Greece

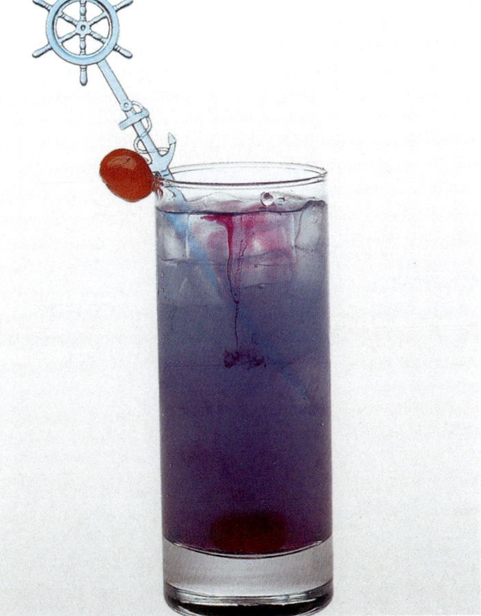

Ingredients

Glass: 285mL/9oz Hi-Ball glass
Mixers: 30mL/1fl oz ouzo
15mL/½fl oz oz Blue Curaçao
15mL/½fl oz Grenadine
top-up with lemonade

Method

Build over ice.
Swizzle stick and straws. Red cherry dropped into glass.
A cool liquid confectionery. Dropping Blue Curaçao and Grenadine into the cocktail after presenting to the customer gives a swirling lollipop effect. Regularly drunk without the Blue Curaçao.

Brazil

Jellyfish

Ingredients

Glass: Cordial (Lexington)

Mixers: 10mL/⅜fl oz Blue Curaçao
10mL/⅜fl oz Sambucca
10mL/⅜fl oz Baileys Irish Cream
2 dashes of Grenadine

Method

Layer in order and pour Grenadine. Watch out for sting at the end of this slippery shooter.

Jeune Homme

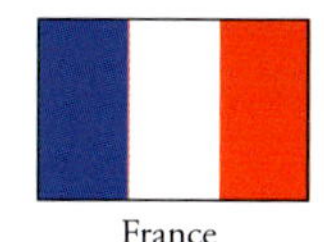

France

Ingredients

Glass: 90mL/3oz Cocktail Glass

Mixers: 30mL/1fl oz dry vermouth
15mL/½fl oz Benedictine
15mL/½fl oz gin
1 dash Angostura Bitter
15mL/½fl oz Cointreau

Method

Shake ingredients and strain into cocktail glass and serve.

Jersey Cow

United Kingdom

Ingredients

Glass: 290mL/9oz Old Fashioned Glass

Mixers: 180mL/6fl oz cola
scoop chocolate ice cream

Method

Stir over ice.
Garnish with a teaspoon of grated chocolate over top.
A choc-cola delight.

South Africa

Joburg

Ingredients

Glass: 150mL/5oz Old Fashioned Spirit Glass

Mixers: 30mL/1fl oz Bacardi
15mL/½fl oz Dubonnet
3 dashes of Orange Bitters

Method

Shake over ice and strain then add ice. Garnish with a twist of orange peel.

Joggers

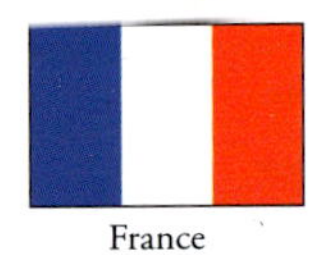

France

Ingredients

Glass: 300mL/10oz Hi-Ball Glass

Mixers: 30mL/1fl oz Benedictine
1 spiral lemon peel
45mL/1½fl oz Cognac
soda water
15mL/½fl oz lemon juice

Method

Half fill hi-ball glass with ice, drop in lemon peel and add lemon juice. Top with Cognac, Benedictine, soda water and serve with straws.

John Collins

U.S.A.

Ingredients

Glass: 300mL/10oz Hi-Ball Glass

Mixers: 30mL/1fl oz gin
1 teaspoon sugar
1 lemon, squeezed
1 dash Angostura Bitter
soda water

Method

Place all ingredients except soda water and lemon in hi-ball glass and stir until sugar is dissolved. Add soda water, garnish with lemon slice and straws and serve.

Jungle Stern

Philippines

Ingredients

Glass:	300mL/10oz Hi-Ball Glass
Mixers:	30mL/1fl oz Midori 4 pineapple pieces 15mL/½fl oz banana liqueur pulp ½ passionfruit 3 pureed strawberries scoop crushed ice

Method
Pour pureed strawberries down the side of hi-ball glass. Blend other ingredients and carefully add to the glass. Garnish with a cherry and pineapple leaves and serve.

Jungle Juice

Trinidad

Ingredients

Glass:	210mL/7oz Hurricane Glass
Mixers:	45mL/1½fl oz white rum 30mL/1fl oz pineapple juice 45mL/1½fl oz Drambuie 30mL/1fl oz cream 45mL/1½fl oz coconut cream ½ banana

Method
Blend until smooth, place in a champagne glass and serve.

U.S.A.

Jupiter Martini

Ingredients

Glass:	140mL/5oz Cocktail Glass
Mixers:	30mL/1fl oz gin 10mL/⅜fl oz dry vermouth 10mL/⅜fl oz Parfait Amour 10mL/⅜fl oz orange juice

Method
Shake over ice and pour. Garnish with a floating small strawberry.

Kahlúa Jaffa

Jamaica

Ingredients

Glass: 140mL/5oz Champagne Saucer
Mixers: 15mL/½fl oz Kahlúa
15mL/½fl oz orange juice
15mL/½fl oz Scotch whiskey
30mL/1fl oz cream

Method
Shake and strain into a champagne saucer, top with mixture of cream and Grand Marnier and serve.

Kakuri

United Kingdom

Ingredients

Glass: 90mL/3oz Cocktail Glass
Mixers: 30mL/1fl oz Pimm's no. 1 cup
5mL/⅛fl oz lemon juice
15mL/½fl oz mango liqueur
15mL/½fl oz bianco vermouth

Method
Shake and strain into cocktail glass and serve.

U.S.A.

Kamikaze

Ingredients
Glass: 140mL/5oz Cocktail Glass
Mixers: 30mL/1fl oz vodka
30mL/1fl oz Cointreau
30mL/1fl oz fresh lemon juice
5mL/⅛fl oz lime cordial

Method
Shake with ice and strain.
Garnish with red cocktail onion on a toothpick in the glass.
Maintain freshness for larger volumes by adding stained egg white. Mix in a jug and keep refrigerated. For the hyper-active.
Cointreau may be replaced with triple sec.

Ketango

Argentina

Ingredients

Glass: 90mL/3oz Cocktail Glass
Mixers: 45mL/1½fl oz vodka
30mL/1fl oz apricot brandy
30mL/1fl oz lime juice

Method
Shake and strain into cocktail glass, garnish with mint and serve.

Keep Going

Chile

Ingredients

Glass: 300mL/10oz Hi-Ball Glass
Mixers: 30mL/1fl oz white rum
15mL/½fl oz grapefruit juice
15mL/½fl oz anisette liqueur
lemonade
30mL/1fl oz cola tonic
½ slice lemon
15mL/½fl oz lime juice

Method
Half fill hi-ball glass with cracked ice, shake ingredients and strain into glass. Garnish with slice of lemon, straws and serve.

Kelly's Comfort

Ireland

Ingredients
Glass: 285mL/9½oz Hi-Ball Glass
Mixers: 30mL/1fl oz Southern Comfort
30mL/1fl oz Baileys Irish Cream
30mL/1fl oz milk
4 strawberries
15mL/½fl oz sugar syrup

Method
Blend over ice and pour. Garnish with a strawberry.

K.G.B

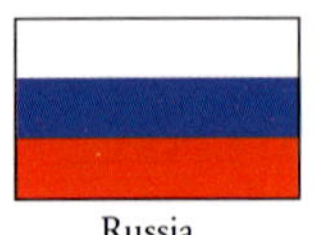

Russia

Ingredients

Glass:	185mL/6oz Old Fashioned Spirit Glass
Mixers:	30mL/1fl oz Kahlúa 30mL/1fl oz Grand Marnier 30mL/1fl oz Baileys Irish Cream

Method

Build over ice.

The first letter of each of the ingredients give this cocktail its name. A late night party drink.

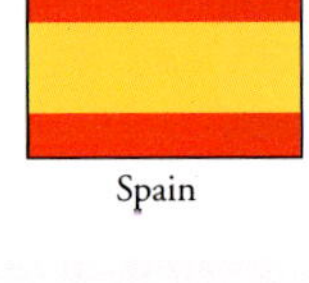
Spain

Kick in the Balls

Ingredients

Glass:	140mL/5oz Champagne Saucer
Mixers:	30mL/1fl oz dark rum 30mL/1fl oz orange juice 30mL/1fl oz melon liqueur 30mL/1fl oz cream 15mL/½fl oz coconut cream

Method

Shake with ice and strain.

Garnish with two melon balls previously marinated in the rum.

Float melon balls. Using a toothpick, eat both balls together and you'll be sure to feel a "Kick in the Balls." Refridgerate melon balls to preserve their freshness.

Kings Cross Nut

Australia

Ingredients

Glass: Coconut
Mixers: 60mL/2fl oz brandy
30mL/1fl oz Tia Maria
1 coconut

Method
Remove the top from the coconut and remove milk. Place half the milk, ice, brandy and Tia Maria in a shaker. Shake, pour into coconut, dust with nutmeg and serve with straws.

Kir Royale

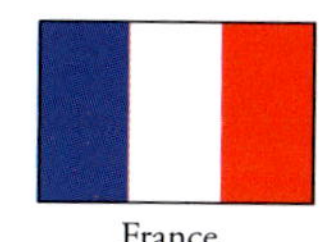
France

Ingredients

Glass: 140mL/5oz Champagne Flute
Mixers: 15mL/½fl oz Crème de Cassis
sparkling white wine

Method
Place Crème de Cassis in a flute glass, top with sparkling wine and serve.

France

Kir

Ingredients
Glass: 190mL/6oz Wine Goblet
Mixers: 15mL/1/2fl oz Crème de Cassis
top-up with dry white wine

Method
Build, no ice.
A superb pre-dinner drink. Use cold dry wines. Do not spoil the drink by using more than 15mL/½fl oz of Crème de Cassis.

Australia

Kiwi

Ingredients

Glass: 285mL Hi-Ball Glass
Mixers: 1 kiwifruit
30mL/1fl oz Bacardi
30mL/1fl oz Midori
15mL/½fl oz Cointreau
45mL/1½fl oz lemon juice
dash sugar syrup

Method

Blend with ice. Garnish with slice of kiwifruit on side of glass.

Kiss My Asteroid

U.S.A.

Ingredients

Glass: 390mL/13oz Hurricane Glass
Mixers: 30mL/1fl oz Midori
pineapple juice
30mL/1fl oz Blue Curaçao
15mL/½fl oz Cointreau

Method

Build Midori, Cointreau and pineapple juice in hurricane glass. Add Blue Curaçao to one large scoop crushed ice and float it on top of the pineapple juice, add straws and serve.

Klu Klux Klanger

U.S.A.

Ingredients

Glass: 150mL/5oz Cocktail Glass
Mixers: 30mL/1fl oz white rum
30mL/1fl oz vodka
30mL/1fl oz Southern Comfort
lemonade

Method

Pour ingredients over crushed ice in a cocktail glass and serve

Lady Brown

United Kingdom

Ingredients

Glass: 150mL/5oz Cocktail Glass
Mixers: 45mL/1½fl oz gin
20mL/⅝fl oz orange juice
20mL/⅝fl oz Grand Marnier
15mL/½fl oz lemon juice

Method
Shake and strain into cocktail glass. Garnish with orange segments and serve.

Lady in Red

U.S.A.

Ingredients

Glass: 140mL/5oz Champagne Saucer
Mixers: 30mL/1fl oz vodka
10mL/⅜fl oz lemon juice
30mL/1fl oz Rubis
1 dash egg white
10mL/⅜fl oz Grenadine
4 strawberries

Method
Blend and pour into a champagne saucer and serve.

Lady M

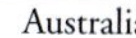
Australia

Ingredients
Glass: 285mL/9oz Hurricane Glass
Mixers: 45mL/1½fl oz Frangelico
45mL/1½fl oz melon liqueur
2 scoops vanilla ice cream

Method
Garnish with strawberry on side of glass sprinkled with grated chocolate. Blend for more than 20 seconds to thoroughly mix ingredients. Be adventurous and try various flavored ice-creams.

Lady Throat Killer

Philippines

Ingredients

Glass: Tall Dutch Cordial
Mixers: 10mL/⅜fl oz Crème de Café
15mL/½fl oz melon liqueur
10mL/⅜fl oz Frangelico

Method

Layer in order. This superb mixture offers an exquisite aftertaste.

Lady's Pleasure

United Kingdom

Ingredients

Glass: 140mL/5oz Champagne Saucer
Mixers: 60mL/2fl oz vodka
1 dash egg white
30mL/1fl oz Galliano

Method

Shake and strain into a champagne glass and serve.

Lambada

Brazil

Ingredients

Glass: Whiskey Shot
Mixers: 15mL/½fl oz mango liqueur
15mL/½fl oz black Sambucca
15mL/½fl oz tequila

Method

Layer in order.

U.S.A.

Lamborghini

Ingredients

Glass: 90mL/3oz Cocktail Glass
Mixers: 20mL/⅝fl oz Kahlúa
20mL/⅝fl oz Cointreau
20mL/⅝fl oz Sambucca
cold fresh cream

Method

Build, no ice. Garnish with grated chocolate flakes.

Layer ingredients in the above order using a spoon, then float fresh cream. As the name suggests, speed is the object of this cocktail. You may like to try drinking each layered ingredient through a straw at a quickening speed; similar to changing the gears in a Lamborghini.

Lamborghini (Flaming)

U.S.A.

Ingredients

Glass: 4-6 Tall Dutch Cordial Glasses
Mixers: 30mL/1fl oz Kahlúa
30mL/1fl oz Cointreau
30mL/1fl oz Sambucca
cold fresh cream

Method

Heat and build.

Warm alcoholic ingredients in a stainless steel saucepan. Be sure to simmer flame to avoid scorching Kahlúa. Stand glasses in a row and allow flame to burn for 10-15 seconds. Pour cold cream into a spoon and float onto the cocktail to extinguish flame. The nightclub version replaces Sambucca for green Chartreuse as it is distinct in color, easier to layer and also flamed.

Last Emperor

Ingredients

China

Glass: 150mL/5oz Cocktail Glass
Mixers: 30mL/1fl oz Canadian whiskey
30mL/1fl oz bianco vermouth
15mL/½fl oz Grand Mariner
30mL/1fl oz orange juice
1 dash Angostura Bitter

Method
Place ingredients in cocktail glass. Add strip of orange peel and serve.

Last Straw

Ingredients

Mauritius

Glass: 140mL Champagne Saucer
Mixers: 30mL/1fl oz Baileys Irish Cream
30mL/1fl oz Cointreau
15mL/½fl oz Rubis
30mL/1fl oz cream

Method
Shake ingredients and strain into cocktail glass. Garnish with strawberries and serve.

Lavender

South Korea

Ingredients
Glass: 210mL/7oz Old Fashioned Glass
Mixers: 90mL/3fl oz dark grape juice
15mL/½fl oz lemon juice
15mL/½fl oz sugar syrup
soda water

Method
Shake with ice and strain.
A lightly "grapesy" drink which is most refreshing before a meal.

Lena

Italy

Ingredients

Glass: 150mL/5oz Cocktail Glass
Mixers: 60mL/2fl oz bourbon
15mL/½fl oz Campari
30mL/1fl oz sweet vermouth
15mL/½fl oz Galleon Liverno
15mL/½fl oz dry vermouth

Method
Stir ingredients and strain into cocktail glass. Garnish with cherry and serve.

Leonardo de Mango

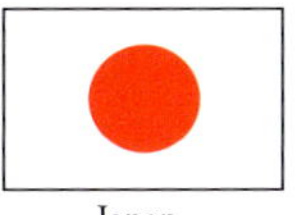

Japan

Ingredients

Glass: 300mL/10oz Hi-Ball Glass
Mixers: 30mL/1fl oz Midori
75mL/2½fl oz apple juice
15mL/½fl oz Baileys Irish Cream
30g/1oz mango
30mL/1fl oz mango liqueur

Method
Blend and pour into hi-ball glass and serve.

Ireland

Leprechaun

Ingredients
Glass: 210mL Old Fashioned Glass
Mixers: 60mL/2fl oz Irish Whiskey
top up with tonic water

Method
Build over ice. Garnish with a lime slice dropped into the glass.

Mexico

Lip Sip Suck

Ingredients

Glass: Whiskey Shot

Mixers: 30mL/1fl oz tequila
lemon in quarters or slices
salt

Method

Pour tequila into glass. On the flat piece of skin between the base of your thumb and index finger, place a pinch of salt. Place a quarter of the lemon by you on the bar. Lick the salt off your hand, shoot the tequila and then suck the lemon in quick succession.

Lieutenant

U.S.A.

Ingredients

Glass: 90mL/3oz Cocktail Glass

Mixers: 15mL/½fl oz apricot brandy
1 teaspoon sugar
30mL/1fl oz bourbon
15mL/½fl oz grapefruit juice

Method

Shake and strain into cocktail glass. Garnish with cherry and serve.

Light Fingers

Czech Republic

Ingredients

Glass: 150mL/5oz Cocktail Glass

Mixers: 60mL/2fl oz white rum
30mL/1fl oz Parfait Amour
30mL/1fl oz anisette liqueur
1 dash Grenadine (add last)

Method

Pour ingredients over half a mixing glass of cracked ice. Stir gently and strain into cocktail glass. Add dash of Grenadine and serve.

Cuba

Lights of Havana

Ingredients

Glass: 285mL/9½oz Hi-Ball Glass
Mixers: 60mL/2fl oz soda water
45mL/1½fl oz Malibu
30mL/1fl oz Midori
60mL/2fl oz orange juice
60mL/2fl oz pineapple juice

Method

Shake over ice and pour. Garnish with a straw and a lime wheel.

Lime Spider

Canada

Ingredients

Glass: 285mL/9½oz Hi-Ball Glass
Mixers: 45mL/1½fl oz lime milk shake syrup
1 tablespoon of sugar
1 small scoop vanilla ice cream
top up with lemonade

Method

Pour over ice and top up with lemonade. Garnish with a banana slice and whipped cream. Serve with spoons and straws.

Lion D'or

France

Ingredients

Glass: 150mL/5oz Cocktail Glass
Mixers: 30mL/1fl oz gin
60mL/2fl oz Grand Marnier
30mL/1fl oz orange juice

Method

Shake and strain into cocktail glass, garnish with orange peel and serve.

Lone Star

Chile

Ingredients

Glass: Cordial (Embassy)
Mixers: 10mL/3/8fl oz Parfait Amour
5mL/1/8fl oz Bacardi
15mL/1/2fl oz cherry brandy

Method
Layer in order and serve.

Long Green

Puerto Rico

Ingredients

Glass: 300mL/10oz Hi-Ball Glass
Mixers: 45mL/1 1/2fl oz Midori
soda water
20mL/5/8fl oz lemon juice

Method
Build ingredients over ice in hi-ball glass. Garnish with lemon wheel, cherry and serve.

Long Island Iced Tea

U.S.A.

Ingredients
Glass: 285mL/9oz Hi-Ball Glass
Mixers: 30mL/1fl oz vodka
30mL/1fl oz lemon juice
30mL/1fl oz tequila
30mL/1fl oz sugar syrup
30mL/1fl oz white rum
dash of cola
30mL/1fl oz Cointreau

Method
Build over ice. Garnish with lemon twist and mint leaves. Serve with straws.
The tea colored cola is splashed into the cocktail making it slightly unsuitable for a "Tea Party." Many variations are concocted using different white spirits.

Long Neck

United Arab Emirates

Ingredients

Glass: 210mL/7oz Old Fashioned
Mixers: 45mL/1½fl oz vodka
30mL/1fl oz Midori
1 scoop crushed ice
30mL/1fl oz lemon juice
1 dash Grenadine (last)

Method
Blend until frozen, place in an old fashioned glass. Add Grenadine and serve.

Love Dori

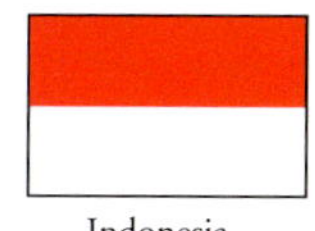

Indonesia

Ingredients

Glass: 150mL/5oz Champagne Saucer
Mixers: 30mL/1fl oz Midori
60mL/2fl oz cream
20mL/⅝fl oz vodka
nutmeg
15mL/½fl oz Galliano Liverno (float)

Method
Shake Midori, vodka and cream, strain into a champagne saucer. Float Galliano Liverno, sprinkle with nutmeg and serve.

U.S.A.

Louisiana Lullaby

Ingredients
Glass: 90mL/3oz Cocktail Glass
Mixers: 30mL/1fl oz dark rum
10mL/⅜fl oz Dubonnet
5mL/⅛fl oz Grand Marnier

Method
Shake over ice and strain. Garnish with a twist of lemon.

Love Potion No. 9

France

Ingredients

Glass: 140mL/5oz Champagne Saucer
Mixers: 30mL/1fl oz Bacardi rum
½ egg white
30mL/1fl oz Cointreau
15mL/½fl oz lemon juice

Method
Shake and strain into a champagne saucer, garnish with cherry and serve.

Lucy's Lament

Jamaica

Ingredients

Glass: 140mL/5oz Champagne Flute
Mixers: 30mL/1fl oz brandy
30mL/1fl oz cream
30mL/1fl oz Tia Maria
15mL/½fl oz Cointreau
3 Maraschino cherries

Method
Shake and strain into a flute glass, drop cherries in and serve.

U.S.A.

Lynchburg Lemonade

Ingredients
Glass: 285mL/9½oz Hi-Ball Glass
Mixers: 20mL/⅝fl oz Jack Daniel's
20mL/⅝fl oz Cointreau
20mL/⅝fl oz fresh lime juice
top up with lemonade or soda

Method
Pour in order then top up with lemonade or soda. Garnish with twisted lemon rind.

Macauley

Canada

Ingredients

Glass: 300mL/10oz Hi-Ball Glass
Mixers: 30mL/1fl oz brandy
1 orange wedge
60mL/2fl oz curaçao
30mL/1fl oz dry vermouth

Method
Shake and strain into hi-ball glass over ice and serve.

Macleay Street

U.S.A.

Ingredients

Glass: 140mL Champagne Saucer
Mixers: 30mL/1fl oz bourbon
1 dash Grenadine
15mL/½fl oz Galliano
orange juice (top up)

Method
Shake and strain into a champagne glass, top with orange juice, stir and serve.

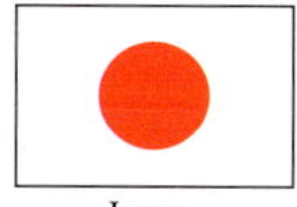

Japan

Madam Butterfly

Ingredients
Glass: 140mL/5oz Margarita Glass
Mixers:
1. 30mL/1fl oz Passoa
15mL/½fl oz melon liqueur
15mL/½fl oz white Crème de Cacao
30mL/1fl oz pineapple juice
2. 30mL/1fl oz cream
15mL/½fl oz melon liqueur

Method
1. Shake with ice and strain.
2. Layer melon liqueur and cream.
Garnish: strawberry and butterfly.
Comments: This cocktail requires two shakers. In one hand, shake the first four ingredients over ice and strain. In the other hand, shake melon liqueur and cream, then layer.

Madras

Ingredients

India

Glass:	210mL/7oz Old Fashioned
Mixers:	30mL/1fl oz vodka
	90mL/3fl oz cranberry juice
	30mL/1fl oz orange juice

Method

Build over ice then top up float orange juice. Garnish with an orange slice.

Magnolia Blossom

Ingredients

U.S.A.

Glass:	90mL/3oz Cocktail Glass
Mixers:	30mL/1fl oz bourbon
	20mL/⅝fl oz cream
	20mL/⅝fl oz lemon juice
	2 dashes Grenadine

Method

Shake then strain into cocktail glass and serve.

Mai-Tai

Tahiti

Ingredients

Glass:	285mL/9oz Hi-Ball Glass
Mixers:	30mL/1fl oz rum
	30mL/1fl oz lemon juice
	15mL/½fl oz Amaretto
	30mL/1fl oz sugar syrup
	½ fresh lime, juiced
	30mL/1fl oz orange curaçao Liqueur

Method

Shake with ice and pour.
Garnish with pineapple spear, mint leaves, tropical flowers if possible, lime shell.
Serve with straws.
A well known rum-based refreshing tropical cocktail. Grenadine is often added to redden a glowing effect while the rum may be floated on top when served without straws.

Maiden's Blush

Ingredients

United Kingdom

Glass: 90mL/3oz Cocktail Glass
Mixers: 60mL/2fl oz gin
30mL/1fl oz Grenadine

Method
Shake and strain into a 3 oz cocktail glass and serve.

Malibu Sting

Ingredients

Jamaica

Glass: 210mL/7 oz Champagne Flute
Mixers: 30mL/1fl oz Malibu
30mL/1fl oz lemonade
30mL/1fl oz gin
30mL/1fl oz Blue Curaçao
crushed ice
60mL/2fl oz pineapple juice

Method
Shake all ingredients except lemonade and pour into a flute glass. Add lemonade, garnish with strawberry on lip of glass and serve.

Malibu Magic

U.S.A.

Ingredients
Glass: 285mL/9oz Hurricane Glass
Mixers: 30mL/1fl oz Malibu
30mL/1fl oz strawberry liqueur
30mL/1fl oz orange juice
3-4 fresh strawberries
60mL/2fl oz cream

Method
Blend with ice and pour.
Garnish with a single strawberry and twisted orange peel.
Shake to the wonders of Californian dreaming.

Mama Rosa

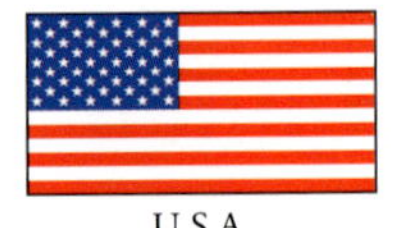
U.S.A.

Ingredients

Glass: 300mL/10oz Georgian Pilsener
Mixers: 30mL/1fl oz Sambucca
30mL/1fl oz cherry Advocaat
top up with soda water

Method
Build over ice then top up with soda. Garnish with a Maraschino cherry and pineapple leaves.

Singapore

Mandarin Sling

Ingredients
Glass: 140mL/5oz Champagne Saucer
Mixers: 20mL/⅝fl oz Kahlúa
20mL/⅝fl oz dark Crème de Cacao
10mL/⅜fl oz chocolate syrup
2 scoops orange sherbert
½ mandarin

Method
Blend without ice. Garnish with a mandarin or orange slice.

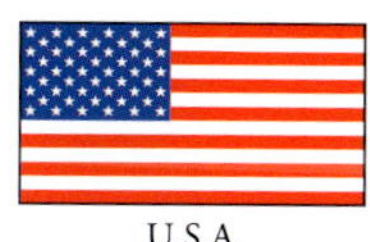

U.S.A.

Manhattan

Ingredients

Glass: 150mL/5oz Cocktail Glass
Mixers: 30mL/1fl oz bourbon
15mL/½fl oz rosso vermouth
dash Angostura Bitter

Method

Stir over ice and strain. Garnish with a red cherry on toothpick in glass.
A pre dinner cocktail. Replace rosso vermouth with Cinzano Dry, add a twist of lemon and you have instantly mixed a Dry Manhattan.
Rye whisky may be substituted for bourbon.

Mango Lantis

PNG

Ingredients

Glass: 150mL/5oz Cocktail Glass
Mixers: 30mL/1fl oz mango liqueur
45mL/1½fl oz orange juice
1 scoop crushed ice
5mL/⅛fl oz lemon juice
1 dash Grenadine (Last)

Method

Blend until frozen and scoop into cocktail glass. Add Grenadine and serve.

Maples

Argentina

Ingredients

Glass: 180mL/6oz Old Fashioned
Mixers: 45mL/1½fl oz gin
60mL/2fl oz pineapple juice
20mL/⅝fl oz white Crème de Cacao
1 dash cream

Method

Shake and strain into an old fashioned glass and serve.

Macroni

Ingredients

France

Glass: 90mL/3oz Cocktail Glass
Mixers: 30mL/1fl oz sweet vermouth
60mL/2fl oz Pernod

Method

Shake and strain into cocktail glass and serve.

Mardi Gras

Brazil

Ingredients

Glass: 90mL/3oz Cocktail Glass
Mixers: 20mL/⅝fl oz Cointreau
30mL/1fl oz banana liqueur
20mL/⅝fl oz Tia Maria

Method

Shake and strain into cocktail glass and serve.

Margarita

Mexico

Ingredients

Glass: 140mL/5oz Margarita Glass, salt-rimmed
Mixers: 30mL/1fl oz tequila
30mL/1fl oz lemon juice
15mL/½fl oz Cointreau
½ egg white, optional

Method

Shake with ice and strain.
Garnish with lemon wheel on edge of glass.
Margarita's can be 'shaken' or 'frozen' - a professional bartender will always ask which method is preferred. A "Frozen Margarita" (Sorbet) contains ⅜ of the blender full of ice. Add water if the mix becomes gluggy.

United Kingdom

Martini

Ingredients

Glass:	90mL/3oz Cocktail Glass
Mixers:	60mL/2fl oz gin
	10mL/⅜fl oz dry vermouth

Method

Stir over ice and strain.
Garnish with lemon twist or olive on toothpick in the glass.
The classically sophisticated black-tie cocktail. Always stirred; however, when shaken it is known as a "Bradford." An olive garnish retains the gin sting whereas a lemon twist makes the cocktail smoother.
Note: a "Dry Martini" has less vermouth.

Martin Luther King

U.S.A.

Ingredients

Glass:	300mL/10 oz Hi-Ball Glass
Mixers:	30mL/1fl oz vodka
	30mL/1fl oz gin
	cola

Method

Shake all ingredients except cola. Strain into hi-ball glass over ice. Top with cola and serve.

Mary Queen of Scots

Scotland

Ingredients

Glass:	140mL Champagne Saucer
Mixers:	30mL/1fl oz Scotch whiskey
	15mL/½fl oz Drambuie
	1 tablespoon castor sugar
	15mL/½fl oz green Chartreuse
	15mL/½fl oz lemon juice

Method

Dip the rim of a cocktail glass in lemon juice then in sugar. Shake Scotch whiskey, Drambuie and Chartreuse with ice and strain into rimmed glass. Garnish with cherry and serve.

Australia

Melon Avalanche

Ingredients

Glass: 285mL/9½oz Hurricane Glass
Mixers: 30mL/1fl oz Blue Curaçao
30mL/1fl oz melon liqueur
15mL/½fl oz triple sec
60mL/2fl oz pineapple juice

Method

Pour Blue Curaçao into glass. Blend other ingredients with ice and pour.
Garnish with a triangle of pineapple on side of glass.

Melon Ball

New Zealand

Ingredients

Glass: 90mL/3oz Cocktail Glass
Mixers: 30mL/1fl oz Midori
30mL/1fl oz strawberry liqueur
30mL/1fl oz banana liqueur

Method

Float liquid ingredients in cocktail glass, place strawberry on lip of glass and serve.

Melon Rock

Australia

Ingredients

Glass: 210mL/7oz Colada Glass
Mixers: 60mL/2fl oz Midori
60g/2oz honeydew melon
30mL/1fl oz lemon juice
10mL/⅜fl oz sugar syrup

Method

Blend and pour into a colada glass, garnish with 1 slice honeydew melon and straws and serve.

Melon Tree

Thailand

Ingredients

Glass: 300mL/10oz Hi-Ball Glass
Mixers: 30mL/1fl oz Midori
120mL/4fl oz milk
30mL/1fl oz peach tree
1 dash cream
30mL/1fl oz Galliano
1 scoop ice cream

Method
Blend and pour into a hi-ball glass and serve with straws.

Merry Widow

Iceland

Ingredients

Glass: 140mL/5oz Cocktail Glass
Mixers: 60mL/2fl oz cherry brandy
60mL/2fl oz Maraschino liqueur

Method
Shake and strain into cocktail glass, garnish with cherry on lip of glass and serve.

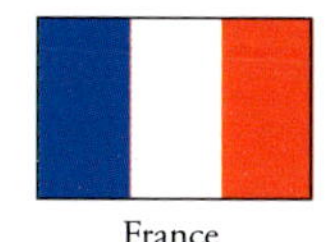

France

Ménage à Trois

Ingredients
Glass: 285mL/9½oz Hurricane Glass
Mixers: 30mL/1fl oz Pernod
30mL/1fl oz Malibu
60mL/2fl oz pineapple juice
15mL/½fl oz coconut cream
1 scoop orange sherbert
1 scoop vanilla ice cream

Method
Blend with ice. Garnish with a plastic swizzle stick with three straws. Voulez-vous soivez avec moi ce soir ? When two's not enough company try this genuine drink that originated from the afternoon cocktail parties held on the crowded houseboats lining the Seine River in Paris. Ideal for three people.

Metropolis

Hong Kong

Ingredients

Glass: 180mL/6oz Old Fashioned
Mixers: 30mL/1fl oz Midori
30mL/1fl oz Baileys Irish Cream

Method

Fill an old fashioned glass with cracked ice, build ingredients and serve.

Mexican Berry

Mexico

Ingredients

Glass: 140mL Champagne Saucer
Mixers: 10mL/⅜fl oz Kahlúa
10mL/⅜fl oz tequila
10mL/⅜fl oz strawberry liqueur

Method

Layer in order in a shot glass and serve.

Mexican Flag

Mexico

Ingredients

Glass: 140mL/5oz Champagne Saucer
Mixers: 60mL/2fl oz tequila
10mL/⅜fl oz sugar syrup
10mL/⅜fl oz lime juice

Method

Shake over ice and pour. Garnish with green and white cocktail onions and a red cherry across the glass on a toothpick.

Mexican Madness

Ingredients

Mexico

Glass: 285mL/9½oz Footed Hi-Ball Glass
Mixers: 30mL/1fl oz tequila
½ banana
30mL/1fl oz Baileys Irish Cream
60mL/2fl oz pineapple juice
15mL/½fl oz Malibu

Method

Blend until smooth and pour into glass and serve.

Mexican Mango

Ingredients

Mexico

Glass: 210mL/7oz Colada Glass
Mixers: 30mL/1fl oz tequila
15mL/½fl oz white curaçao
30mL/1fl oz mango liqueur
60mL/2fl oz orange juice

Method

Blend with ice and pour into a colada glass. Add straws and serve.

Mexican Runner

Mexico

Ingredients

Glass: 140mL Cocktail Glass
Mixers: 30mL/1fl oz tequila
15mL/½fl oz Tia Maria
15mL/½fl oz Grand Marnier
15mL/½fl oz blackberry liqueur
30mL/1fl oz lemon juice
½ banana
2 strawberries

Method

Blend over ice and pour. Garnish with a strawberry with umbrella parasol. Developed after the 1968 Olympics where an all American black 4 x 400 metre relay team won the gold medal breaking the world record.

Miami Advice

U.S.A.

Ingredients

Glass: 90mL/3oz Cocktail Glass
Mixers: 30mL/1fl oz Malibu
30mL/1fl oz banana liqueur
cream

Method

Layer in cocktail glass, place banana slice on lip of glass and serve.

Midnight Rose

Netherlands

Ingredients

Glass: 150mL/5oz Cocktail Glass
Mixers: 30mL/1fl oz Advocaat
cream
15mL/½fl oz strawberry liqueur
½ strawberry
15mL/½fl oz kirsch

Method

Shake and strain into cocktail glass, garnish with strawberry and serve.

Italy

Michaelangelo

Ingredients

Glass: 285mL/9½oz Hi-Ball Glass
Mixers: 90g/3oz zucchini
90mL/3oz tomato juice
1 thinly sliced onion
1 dash Italian seasoning

Method

Blend with ice then pour. Garnish with a zucchini slice.

U.S.A.

Midnight Sax

Ingredients

Glass: 450mL/15oz Gibraltar Cooling Glass

Mixers: 30mL/1fl oz Midori
30mL/1fl oz Southern Comfort
30mL/1fl oz orange and mango fruit juices
top up with ginger ale

Method

Pour over ice and stir, then top up with ginger ale. Garnish with slices of oranges in the glass and orange rind on the side.

Midori Alexander

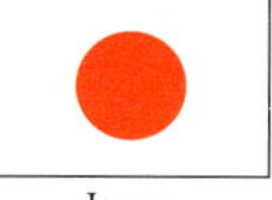

Japan

Ingredients

Glass: 150mL/5oz Cocktail Glass

Mixers: 30mL/1fl oz Midori
30mL/1fl oz white curaçao
60mL/2fl oz cream

Method

Shake and strain into cocktail glass, sprinkle with nutmeg and serve.

Midori Colada

U.S.A.

Ingredients

Glass: 300mL/10oz Tulip Glass

Mixers: 30mL/1fl oz Midori
90mL/3fl oz pineapple juice
30mL/1fl oz white rum
1 slice pineapple
30mL/1fl oz coconut cream
1 scoop crushed ice
30mL/1fl oz cream

Method

Blend until smooth and pour into tulip glass, garnish with pineapple wedge, straws and serve.

Midori Mist

Ingredients

Australia

Glass: 140mL/5oz Champagne Flute
Mixers: 30mL/1fl oz Midori
sparkling white wine

Method

Build ingredients into a flute glass and serve.

Midori Splice

Ingredients

New Zealand

Glass: Brandy Balloon
Mixers: 45mL/1½fl oz Midori
15mL/½fl oz cream (float)
30mL/1fl oz Malibu
cracked ice
20mL/4fl oz pineapple juice

Method

Build ingredients in brandy balloon, float cream and serve.

Mint Julep

U.S.A.

Ingredients

Glass: 285mL/9½oz Tom Collins Glass
Mixers: 60mL/2fl oz Bourbon
1 teaspoon sugar
2-3 dashes cold water or club soda
8 sprigs of fresh mint
crushed or shaved ice

Method

Muddle sugar, water and 5 mint sprigs in a glass. Pour into thoroughly frosted glass and pack with ice. Add bourbon and mix (with a chopping motion using a long-handled bar spoon). Garnish with remaining mint and serve with a straw. Tear mint leaves slightly before sugaring for greater aroma.

Luxembourg

Mintlup

Ingredients

Glass: 310mL/10oz Hi-Ball Glass

Mixers: large sprig of crushed mint
15mL/½fl oz lime juice
90mL/3fl oz dry ginger ale
90mL/3fl oz lemon & lime mineral water

Method

Build over ice.
Garnish with mint leaf on lemon slice.

Miss Aileen

Netherlands

Ingredients

Glass: 90mL/3oz Cocktail Glass

Mixers: 30mL/1fl oz Advocaat
30mL/1fl oz Galliano
30mL/1fl oz Vandermint

Method

Shake and strain into cocktail glass and serve.

Mission Impossible

U.S.A.

Ingredients

Glass: 120mL/4oz Cocktail Glass

Mixers: 30mL/1fl oz Cointreau
30mL/1fl oz Midori
30mL/1fl oz strawberry liqueur
30mL/1fl oz banana liqueur

Method

Layer in a 4 oz cocktail glass and serve.

Mississippi Mud

U.S.A.

Ingredients

Glass: 140mL Champagne Saucer
Mixers: 30mL/1fl oz Kahlúa
cola
30mL/1fl oz Southern Comfort
1 small scoop ice cream

Method
Place Kahlúa, Southern Comfort and ice cream in a 10 oz hi-ball glass. Top with cola.
Sprinkle grated chocolate over the top. Add two straws and serve.

Mocha Mint

Mexico

Ingredients

Glass: 90mL/3oz Cocktail Glass
Mixers: 20mL/⅝fl oz Kahlúa
20mL/⅝fl oz white Crème de Menthe
20mL/⅝fl oz white Crème de Cacao

Method
Shake with ice and strain. Garnish with peppermint chocolate flakes.

Australia

Mockatini

Ingredients
Glass: 90mL/3oz Cocktail Glass
Mixers: 15mL/½fl oz lime juice
dash lemon juice
60mL tonic water

Method
Stir with ice and strain. Garnish with a green olive on a toothpick or a lemon twist.
The classic cocktail, non-alcoholic version.

Molfetta Madness

Ingredients

Belgium

Glass: 120mL/4oz Cocktail Glass
Mixers: 30mL/1fl oz Sambucca
20mL/⅝fl oz cream
30mL/1fl oz mandarin liqueur
30mL/1fl oz orange juice

Method
Shake and strain into cocktail glass.
Garnish with orange slice and serve.

Monk's Madness

Ingredients

Thailand

Glass: 150mL/5oz Cocktail Glass
Mixers: 20mL/⅝fl oz cream
strawberry liqueur
60mL/2fl oz cream
30mL/1fl oz Crème de Cacao
cracked ice
60mL/2fl oz Benedictine

Method
Shake and strain into cocktail glass frosted with shaved chocolate.

Monkey Gland

Zimbabwe

Ingredients
Glass: 120mL/4oz Cocktail Glass
Mixers: 30mL/1fl oz gin
10mL/⅜fl oz apple juice
5mL/⅛fl oz Parfait Amour
5mL/⅛fl oz Grenadine

Method
Shake with ice and strain
Garnish with an orange twist.
Variation: substitute 20mL Pernod for the Parfait Amour and Grenadine.

Monkey's Punch

U.S.A.

Ingredients

Glass: Cordial (Lexington)
Mixers: 10mL/⅜fl oz Kahlúa
15mL/½fl oz Crème de Menthe
10mL/⅜fl oz Baileys Irish Cream

Method
Layer in order then shoot.

Monaco

Monte Carlo

Ingredients
Glass: 90mL/3oz Cocktail Glass
Mixers: 30mL/1fl oz rye whisky
10mL/⅜fl oz Benedictine
2 dashes of Angostura Bitter

Method
Shake with ice and strain.

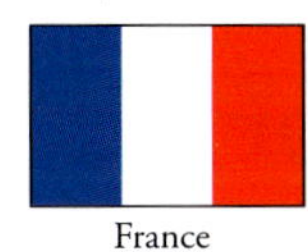
France

Montmartre

Ingredients

Glass: 90mL/3oz Cocktail Glass
Mixers: 10mL/⅜fl oz Cointreau
30mL/1fl oz Gilbey's Gin
10mL/⅜fl oz Cinzano Sweet Vermouth

Method

Coat glass with Cointreau then pour gin Gilbey's Gin andsweet vermouth Cinzano Sweet Vermouth over ice. Garnish with a red cherry.
From the world renowned painters courtyard next to Sacré Coeur that overlooks Paris.

Moomba

Australia

Ingredients

Glass: 150mL/5oz Champagne Saucer
Mixers: 30mL/1fl oz Bacardi rum
1 dash Grenadine
30mL/1fl oz Grand Marnier
15mL/½fl oz orange juice
10mL/⅜fl oz lemon juice

Method

Shake and strain into cocktail glass, garnish with orange peel and serve.

Moonbeam

U.S.A.

Ingredients

Glass: 150mL/5oz Cocktail Glass
Mixers: 30mL/1fl oz Midori
30mL/1fl oz cream
20mL/⅝fl oz vodka
15mL/½fl oz Grand Marnier

Method

Shake and strain into cocktail glass, garnish with kiwifruit and serve.

Moon Crater

Ingredients

Finland

Glass: 300mL/10oz Hi-Ball Glass
Mixers: 30mL/1fl oz vodka
30mL/1fl oz Advocaat
1 Maraschino cherry
orange soda
fresh cream (float)

Method

Place vodka and Advocaat in a hi-ball glass, top with orange soda. Float cream, dust with nutmeg and garnish with cherry and serve.

Morning Glory

Saudi Arabia

Ingredients

Glass: 300mL/10oz Hi-Ball Glass
Mixers: 30mL/1fl oz Scotch whisky
30mL/1fl oz brandy
10mL/⅜fl oz Pernod
10mL/⅜fl oz white curaçao
dashes Angostura Bitter
top up with soda

Method

Shake with ice and pour then top up with soda. Garnish with an orange twist.

Moroccan Cocktail

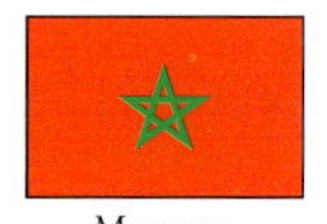

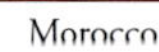

Morocco

Ingredients

Glass: 90mL/3oz Cocktail Glass
Mixers: 30mL/1fl oz gin
30mL/1fl oz Cointreau
5mL/⅙fl oz orange curaçao

Method

Shake with ice and strain. Garnish with a lemon wheel.

Russia

Moscow Mule

Ingredients

Glass: 285mL/9oz Hi-Ball Glass

Mixers: 30mL/1fl oz vodka
15mL/½fl oz lime cordial
top-up with ginger beer

Method

Build over ice.
Garnish with slice of lemon and mint, straws and swizzle stick.
A long, cool, refreshing cocktail. It tastes a lot better if the juice of half a lime is squeezed into the cocktail in place of the lime cordial.

Moulin Rouge

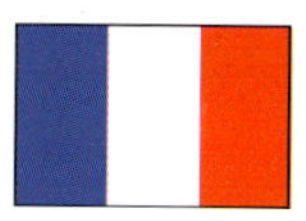

France

Ingredients

Glass: 140mL/5oz Champagne Saucer

Mixers: 30mL/1fl oz gin
20mL/⅝fl oz apricot brandy
20mL/⅝fl oz lemon juice
1 teaspoon Grenadine
sparkling white wine

Method

Shake and strain into a champagne saucer, top with sparkling white wine.
Garnish with orange slice and serve.

Mount Cook Sunset

New Zealand

Ingredients

Glass: 140mL/5oz Champagne Saucer

Mixers: 45mL/1½fl oz vodka
15mL/½fl oz lemon juice
15mL/½fl oz Maraschino liqueur
15mL/½fl oz orange juice
1 dash Grenadine

Method

Shake and strain into a champagne saucer and serve.

Mount Temple

Israel

Ingredients

Glass: 90mL/3oz Cocktail Glass
Mixers: 30mL/1fl oz Kahlúa
30mL/1fl oz Tequila
30mL/1fl oz Coconut Liqueur

Method

Build over ice.
Garnish with a dollop of cream in centre of glass.

Mount Fuji

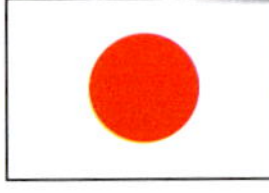
Japan

Ingredients

Glass: 140mL/5oz Champagne Saucer
Mixers: 30mL/1fl oz gin
15mL/½fl oz lemon juice
10mL/⅜fl oz heavy cream
1 egg white

Method

Blend with ice and strain.
Garnish with a round slice of banana and mint leaves.

Myra

U.S.A.

Ingredients

Glass: 90mL/3oz Cocktail Glass
Mixers: 15mL/½fl oz vodka
30mL/1fl oz dry red wine
15mL/½fl oz sweet vermouth

Method

Place ingredients in a mixing glass and stir gently. Strain into cocktail glass and serve.

Napolean

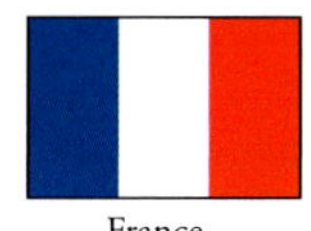
France

Ingredients

Glass: 90mL/3oz Cocktail Glass
Mixers: 45mL/1½fl oz gin
1 dash white curaçao
1 dash Fernet Branca

Method
Stir and strain into cocktail glass and serve.

New Yorker

U.S.A.

Ingredients

Glass: 90mL/3oz Cocktail Glass
Mixers: 15mL/½fl oz gin
1 dash Cointreau
45mL/1½fl oz French vermouth
15mL/½fl oz sweet sherry

Method
Stir and strain into cocktail glass and serve.

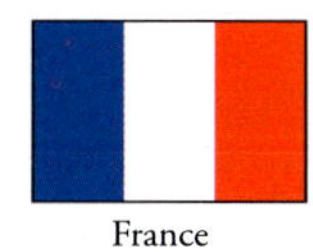
France

Negroni

Ingredients
Glass: 90mL/3oz Cocktail Glass
Mixers: 20mL/⅝fl oz Campari
20mL/⅝fl oz sweet vermouth
10mL/⅜fl oz gin

Method
Shake with ice and strain. Garnish with a twist of lemon and orange peel.

Australia

Nick's Health Drink

Ingredients

Glass: 290mL/9oz Poco Grande Glass

Mixers: 60mL/2fl oz V8 juice
60mL/2fl oz orange juice
120mL/4fl oz natural yoghurt

Method

Shake with ice and strain.

Nickel Fever

Ingredients

U.S.A.

Glass: 150mL/5oz Cocktail Glass

Mixers: 20mL/⅝fl oz Southern Comfort
45mL/1½fl oz cream
20mL/⅝fl oz Galliano
45mL/1½fl oz orange juice
10mL/⅜fl oz Blue Curaçao

Method

Shake and strain into cocktail glass and serve.

Night of Passion

Ingredients

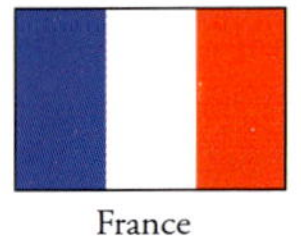

France

Glass: 290mL/9oz Poco Grande Glass

Mixers: 60mL/2fl oz gin
20mL/⅝fl oz lemon juice
30mL/1fl oz Cointreau
60mL/2fl oz passionfruit juice
60mL/2fl oz peach nectar

Method

Shake and strain into a rocks glass and serve.

Israel

Noah's Ark

Ingredients

Glass: Cordial (Lexington)
Mixers: 10mL/⅜fl oz Blue Curaçao
10mL/⅜fl oz cream
10mL/⅜fl oz lemonade

Method

Shake Blue Curaçao with cream, then layer lemonade. Optionally, place half a lychee nut in glass before pouring.

Norman Conquest

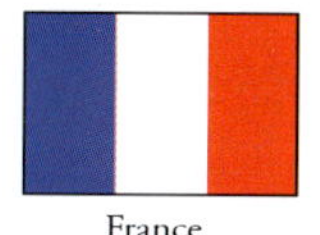
France

Ingredients

Glass: 90mL/3oz Cocktail Glass
Mixers: 60mL/2fl oz Calvados
10mL/⅜fl oz Grenadine
20mL/⅝fl oz lemon juice

Method

Shake and strain into cocktail glass and serve.

Nude Bomb

Canada

Ingredients

Glass: Cordial (Lexington)
Mixers: 10mL/⅜fl oz Kahlúa
10mL/⅜fl oz banana liqueur
10mL/⅜fl oz Amaretto

Method

Layer in order in a shot glass and serve.

Nutty Irishman

Ireland

Ingredients

Glass: 180mL/6oz Old Fashioned Glass

Mixers: 30mL/1fl oz Frangelico
30mL/1fl oz Baileys Irish Cream
15mL/½fl oz fresh lime juice
top up with fresh milk

Method

Build over ice. Garnish with sprinkled nutmeg or chocolate flakes.

Oceanic

Indonesia

Ingredients

Glass: 140mL/5oz Champagne Saucer

Mixers: 45mL/1½fl oz Scotch whiskey
15mL/½fl oz Bianco vermouth
cracked ice
30mL/1fl oz Kahlúa

Method

Mix in a mixing glass and strain into a champagne glass. Garnish with a spiral of orange peel and serve.

Off the Leach

Italy

Ingredients

Glass: 140mL/5oz Champagne Saucer

Mixers: 90mL/3fl oz brandy
30mL/1fl oz sweet vermouth

Method

Mix in a mixing glass and strain into a champagne glass. Garnish with a Maraschino cherry and serve.

Oil Fever

Ingredients

Jamaica

Glass: 140mL/5oz Cocktail Glass
Mixers: 60mL/2fl oz dark rum
60mL/2fl oz Tia Maria

Method
Shake with ice and strain into cocktail glass. Garnish with orange twist.

Old Pal

U.S.A.

Ingredients

Glass: 140mL/5oz Champagne Saucer
Mixers: 30mL/1fl oz bourbon
15mL/½fl oz dry vermouth
15mL/½fl oz Campari

Method
Mix in a mixing glass and strain into a 3 oz cocktail glass. Garnish with lemon peel and serve.

Old Fashioned - Scotch

U.S.A.

Ingredients
Glass: 285mL/9oz Old Fashioned Glass
Mixers: 30mL/1fl oz Scotch whisky
Angostura Bitter
sugar cube
soda water

Method
Garnish: 1/2 slice of orange and lemon and a cherry. A swizzle stick may be used. Splash bitters evenly over the sugar cube before adding ice, Scotch and topping up with soda. A soothing 'knocking-off' drink after 5 pm. Ensure cherries are dry. If cherries are moist, the juice may taint the flavor, thereby marring the appearance of the Scotch.
Bourbon and Rye Whisky may be served in the "Old Fashioned" way.

U.S.A.

Ole

Ingredients

Glass: 90mL/3oz Cocktail Glass
Mixers: 30mL/1fl oz tequila
30mL/1fl oz banana liqueur
10mL/⅜fl oz Blue Curaçao

Method

Stir over ice and strain.
Garnish with lemon wheel
Stir the tequila and banana liqueur gently over ice to avoid 'bruising' and strain into the glass, then drop Blue Curaçao. It not only looks good but is great to drink. Easy to make if you're in a hurry.

Old San Fransisco

Australia

Ingredients

Glass: 150mL/5oz Cocktail Glass
Mixers: 30mL/1fl oz kirsch
2 dashes Grenadine
30mL/1fl oz vodka
fresh cream
2 dashes lime cordial
½ tsp instant coffee

Method

Mix kirsch, vodka and Grenadine with ice and strain into cocktail glass and add cordial. Mix coffee with cream and float on top and serve.

Opal Royale

Austria

Ingredients

Glass: 150mL/5oz Cocktail Glass
Mixers: 30mL/1fl oz black Sambucca
30mL/1fl oz cream
30mL/1fl oz brandy
15mL/½fl oz white Crème de Menthe

Method

Shake and strain all ingredients except cream. Strain into cocktail glass and float cream. Garnish with cherry and serve.

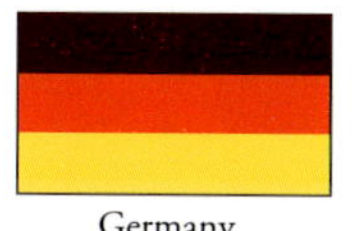
Germany

Oppenheim Cocktail

Ingredients

Glass: 120mL/4oz Cocktail Glass

Mixers: 30mL/1fl oz Bourbon
20mL/⅝fl oz Grenadine
20mL/⅝fl oz rosso vermouth
5mL/⅛fl oz Pernod

Method

Stir over ice and strain. Garnish with lemon and orange peel and a parasol.

Orange Blossom

United Kingdom

Ingredients

Glass: 90mL/3oz Cocktail Glass

Mixers: 30mL/1fl oz gin
60mL/2fl oz orange juice

Method

Shake and strain into a cocktail glass and serve.

Orange Bus

PNG

Ingredients

Glass: 180mL/6oz Old Fashioned

Mixers: 30mL/1fl oz mango liqueur
30mL/1fl oz banana liqueur
90mL/3fl oz orange juice

Method

Shake and strain into an old fashioned glass and serve.

Orange Nog

Scotland

Ingredients

Glass: 285mL Hi-Ball Glass

Mixers: 1 egg
120m/4fl oz milk
120m/4fl oz orange juice
10mL/⅜fl oz sugar syrup

Method

Blend over ice and pour. Garnish with a sprinkle of ground nutmeg and twisted orange peel.

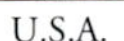

U.S.A.

Oramato

Ingredients

Glass: 240mL/8oz Footed Hi-Ball Glass

Mixers: 90mL/3oz tomato juice
120mL/4fl oz orange juice

Method

Shake with ice and pour. Garnish with an orange peel curl.

U.S.A.

Orgasm

Ingredients

Glass:	210mL/7oz Old Fashioned Spirit Glass
Mixers:	30mL/1fl oz Baileys Irish Cream 30mL/1fl oz Cointreau

Method
Build over ice.
Garnish: Strawberry or cherries, optional
A "Multiple Orgasm" is made with the addition of 30mL of fresh cream or milk.
A "Screaming Multiple Orgasm" has the addition of 15mL Galliano along with 30mL fresh cream or milk.

Orgasm Shooter

U.S.A.

Ingredients

Glass:	Tall Dutch Cordial
Mixers:	20mL/⅝fl oz Baileys Irish Cream 20mL/⅝fl oz Coinreau

Method
Layer in order then shoot.

Oyster Shooter

Australia

Ingredients

Glass: Cordial (Embassy)
Mixers: 10mL/⅜fl oz vodka
10mL/⅜fl oz tomato juice
5mL/⅛fl oz cocktail sauce
Worcestershire Sauce to taste
Tabasco Sauce to taste
1 fresh oyster

Method

Pour tomato juice onto the vodka, float the cocktail sauce, dash sauces to taste and drop in oyster.
An early morning wake-up call, replenishing energy lost the night before. Also referred to as a heart starter.

Outer Space

Ingredients

Russia

Glass: 150mL/5oz Cocktail Glass
Mixers: 45mL/1½fl oz vodka
10mL/⅜fl oz lime juice
45mL/1½fl oz Bacardi rum
20mL/⅝fl oz Galliano

Method

Shake and strain into cocktail glass, garnish and serve.

Pablo

Ingredients

Portugal

Glass: 90mL/3oz Cocktail Glass
Mixers: 30mL/1fl oz Bacardi rum
10mL/⅜fl oz Cointreau
1 Maraschino cherry
10mL/⅜fl oz Advocaat

Method

Shake and strain into cocktail glass, garnish with pineapple, cherry and serve.

Paddy's Peril

Ireland

Ingredients

Glass: 150mL/5oz Cocktail Glass
Mixers: 60mL/2fl oz Baileys Irish Cream
1 dash Grenadine
30mL/1fl oz vodka
crushed ice
coconut milk

Method
Shake and strain into cocktail glass and serve.

Paint Box

Netherlands

Ingredients

Glass: 90mL/3oz Cocktail Glass
Mixers: 30mL/1fl oz cherry Advocaat
30mL/1fl oz Advocaat
30mL/1fl oz Blue Curaçao

Method
Layer in cocktail glass and serve.

Cook Is

Pago Pago

Ingredients
Glass: 250mL/8oz Old Fashioned
Mixers: 30mL/1fl oz Bacardi Gold Rum
10mL/⅜fl oz lime juice
10mL/⅜fl oz pineapple juice
5mL/⅛fl oz green Chartreuse
5mL/⅛fl oz Cointreau

Method
Shake with ice and strain over 3 cubes of ice. Garnish with a pineapple wedge and a cherry.

Fiji

Palm Sundae

Ingredients

Glass: 285mL/9oz Hurricane Glass
Mixers: 45mL/11/2fl oz peach liqueur
30mL/1fl oz coconut liqueur
15mL/1/2fl oz banana liqueur
60mL/2fl oz tropical fruit juice
3 fresh strawberries

Method

Blend with ice and pour.
Garnish with orange wedge, pineapple leaves and Maraschino cherry.
Peach liqueur is dynamically exquisite in this specially designed cocktail recipe. The succulent peach flavor is another member in the new generation of natural tropical fruit cocktails.

Palm Tree

Ingredients

Mauritius

Glass: 150mL/5oz Margarita Glass
Mixers: 15mL/½fl oz Grand Marnier
15mL/½fl oz mango liqueur
15mL/½fl oz Cognac
30mL/1fl oz cream
15mL/½fl oz Bacardi rum
15mL/½fl oz Malibu
15mL/½fl oz peach liqueur

Method

Shake and strain into margarita glass, garnish with cherry, pineapple leaves and serve.

Palomino

Ingredients

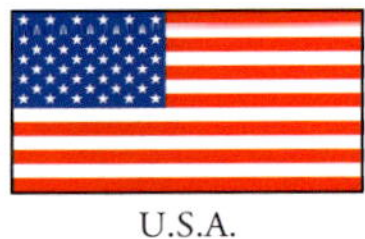
U.S.A.

Glass: 150mL/5oz Cocktail Glass
Mixers: 20mL/⅝fl oz Galliano
30mL/1fl oz Kahlúa
45mL/1½fl oz cream

Method

Shake with ice and strain into cocktail glass and serve.

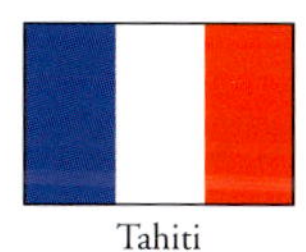
Tahiti

Papaya Sling

Ingredients

Glass: 285mL/9oz Hi-Ball Glass
Mixers: 30mL/1fl oz Gilbey's Gin
15mL/½fl oz lime juice
20mL/⅝fl oz papaya juice or syrup
2 dashes of Angostura Bitter

Method

Shake with ice and pour then top up with soda. Garnish with lime slice.

Paradise

Bermuda

Ingredients

Glass: 210mL/7oz Old Fashioned
Mixers: 45mL/1½fl oz Midori
½ kiwifruit
120mL/4fl oz pineapple juice

Method

Blend until smooth, pour into an old fashioned glass and serve.

Paris By Night

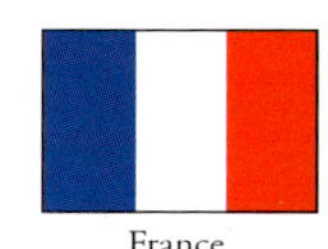
France

Ingredients

Glass: 300mL/10oz Hi-Ball Glass
Mixers: 30mL/1fl oz Pernod
30mL/1fl oz Strega
lemonade

Method

Place all ingredients except lemonade in hi-ball glass, top with lemonade. Garnish with Maraschino cherry, add straws and serve.

Paris Beach

France

Ingredients

Glass: 90mL/3oz Cocktail Glass
Mixers: 60mL/2fl oz peach liqueur
10mL/⅜fl oz Pernod

Method
Pour over ice in cocktail glass and serve.

Passionate Scene

Australia

Ingredients

Glass: 300mL/10oz Hi-Ball Glass
Mixers: 45mL/1½fl oz strawberry liqueur
1 teaspoon passionfruit pulp
60mL/2fl oz orange juice
5mL/⅛fl oz lemon juice

Method
Pour ingredients into hi-ball glass, float passionfruit pulp and serve.

Passionate

Brazil

Ingredients
Glass: 230mL/7oz Hurricane Glass
Mixers: 1 teaspoon passionfruit pulp
45mL/1½fl oz Bacardi
60mL/2fl oz grapefruit juice
dash lime juice
dash Grenadine
mineral water to top-up

Method
Blend with ice and pour.
Garnish with lime slice on side of glass.

Peach Explosion

Maldives

Ingredients

Glass: 150mL/5oz Cocktail Glass

Mixers: 45mL/1 1/2fl oz peach liqueur
45mL/1 1/2fl oz vodka

Method

Pour over ice in cocktail glass and serve.

Peach Bomb

Ivory Coast

Ingredients

Glass: 90mL/3oz Cocktail Glass

Mixers: 45mL/1 1/2fl oz peach liqueur
5mL/1/8fl oz lemon juice
15mL/1/2fl oz vodka

Method

Stir ingredients and pour over ice in a cocktail glass and serve.

Malaysia

Peach Almond Shake

Ingredients

Glass: 295mL/300mL Poco Grande Glass

Mixers: 60mL/2fl oz Peach Liqueur
1 whole peeled peach
30mL/1fl oz Amaretto
2 scoops of vanilla ice cream
top up with lemonade

Method

Blend with ice and pour then top up with lemonade. Garnish with a peach slice and shredded almonds and a straw.

Peach Magic

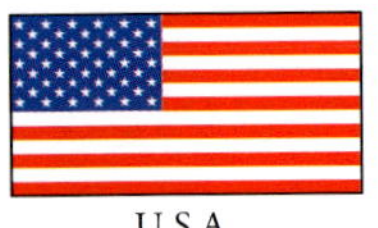
U.S.A.

Ingredients

Glass: 440mL/14oz Hurricane Glass
Mixers: 1 peach or apricot, stoned
30mL/1fl oz peach liqueur
30mL/1fl oz vodka
90mL/3fl oz orange and mango juice
90mL/3fl oz apple juice
top-up with dry ginger ale

Method

Blend over ice and pour.
Garnish with watermelon slice and stemmed Maraschino cherry.

Peach Marnier

Switzerland

Ingredients

Glass: 300mL/10oz Hi-Ball Glass
Mixers: 30mL/1fl oz Grand Marnier
2 peaches (skinned and sliced)
30mL/1fl oz white rum
crushed ice
20mL/⅝fl oz sugar syrup
30mL/1fl oz pineapple juice

Method

Blend with crushed ice until smooth, pour into hi-ball glass. Garnish with a pineapple slice, straws and serve.

Peach Me

U.S.A.

Ingredients

Glass: Brandy Balloon
Mixers: 30mL/1fl oz Southern Comfort
30mL/1fl oz cream
30mL/1fl oz Calvados
1 dash Grenadine
60mL/2fl oz orange juice
2 peach halves

Method

Blend until smooth and pour into a brandy balloon and serve.

United Kingdom

Pearl Necklace

Ingredients

Glass: Cordial (Embassy)
Mixers: 15mL/½fl oz melon liqueur
15mL/½fl oz Pimm's No. 1 Cup

Method

Layer in order.
A dash of lemonade dilutes the zappy aftertaste.

Pearl Harbour

U.S.A.

Ingredients

Glass: Brandy Balloon
Mixers: 30mL/1fl oz sake
lemonade
30mL/1fl oz Blue Curaçao
cracked ice

Method

In a brandy Balloon place 1 scoop of cracked ice. Pour in sake and Curaçao, top with lemonade and serve with straws.

Petite Fleur

France

Ingredients

Glass: 140mL/5oz Champagne Saucer
Mixers: 60mL/2fl oz Bacardi rum
cracked ice
30mL/1fl oz Cointreau
30mL/1fl oz grapefruit juice

Method

Shake and strain into a champagne glass, garnish with cherry and serve.

Photo Finish

United Arab Emirates

Ingredients

Glass: 150mL/5oz Cocktail Glass
Mixers: 45mL/1½fl oz Bacardi rum
10mL/⅜fl oz lime juice
45mL/1½fl oz apricot brandy
30mL/1fl oz dry vermouth

Method
Shake and strain into cocktail glass, garnish with twist of lemon peel and serve.

Piaff

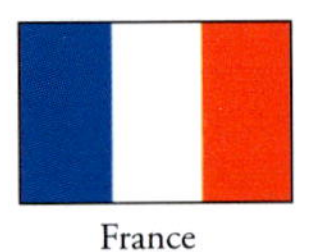
France

Ingredients

Glass: 150mL/5oz Cocktail Glass
Mixers: 30mL/1fl oz brandy
20mL/⅝fl oz sugar syrup
30mL/1fl oz white curaçao
1 egg
15mL/½fl oz lemon juice

Method
Shake and strain into a cocktail glass and serve.

United Kingdom

Picadilly Punch

Ingredients
Glass: 90mL/3oz Cocktail Glass - Preheated
Mixers: 30mL/1fl oz cognac
10mL/⅜fl oz sugar
15mL/½fl oz lemon juice
1 clove
cinnamon stick
ground nutmeg

Method
Simmer all ingredients except for cognac. Pour cognac into ladle and ignite before infusing the punch mix. Stir and serve. Garnish with an orange slice and a red cherry.

Spain

Picasso

Ingredients

Glass: 90mL/3oz Cocktail Glass

Mixers: 30mL/1fl oz cognac
10mL/⅜fl oz Dubonnet
10mL/⅜fl oz lime juice
15mL/½fl oz sugar syrup

Method

Shake over ice and strain. Garnish with an orange twist.

Pickled Brain

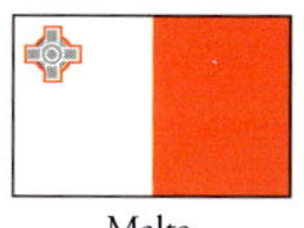

Malta

Ingredients

Glass: Whiskey Shot

Mixers: 15mL/½fl oz Kahlúa
15mL/½fl oz sweet vermouth
15mL/½fl oz dry vermouth

Method

Layer in order in a shot glass and serve.

Pick-Me-Up

Italy

Ingredients

Glass: 90mL/3oz Cocktail Glass

Mixers: 30mL/1fl oz cognac
30mL/1fl oz sweet vermouth
30mL/1fl oz dry vermouth

Method

Stir and strain into a cocktail glass and serve.

Pimms No. 1 Cup

United Kingdom

Ingredients

Glass: 285mL/9oz Hi-Ball Glass
Mixers: 45mL/1½fl oz Pimm's No. 1 Cup
top-up with either lemonade or dry ginger or equal parts of both

Method

Build over ice.
Garnish with orange and lemon slice, cherries, cucumber skin, swizzle stick and straws.
A slice of orange can detract from the sweet aftertaste. Slicing the inside of the cucumber skin allows the small drops to keep the drink chilled. Originally 6 Pimm's numbers were commonly consumed, today there are only two. Pimm's No.1 - Gin base, Pimm's No. 2 - Vodka base.

U.S.A.

Pina Colada

Ingredients

Glass: 285mL/9oz Hi-Ball Glass
Mixers: 30mL/1fl oz white rum
30mL/1fl oz Malibu
30mL/1fl oz coconut cream
30mL/1fl oz sugar syrup
125mL/4fl oz pineapple juice

Method

Shake with ice and pour.
Garnish with pineapple wedge - three leaves and a cherry, straws & swizzle stick.
Another tropical Hawaiian cocktail which is distinguished by including coconut cream.

Pinchgut Peril

Ingredients

Singapore

Glass: 300mL/10oz Hi-Ball
Mixers: 30mL/1fl oz Scotch whiskey
15mL/½fl oz gin
15mL/½fl oz lime juice
pineapple pieces
1 dash Grenadine

Method
Blend whiskey, gin, lime juice, Grenadine and pineapple pieces until smooth. Pour over shaved ice into a 10 oz hi-ball glass. Garnish with pineapple wedge, orange slice, straws and serve.

Pineapple Bomber

U.S.A.

Ingredients

Glass: 140mL Champagne Saucer
Mixers: 45mL/1½fl oz Southern Comfort
15mL/½fl oz Amaretto
90mL/3fl oz pineapple juice

Method
Shake and strain into a cocktail glass, garnish with pineapple wedge and serve.

Pineapple Plantation

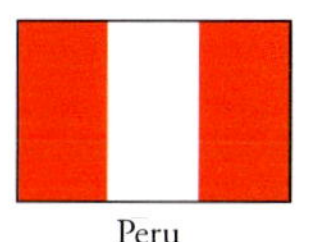

Peru

Ingredients

Glass: 285mL/9½oz Footed Hi-Ball
Mixers: 30mL/1fl oz Amaretto
30mL/1fl oz Southern Comfort
90mL/3fl oz pineapple juice
top up with lemonade

Method
Blend with ice and pour then top up with lemonade. Garnish with a pineapple wedge and a cherry.

Pink Angel

Australia

Ingredients

Glass: 150mL/5oz Champagne Saucer

Mixers: 30mL/1fl oz white rum
1 egg white
15mL/½fl oz Advocaat
30mL/1fl oz fresh cream
15mL/½fl oz cherry brandy

Method
Shake and strain into a 5 oz champagne glass and serve.

Pink Elephant

Denmark

Ingredients

Glass: 150mL/5oz Champagne Saucer

Mixers: 30mL/1fl oz vodka
30mL/1fl oz cream
30mL/1fl oz Galliano Liverno
1 dash Grenadine
30mL/1fl oz almond liqueur
cracked ice
30mL/1fl oz orange juice

Method
Shake and strain into a champagne saucer, sprinkle with nutmeg and serve.

Pink Gin

United Kingdom

Ingredients

Glass: 285mL/9½oz Hurricane Glass

Mixers: 3 dashes Angostura Bitter
45mL/1½fl oz gin
water

Method
Put dashes of bitters into glass. Rotate in the glass. Throw out the bitters. Add ice cubes, gin and water, and serve.

U.S.A.

Pink Panther

Ingredients

Glass: 150mL/5oz Champagne Saucer

Mixers: 20mL/⅝fl oz bourbon
30mL/1fl oz vodka
15mL/½fl oz Malibu
45mL/1½fl oz cream
dash Grenadine

Method

Shake with ice and strain
Garnish with a cherry and mint.

Pink Lady

United Kingdom

Ingredients

Glass: 150mL/5oz Champagne Saucer

Mixers: 60mL/2 oz gin
30mL/1fl oz fresh cream
15mL/½fl oz Grenadine
30mL/1fl oz brandy

Method

Shake and strain into champagne saucer and serve.

Pink Pussy

Italy

Ingredients

Glass: 300mL/10oz Hi-Ball Glass

Mixers: 30mL/1fl oz Campari
bitter lemon
1 dash egg white
15mL/½fl oz peach brandy

Method

Shake all ingredients except bitter lemon and strain into hi-ball glass. Top with bitter lemon, garnish with slice of lemon, straws and serve.

New Zealand

Pipsqueak

Ingredients

Glass: Cordial (Embassy)
Mixers: 20mL/⅝fl oz Frangelico
10mL/⅜fl oz vodka
5mL/⅛fl oz lemon juice

Method

Layer in order, then stir.

Pirates Plunder

Jamaica

Ingredients

Glass: 300mL/10oz Hi-Ball Glass
Mixers: 30mL/1fl oz Tia Maria
30mL/1fl oz coconut cream
30mL/1fl oz white rum
90mL/3fl oz pineapple juice
20mL/⅝fl oz Malibu
1 slice pineapple

Method

Blend until smooth and pour into a hi-ball glass and serve with straws.

P.J.

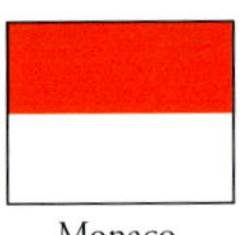
Monaco

Ingredients

Glass: 150mL/5oz Cocktail Glass
Mixers: 30mL/1fl oz vodka
1 dash egg white
30mL/1fl oz Campari
30mL/1fl oz orange juice

Method

Shake and strain into cocktail glass, garnish with cherry and serve.

Plantation Night

Puerto Rico

Ingredients

Glass:	180mL/6oz Champagne Flute
Mixers:	30mL/1fl oz Kahlúa 30mL/1fl oz strawberry liqueur 30mL/1fl oz banana liqueur 1 banana 45mL/1½fl oz cream

Method
Blend until smooth and pour into a flute glass and serve.

Playground

U.S.A.

Ingredients

Glass:	90mL/3oz Cocktail Glass
Mixers:	30mL/1fl oz Baileys Irish Cream 30mL/1fl oz Malibu 30mL/1fl oz banana liqueur

Method
Layer in a cocktail glass and serve.

Nepal

Planters Punch

Ingredients

Glass:	150mL/5oz Cocktail Glass
Mixers:	30mL/1fl oz dark rum 30mL/1fl oz lemon or lime juice 60mL/2fl oz orange juice 5mL/⅙fl oz Grenadine

Method
Build over ice then add dash of Grenadine. Garnish with fruit slices.

Polish Sidecar

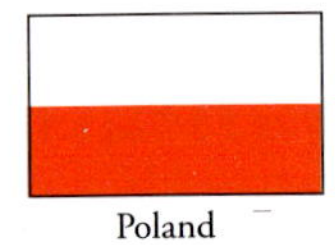
Poland

Ingredients

Glass:	90mL/3oz Cocktail Glass
Mixers:	20mL/⅝fl oz gin
	20mL/⅝fl oz lemon juice
	10mL/⅜fl oz blackberry liqueur

Method
Shake with gin and lemon juice with ice and pour then float blackberry liqueur. Garnish with blackberries or raspberries.

Tahiti

Polynesia

Ingredients

Glass:	135mL/4½oz Tulip Champagne Glass
Mixers:	30mL/1fl oz white rum
	30mL/1fl oz passionfruit liqueur
	10mL/⅜fl oz lime juice
	half egg white

Method
Blend with ice and pour. Garnish with passionfruit.

Port in a Storm

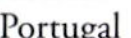

Portugal

Ingredients

Glass: 180mL/6oz Wine Goblet
Mixers: 45mL/1½fl oz port
⅜ strip orange peel
60mL/2fl oz red wine
15mL/½fl oz brandy
1 sprig mint

Method

Fill a large goblet glass with ice. Stir liquid ingredients and pour over ice. Garnish with sprig of mint and serve.

Porto Flip

Portugal

Ingredients

Glass: 150mL/5oz Cocktail Glass
Mixers: 45mL/1½fl oz port
1 egg yolk
10mL/⅛fl oz cognac
10mL/⅛fl oz sugar syrup

Method

Shake and strain into a cocktail glass, sprinkle with nutmeg and serve.

Prairie Oyster

U.S.A.

Ingredients

Glass: 90mL/3oz Cocktail Glass
Mixers: 30mL/1fl oz brandy
salt and pepper
Worcestershire Sauce
Tabasco Sauce
1 egg yolk

Method

Build, no ice.
The spices relieve a sore head and the brandy replenishes lost energy. Brandy may be replaced with any spirit of your choice, however cold vodka is medically soothing. Best before breakfast.

Pretty Woman

Australia

Ingredients

Glass: 285mL/9oz Hurricane Glass
Mixers: Blender 1
30mL/1fl oz melon liqueur
30mL/1fl oz Malibu
Blender 2
30mL/1fl oz strawberry liqueur
3-4 strawberries

Method

Blend with ice in two separate blenders and pour. Garnish with strawberry and umbrella on side of glass.
Remember to tilt the glass when pouring the two sets of ingredients into the glass. Choosing a long glass will assist you. Very alcoholic as there is no juice.
A kaleidoscope of color for you to enjoy.

Wales

Prince of Wales

Ingredients

Glass: 150mL/5oz Champagne Saucer
Mixers: 15mL/½fl oz Madeira
15mL/½fl oz brandy
5mL/⅛fl oz Cointreau
1-2 dashes of Angostura Bitter
top up with Champagne

Method

Shake with ice and strain then top up with champagne. Garnish with an orange slice.

Purple Shell

United Kingdom

Ingredients

Glass: 150mL/5oz Champagne Saucer

Mixers: 60mL/3fl oz gin
15mL/½fl oz Parfait Amour
45mL/1½fl oz fresh cream

Method
Shake and strain into a champagne glass and serve.

Purple Waters

U.S.A.

Ingredients

Glass: 150mL/5oz Champagne Saucer

Mixers: 20mL/⅝fl oz Bacardi rum
15mL/½fl oz Parfait Amour
15mL/½fl oz orange curaçao
15mL/½fl oz yellow Chartreuse

Method
Layer in order in a cocktail glass and serve.

South Korea

P.S. I Love You

Ingredients

Glass: 150mL/5oz Champagne Saucer

Mixers: 30mL/1fl oz Amaretto
30mL/1fl oz Kahlúa
30mL/1fl oz Baileys Irish Cream
5mL/⅙fl oz Grenadine

Method
Build over ice and stir. Garnish with sprinkled nutmeg.

Puerto Rican Pink Lady

Puerto Rico

Ingredients

Glass: 135mL/4½oz Tulip Champagne Glass, sugar rimmed
Mixers: 30mL/1fl oz white rum
10mL/⅜fl oz lemon juice
10mL/⅜fl oz Grenadine
half egg white

Method

Blend with ice and strain. Garnish with a strawberry splashed with Grenadine.

Seychelles

Purple People Eater

Ingredients

Glass: 120mL/4oz Cocktail Glass
Mixers: 30mL/1fl oz Parfait Amour
30mL/1fl oz gin
10mL/⅜fl oz lemon juice

Method

Shake over ice and strain. Garnish with a strawberry and pink parasol.

Canada

Quebec

Ingredients

Glass: 120mL/4oz Cocktail Glass

Mixers: 30mL/1fl oz Canadian Club Whisky
10mL/⅜fl oz dry vermouth
10mL/⅜fl oz Amer Picon
10mL/⅜fl oz Maraschino liqueur

Method

Shake over ice and strain. Garnish with a cocktail onion.
Amer Picon is a French brand of bitters that derives much of its flavor from gentian root and oranges. 3mL Angostura Bitter may be substituted.

Queen Bee

United Kingdom

Ingredients

Glass: 90mL/3oz Cocktail Glass
Mixers: 30mL/1fl oz gin
1 dash Pernod
30mL/1fl oz Cointreau

Method

Shake and strain into cocktail glass and serve.

Queen Elizabeth

United Kingdom

Ingredients

Glass: 90mL/3oz Cocktail Glass
Mixers: 30mL/1fl oz gin
15mL/½fl oz lemon juice
15mL/½fl oz Cointreau
1 dash Pernod

Method

Shake and strain into a cocktail glass, garnish with cherry and serve.

Queen's Peg

United Kingdom

Ingredients

Glass: 180mL/6oz Wine Goblet
Mixers: 30mL/1fl oz gin
1 large ice cube
sparkling white wine

Method

Place ice cube in a goblet glass, add gin and top with wine before serving.

Queen's

United Kingdom

Ingredients

Glass: 150mL/5oz Cocktail Glass
Mixers: 30mL/1fl oz gin
30mL/1fl oz pineapple juice
30mL/1fl oz dry vermouth
30mL/1fl oz sweet vermouth

Method

Shake and strain into cocktail glass, garnish with cherry, pineapple wedge and serve.

Quenchie

Trinidad

Ingredients

Glass: 390mL/13oz Poco Grande Glass
Mixers: 120mL/4fl oz orange juice
150mL/5fl oz lemonade
45mL/1½fl oz passionfruit pulp
45mL/1½fl oz white rum

Method

Build over ice and stir.
Garnish with a slice of orange, slice of lemon with 2 Maraschino cherries on toothpicks, serve with swizzle sticks and straws.

R & R

Australia

Ingredients

Glass: 90mL/3oz Cocktail Glass
Mixers: 30mL/1fl oz Cointreau
30mL/1fl oz Midori
30mL/1fl oz tequila

Method

Layer in order in a 3 oz cocktail glass and serve.

Rabbit's Revenge

U.S.A.

Ingredients

Glass: 180mL/6oz Old Fashioned
Mixers: 45mL/1½fl oz bourbon
tonic water
3 dashes Grenadine
30mL/1fl oz pineapple juice

Method

Shake ingredients except tonic water and strain into an old fashioned glass. Top with tonic water, garnish with orange slice and serve with straws

---

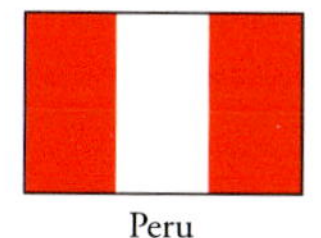
Peru

Rabbit-Punch

Ingredients

Glass: Whiskey Shot
Mixers: 10mL/⅜fl oz Campari
10mL/⅜fl oz dark Crème de Cacao
10mL/⅜fl oz Malibu
10mL/⅜fl oz Baileys Irish Cream

Method

Pour in order then layer Baileys.

Raffles Singapore Sling

Singapore

Ingredients

Glass: 285mL/9oz Hi-Ball Glass
Mixers: 30mL/1fl oz gin
30mL/1fl oz orange juice
30mL/1fl oz cherry brandy
30mL/1fl oz lime juice
15mL/½fl oz triple sec
30mL/1fl oz pineapple juice
dash Angostura Bitter
15mL/½fl oz Benedictine

Method

Shake with ice and pour. Garnish with orange slice, mint, a cherry, swizzle stick and straws.
This recipe is the original Singapore version. With its fruit juices. it tastes totally different from some gin slings commonly served in bars.

Raging Bull

Zimbabwe

Ingredients

Glass: 180mL/6oz Old Fashioned
Mixers: 30mL/1fl oz Afrikoko
30mL/1fl oz Sabra
milk (top up)

Method

Pour over ice in an old fashioned glass, top with milk and serve.

Raider

U.S.A.

Ingredients

Glass: Whiskey Shot
Mixers: 15mL/½fl oz Baileys Irish Cream
15mL/½fl oz Cointreau
15mL/½fl oz Grand Marnier

Method

Layer in order in a shot glass and serve.

Hong Kong

Rainbow Sherbet

Ingredients

Glass: 195mL/8½oz Tulip Wine Glass

Mixers: 15mL/½fl oz Midori
15mL/½fl oz banana liqueur
15mL/½fl oz strawberry Liqueur
60mL/2fl oz orange juice
15mL/½fl oz Grenadine
2 scoops orange sherbert
blue vegetable dye

Method

Blend without ice. Garnish with assorted fruit and a dash of blue vegetable dye.

RAM

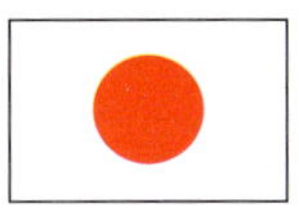

Japan

Ingredients

Glass: 150mL/5oz Champagne Saucer

Mixers: 30mL/1fl oz Malibu
45mL/1½fl oz orange juice
15mL/½fl oz Galliano
whipped cream

Method

Shake ingredients except whipped cream and strain into a champagne saucer. Float whipped cream and serve.

Ramona

U.S.A.

Ingredients

Glass: 150mL/5oz Champagne Saucer

Mixers: 60mL/2fl oz Bacardi rum
2 teaspoon castor sugar
30mL/1fl oz Cointreau
60mL/2fl oz lemon juice
soda water

Method

Shake all ingredients except soda water and strain over ice in a 10 oz hi-ball glass. Top with soda water, garnish with lemon slice, straws and serve.

Rasputin's Revenge

Russia

Ingredients

Glass: 140mL Champagne Saucer
Mixers: 60mL/2fl oz vodka
30mL/1fl oz orange juice

Method
Shake and strain over ice in a rocks glass and serve.

Ray Long

Canada

Ingredients

Glass: 90mL/3oz Cocktail Glass
Mixers: 30mL/1fl oz bianco vermouth
15mL/½fl oz Pernod
15mL/½fl oz brandy
1 dash Angostura Bitter

Method
Mix ingredients and strain into a cocktail glass and serve.

Australia

Ready, Set, Go!

Ingredients
Glass: Tall Dutch Cordial
Mixers: 15mL/½fl oz strawberry liqueur
15mL/½fl oz banana liqueur
15mL/½fl oz melon liqueur

Method
Layer in order.

U.S.A.

Red Eye

Ingredients

Glass: 140mL Cocktail Glass

Mixers: 210mL/7fl oz beer
90mL/3fl oz tomato juice

Method

Build, no ice.

Red Cucumber Bowl

India

Ingredients

Glass: 180mL/6oz Old Fashioned

Mixers: 150mL/5fl oz red wine
1 pinch ground cloves
15mL/½fl oz Maraschino liqueur
2 thin slices cucumber
1 pinch cinnamon

Method

Shake ingredients except cucumber. Strain into old fashioned glass, garnish with cucumber and serve.

Red Lights

Iceland

Ingredients

Glass: 300mL/10oz Hi-Ball Glass

Mixers: 20mL/⅝fl oz gin
15mL/½fl oz Cointreau
15mL/½fl oz Galliano
60mL/2fl oz orange juice

Method

Shake and strain into a hi-ball glass and serve.

Rendezvous

France

Ingredients

Glass: 150mL/5oz Champagne Flute

Mixers:
- 30mL/1fl oz Cointreau
- 30mL/1fl oz vodka
- 15mL/½fl oz Rubis
- lemonade (top up)

Method

Shake and strain into a flute glass, top with lemonade and serve.

Rhett Butler

U.S.A.

Ingredients

Glass: 300mL/10oz Hi-Ball Glass

Mixers:
- 30mL/1fl oz Southern Comfort
- 5mL/⅛fl oz lime cordial
- 30mL/1fl oz orange curaçao
- soda water (top up)
- 15mL/½fl oz lemon juice

Method

Build ingredients over ice in hi-ball glass, top with soda water. Garnish with orange wheel and serve with straws.

Rhythm of Love

Fiji

Ingredients

Glass: Cordial (Embassy)

Mixers:
- 10mL/⅜fl oz Midori
- small piece of kiwifruit
- 10mL/⅜fl oz Crème de Cassis
- float cream

Method

Squeeze kiwifruit onto Midori into glass, then layer in order.

Rio Lady

Brazil

Ingredients

Glass: 150mL/5oz Champagne Saucer
Mixers: 30mL/1fl oz white Crème de Cacao
60mL/2fl oz cream
15mL/½fl oz goldwasser

Method

Shake and strain into a champagne saucer and serve.

Ritz

United Kingdom

Ingredients

Glass: 150mL/5oz Epson Glass
Mixers: 30mL/1fl oz brandy
15mL/½fl oz Cointreau
cracked ice
15mL/½fl oz orange juice
chilled Champagne (top up)

Method

Shake and strain into epsom glass, top with champagne and serve.

Scotland

Rob Roy

Ingredients

Glass: 120mL/4oz Cocktail Glass
Mixers: 30mL/1fl oz Scotch whisky
30mL/1fl oz rosso vermouth
5mL/⅛fl oz sugar syrup

Method

Shake over ice and strain. Garnish with a red cherry.

Rock Lobster

U.S.A.

Ingredients

Glass:	140mL/5oz Margarita Glass
Mixers:	45mL/1½fl oz Grand Marnier
	15mL/½fl oz Amaretto
	milk and cream
	sprinkle cinnamon

Method
Build over ice.

Australia

Rocket Fuel

Ingredients

Glass:	210mL/7oz Old Fashioned Glass
Mixers:	15mL/½fl oz rum
	15mL/½fl oz gin
	15mL/½fl oz vodka
	30mL/1fl oz lemonade
	15mL/½fl oz tequila

Method
Build over ice.

Rolls Royce

United Kingdom

Ingredients

Glass: 90mL/3oz Cocktail Glass
Mixers: 30mL/1fl oz dry gin
10mL/⅜fl oz Benedictine
15mL/½fl oz dry vermouth
15mL/½fl oz sweet vermouth

Method
Stir and strain into a 3 oz cocktail glass and serve.

Roman Driver

Italy

Ingredients

Glass: 150mL/5oz Champagne Saucer
Mixers: 30mL/1fl oz Galleon Liverno
1 dash Grenadine
15mL/½fl oz vodka
20mL/⅝fl oz cream
20mL/⅝fl oz almond syrup

Method
Shake and strain into a champagne saucer and serve.

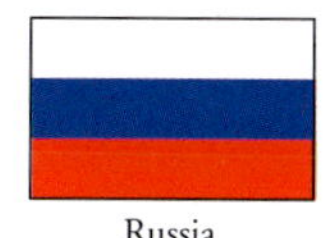
Russia

Russian Tea

Ingredients
Glass: 250mL/8oz Irish Coffee Glass
Mixers: 4 teaspoons of ground tea
120mL/4fl oz orange juice
15mL/½fl oz lemon juice
45mL/1½fl oz vodka
1 cinnamon stick
whole cloves
sugar to taste

Method
Boil the cinnamon stick and whole cloves in water for 2 minutes, add tea and allow to simmer for 2 more minutes. Strain into glass before adding juices, vodka and sugar. Garnish with an orange slice.

Rusty Bucket

Portugal

Ingredients

Glass: 150mL/5oz Cocktail Glass
Mixers: 30mL/1fl oz port wine
cola

Method
Build over ice in cocktail glass.

Rusty Nail

Scotland

Ingredients

Glass: 180mL/6oz Old Fashioned
Mixers: 30mL/1fl oz Scotch whiskey
30mL/1fl oz Drambuie

Method
Fill an old fashioned glass with cracked ice. Add ingredients and serve.

Scotland

Rusty Nail No. 2

Ingredients
Glass: 180mL/6oz Old Fashioned
Mixers: 30mL/1fl oz Scotch whiskey
30mL/1fl oz Drambuie
lemon peel

Method
Fill an old fashioned glass with cracked ice and lemon peel. Add ingredients and serve.

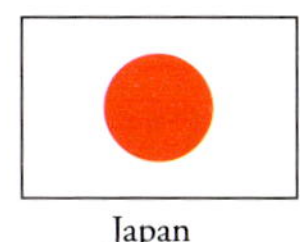

Japan

Rusty Spade

Ingredients

Glass: 140mL/5oz Margarita Glass
Mixers: 1 mango
30mL/1fl oz strawberry liqueur
1 passionfruit
dash of cream
ice

Method
Blend with ice with strawberry fan on side of glass.

Ryans's Rush

Australia

Ingredients
Glass: Cordial (Embassy)
Mixers: 10mL/⅜fl oz Kahlúa
10mL/⅜fl oz Baileys Irish Cream
10mL/⅜fl oz rum

Method
Layer in order.
An easy one. Don't be lulled by the pleasant taste, this one has a real kick.

Sail Away

New Zealand

Ingredients

Glass: 150mL/5oz Cocktail Glass
Mixers: 30mL/1fl oz Midori
30mL/1fl oz lime juice
15mL/½fl oz peach liqueur
1 dash lemon juice
30mL/1fl oz vodka

Method
Shake ingredients and strain into cocktail glass. Garnish with a lime wheel and serve.

Saint Petersburg

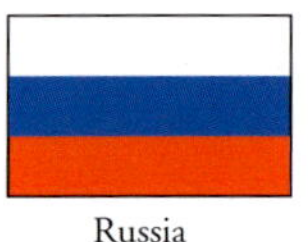
Russia

Ingredients

Glass: 150mL/5oz Cocktail Glass
Mixers: 30mL/1fl oz vodka
30mL/1fl oz Blue Curaçao
lemonade (top up)

Method
Shake vodka and curaçao and strain into cocktail glass. Top with lemonade and serve.

Saint Moritz

Switzerland

Ingredients
Glass: 150mL/5oz Old Fashioned Glass
Mixers: 30mL/1fl oz schnapps
30mL/1fl oz cream

Method
Build with ice. Garnish with a layer of heavy cream.
Traditionally this drink is made with Chambord (a raspberry flavored liqueur from France) instead of schnapps.

Saint Vincent

St Vincent

Ingredients

Glass: 150mL/5oz Champagne Saucer
Mixers: 30mL/1fl oz gin
30mL/1fl oz cream
30mL/1fl oz Galliano
dash Grenadine

Method
Shake and strain into champagne glass and serve.

Sake Special

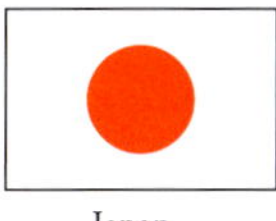
Japan

Ingredients

Glass: 90mL/3oz Cocktail Glass
Mixers: 30mL/1fl oz sake
2 dashes Angostura Bitter
60mL/2fl oz gin

Method
Mix ingredients in a mixing glass, strain into cocktail glass and serve.

Saketini

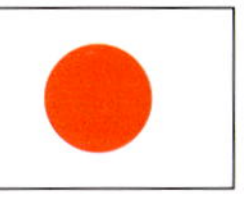
Japan

Ingredients
Glass: 90mL/3oz Cocktail Glass
Mixers: 30mL/1fl oz gin
10mL/⅜fl oz sake

Method
Shake over ice and pour. Garnish with an olive.

Panama

Salty Dog

Ingredients

Glass: 285mL/9oz Hi-Ball Glass - salt-rimmed

Mixers: 45mL/1½fl oz vodka
top-up with grapefruit juice

Method

Build over ice.
Slowly re-emerging as the long, cool cocktail it was renowned for in its heyday. Unfortunately, a limited number of bars stock grapefruit juice, which restricts availability. But as the saying goes "Every dog has his day." Straws are unnecessary, drink the cocktail from the salt rim.

Salubrious Salutations

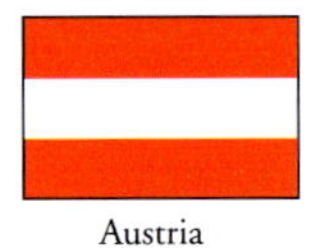
Austria

Ingredients

Glass: 90mL/3oz Cocktail Glass

Mixers: 15mL/½fl oz Galliano
15mL/½fl oz Benedictine
15mL/½fl oz Drambuie
30mL/1fl oz cream
15mL/½fl oz gin

Method

Shake and strain into cocktail glass and serve.

Sambucca Shaker

Italy

Ingredients

Glass: 210mL/7oz Old Fashioned

Mixers: 30mL/1fl oz Sambucca

Method

Pour Sambucca then light. Cup your hand entirely over the rim while it flames, creating suction. Shake the glass, place under your nose, take hand from glass to inhale the fumes, then shoot.

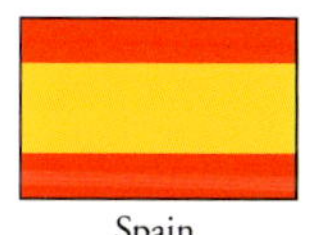
Spain

Sangria

Ingredients

Glass: 180mL/6oz Wine Glass
Mixers: 20mL/⅝fl oz Cointreau
20mL/⅝fl oz brandy
20mL/⅝fl oz Bacardi
orange, lime, lemon and strawberry pieces
sugar syrup
spanish red wine

Method
Pour in order.
Thinly slice orange and lime and place in bowl. Pour in sugar syrup and allow to stand for several hours. Add red wine.

Satin Pillow

United Arab Emirates

Ingredients
Glass: 150mL/5oz Cocktail Glass
Mixers: 5mL/⅛fl oz strawberry liqueur
10mL/⅜fl oz Cointreau
15mL/½fl oz Frangelico
15mL/½fl oz Tia Maria
20mL/⅝fl oz pineapple juice
20mL/⅝fl oz cream

Method
Blend with ice and pour.
Cut a strawberry in half and place on side of glass then swirl cream over strawberry halves.

Saturday Night

Canada

Ingredients

Glass: 180mL/6oz Colada Glass
Mixers: 15mL/½fl oz banana liqueur
60mL/2fl oz lemon juice
30mL/1fl oz gin
15mL/½fl oz Blue Curaçao
60mL/2fl oz cream

Method
Shake and strain into a colada glass, garnish with lime wheel, cherry and serve.

Sayonara

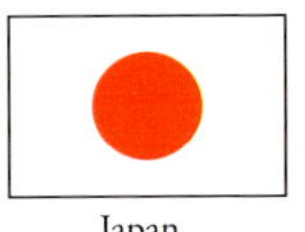
Japan

Ingredients

Glass: 150mL/5oz Cocktail Glass
Mixers: 30mL/1fl oz Midori
75mL/2½fl oz cream
30mL/1fl oz Advocaat

Method
Shake well, strain into cocktail glass and serve.

Sweden

Scandinavian Glogg

Ingredients
Glass: 180mL/6oz Wine Glass
Mixers: 30mL/1fl oz vodka
60mL/2fl oz red wine
3 blanched almonds
3 raisins
grated orange peel
1 dried fig
4 cardamon seeds
1 cinnamon stick
1 clove
1 sugar cube per serve

Method
Simmer all ingredients in a saucepan for a few minutes except for sugar cubes, then pour.

U.S.A.

Scarlett O'Hara

Ingredients

Glass: 120mL/4oz Cocktail Glass
Mixers: 30mL/1fl oz Southern Comfort
30mL/1fl oz cranberry juice
15mL/½fl oz lime juice

Method

Blend with ice and strain. Garnish with a Maraschino cherry and a lime slice.
The famous character from Margaret Mitchell's epic novel "Gone With the Wind."

Scorpion

United Arab Emirates

Ingredients

Glass: 140mL Cocktail Glass
Mixers: 15mL/½fl oz dark rum
15mL/½fl oz cognac
15mL/½fl oz Sambucca
15mL/½fl oz Orgeat
45mL/1½fl oz orange juice
15mL/½fl oz lemon juice

Method

Blend with ice. Garnish with a lime wheel with cherry.
This perilous animal and cocktail come from the trading capital of the Middle East. Remember they have a sting in their tail. Orgeat is an almond-flavored non-alcoholic syrup. Amaretto may be used as a substitute.

Scotch Frog

Austria

Ingredients

Glass: 150mL/5oz Champagne Saucer

Mixers: 60mL/2fl oz vodka
15mL/½fl oz lime cordial
30mL/1fl oz Galliano Liverno
1 dash Angostura Bitter

Method

Shake and strain into a champagne saucer, garnish with cherry and serve.

Scotch Mate

Scotland

Ingredients

Glass: 150mL/5oz Champagne Saucer

Mixers: 15mL/½fl oz Scotch whiskey
30mL/1fl oz sweet vermouth
30mL/1fl oz Galliano Liverno
30mL/1fl oz orange juice

Method

Shake and strain into a champagne saucer, garnish with orange peel and serve.

Scotch Mist

Scotland

Ingredients

Glass: 150mL/5 oz Old Fashioned Spirit Glass

Mixers: 30mL/1fl oz Scotch whisky
twist of lemon

Method

Shake over ice and pour. Garnish with a lemon rind (optional).

Scotch Solace

Scotland

Ingredients

Glass: 300mL/10oz Hi-Ball Glass
Mixers: 30mL/1fl oz Scotch whiskey
150mL/5fl oz milk
15mL/½fl oz Cointreau
30mL/1fl oz cream
1 teaspoon honey
1 teaspoon grated orange peel

Method
Fill hi-ball glass with cracked ice, add whiskey, Cointreau, honey and stir. Add milk, cream, orange peel and serve with straws.

Screaming Lizard

Panama

Ingredients

Glass: 180mL/6oz Old Fashioned
Mixers: 30mL/1fl oz Crème de Menthe
1 dash soda water
30mL/1fl oz Chartreuse

Method
Pour ingredients over ice in an old fashioned glass and serve.

U.S.A.

Screwdriver

Ingredients
Glass: 210mL/7oz Old Fashioned Glass
Mixers: 45mL/1½fl oz vodka
45mL/1½fl oz orange juice

Method
Build over ice. Garnish with orange twist or spiral.
A Comfortable Screw is made with 30mL/1fl oz Vodka, 15mL/½fl oz Southern Comfort and topped with orange juice.
A Slow Comfortable Screw has the addition of 15mL/½fl oz gin.
A Long Slow Comfortable Screw is a longer drink served in a 285mL/9½fl oz Hi-Ball Glass.
A Long Slow Comfortable Screw Up Against A Wall has the addition of 15mL/½fl oz Galliano floated.

Sea Breeze

Ingredients

Cayman Is

Glass: 150mL/5oz Cocktail glass
Mixers: 15mL/½fl oz Malibu
60mL/2fl oz pineapple juice
15mL/½fl oz Blue Curaçao
30mL/1fl oz gin
30mL/1fl oz cream

Method
Shake and strain into cocktail glass, garnish with kiwifruit and serve.

Seduction

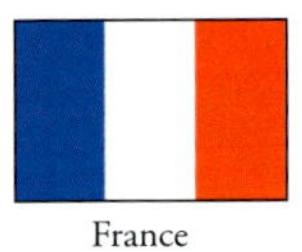

France

Ingredients

Glass: 140mL/5oz Margarita Glass
Mixers: 20mL/⅝fl oz Grand Marnier
30mL/1fl oz cream
15mL/½fl oz Cointreau
10mL/⅜fl oz orange bitters
20mL/⅝fl oz banana liqueur
1 banana

Method
Blend until smooth and pour into a margarita glass and serve.

Sex on the Beach

U.S.A.

Ingredients
Glass: 210mL/7oz Fancy Cocktail Glass
Mixers: 15mL/½fl oz Kahlúa
30mL/1fl oz Malibu
30mL/1fl oz pineapple liqueur
60mL/2fl oz cream

Method
Shake with ice and strain.
Garnish with pineapple wedge on side of glass.

Shady Lady

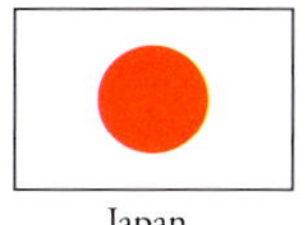
Japan

Ingredients

Glass: 300mL/10oz Hi-Ball Glass
Mixers: 30mL/1fl oz Midori
30mL/1fl oz tequila
1 slice lime
90mL/3fl oz grapefruit juice
1 Maraschino cherry

Method
Shake and pour over ice in a hi-ball glass, garnish with lemon, lime, cherry and serve.

Shandy

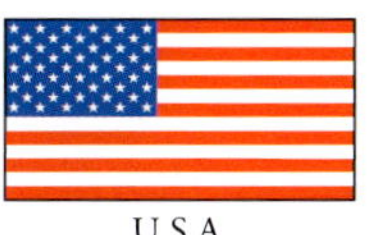
U.S.A.

Ingredients

Glass: 300mL/10oz Beer Glass
Mixers: 150mL/5oz beer
150mL/5oz lemonade

Method
Half fill beer glass with lemonade, top with beer and serve.

China

Shanghai Punch

Ingredients
Glass: 350mL/12oz Fancy Hi-Ball Glass
Mixers: 30mL/1fl oz cognac
30mL/1fl oz dark rum
45mL/1½fl oz orange juice
20mL/⅝fl oz Cointreau
20mL/⅝fl oz lemon juice
almond extract
fresh tea
grated orange and lemon peels
cinnamon sticks

Method
Boil tea and add ingredients then stir.

Sheep's Head

New Zealand

Ingredients

Glass: 150mL/5oz Old Fashioned
Mixers: 15mL/½fl oz sweet vermouth
45mL/1½fl oz bourbon
1 piece lemon peel
15mL/½fl oz Benedictine

Method

Stir and strain into a small tumbler glass, garnish with lemon peel, cherry and serve.

Sherry

United Kingdom

Ingredients

Glass: 90mL/3oz Cocktail Glass
Mixers: 30mL/1fl oz gin
30mL/1fl oz lemon juice
30mL/1fl oz sweet sherry

Method

Shake and strain into cocktail glass and serve.

U.S.A.

Shirley Temple

Ingredients

Glass: 310mL/10oz Hi-Ball Glass
Mixers: 15mL/½fl oz Grenadine
ginger ale or lemonade to top-up

Method

Build over ice.
Slice of orange, serve with swizzle stick and two straws.
For a tangy variation to this drink try a Shirley Temple No.2. Use the following: 60mL/2 fl oz pineapple juice to a glass half full of ice. Top with lemonade, float 15mL/½fl oz passionfruit pulp on top and garnish with pineapple wedge and cherry.

Shocking Blue

PNG

Ingredients

Glass: 300mL/10oz Hi-Ball Glass
Mixers: 30mL/1fl oz Blue Curaçao
30mL/1fl oz lemonade
30mL/1fl oz Midori
30mL/1fl oz banana liqueur

Method
Fill a hi-ball glass with ice and gently layer ingredients. Garnish with lime wheel and serve.

Shooting Star

U.S.A.

Ingredients

Glass: 180mL/6oz Colada Glass
Mixers: 30mL/1fl oz Midori
30mL/1fl oz cream
30mL/1fl oz peach liqueur
30g/1oz rockmelon
15mL/½fl oz orange curaçao

Method
Blend until smooth and pour into a colada glass.

Short Leg

Belgium

Ingredients
Glass: 285mL/9oz Hi-Ball Glass
Mixers: 30mL/1fl oz Cointreau
30mL/1fl oz gin
60mL/2fl oz orange juice
15mL/½fl oz lemon juice

Method
Build over ice.

Sicilian Kiss

Italy

Ingredients

Glass: 150mL/5oz Old Fashioned
Mixers: 30mL/1fl oz Southern Comfort
30mL/1fl oz Amaretto

Method
Build with ice.

U.S.A.

Sidecar

Ingredients
Glass: 90mL/3oz Cocktail Glass
Mixers: 30mL/1fl oz brandy
20mL/⅝fl oz Cointreau
30mL/1fl oz lemon juice

Method
Shake with ice and strain. Lemon twist optional.
A zappy pre-dinner cocktail. The lemon juice purifies the brandy and ferments the Cointreau. Too much lemon juice will leave an acidic after taste.

Simply Peaches

U.S.A.

Ingredients

Glass: 240mL/8oz Colada Glass
Mixers: 45mL/1½fl oz peach liqueur
2 peach halves
30mL/1fl oz Cointreau
2 scoops ice cream
75mL/2½fl oz peach nectar

Method
Blend until smooth and pour into a colada glass. Float a small scoop of ice cream, add straws and serve.

Sing Sing

Malaysia

Ingredients

Glass: 150mL/5oz Cocktail Glass
Mixers: 60mL/2fl oz Scotch whiskey
30mL/1fl oz sweet vermouth
30mL/1fl oz orange curaçao

Method
Stir and strain into cocktail glass, garnish with twist of orange peel and serve.

Australia

Slippery Nipple

Ingredients
Glass: Cordial (Embassy)
Mixers: 30mL/1fl oz Sambucca
15mL/½fl oz Baileys Irish Cream

Method
Layer in order.
One of the originals, very well received. Cream floated on the Baileys becomes a "Pregnant Slippery Nipple". Grand Marnier included makes a "Slipadicthome".

Slow Comfortable Screw

U.S.A.

Ingredients

Glass: 300mL/10oz Hi-Ball
Mixers: 30mL/1fl oz vodka
15mL/½fl oz sloe gin
15mL/½fl oz Southern Comfort
orange juice (top up)

Method

Build over ice in hi-ball glass, top with orange juice and serve with straws.

Slow Comfortable Screw No. 2

U.S.A.

Ingredients

Glass: 300mL/10oz Hi-Ball
Mixers: 30mL/1fl oz gin
60mL/2fl oz Southern Comfort
120mL/4fl oz orange juice

Method

Shake and strain into a hi-ball glass, garnish with orange wheel, cherry, straws and serve.

Slyde Your Thigh

Australia

Ingredients

Glass: 180mL/6oz Fancy Old Fashioned
Mixers: 30mL/1fl oz banana liqueur
30mL/1fl oz Crème de Cacao
30mL/1fl oz Midori
60mL/2fl oz cream

Method

Shake with ice and pour into old fashioned glass and serve.

Smog City

Mexico

Ingredients

Glass: 300mL/10oz Hi-Ball Glass
Mixers: 30mL/1fl oz tequila
60mL/2fl oz cream
30mL/1fl oz Crème de Cacao
cola (top up)

Method
Half fill a hi-ball glass with cracked ice, add liquid ingredients and lop with cola. Add straws, swizzle stick and serve.

Smooth Boy

Fiji

Ingredients

Glass: 90mL/3oz Cocktail Glass
Mixers: 30mL/1fl oz Midori
30mL/1fl oz coconut cream
15mL/½fl oz Tia Maria
330mL/1fl oz cream
75mL/2½fl oz pineapple juice

Method
Shake and strain into two cocktail glasses. Garnish with orchids (if available) and serve.

Australia

Snake in the Grass

Ingredients
Glass: 120mL/4oz Cocktail Glass
Mixers: 60mL/2fl oz Baileys
30mL/1fl oz Crème de Menthe
cream (optional)

Method
Shake with ice and pour into cocktail glass.

Snake Bite Shooter

Portugal

Ingredients

Glass: Cordial (Embassy)

Mixers: 20mL/⅝fl oz Crème de Cafe
10mL/⅞fl oz green Chartreuse

Method

Layer in order and shoot.

Snake Bite

Ingredients

United Kingdom

Glass: 120mL/4oz Cocktail Glass

Mixers: 60mL/2fl oz gin
60mL/2fl oz Crème de Menthe

Method

Shake and strain into cocktail glass.

Snoopy's Gleam

Ingredients

U.S.A.

Glass: 90mL/3oz Cocktail Glass

Mixers: 30mL/1fl oz bourbon
15mL/½fl oz orange curaçao
10mL/⅜fl oz Grenadine
15mL/½fl oz orange soda (float)

Method

Shake and strain into cocktail glass, garnish with orange peel, cherry and serve.

Norway

Snowball

Ingredients

Glass: 285mL/9½oz Hi-Ball Glass
Mixers: 30mL/1fl oz Advocaat liqueur
top-up with lemonade
dash of lime cordial
cream, optional

Method

Build over ice.
Garnish with red cherry, swizzle sticks and straws.
Place ice in the glass after mixing the Advocaat with lemonade before floating cream on top. The pressure of a post mix gun will create the desired 'snowball' effect.

Snow Drop

Scotland

Ingredients

Glass: 150m/5oz Champagne Saucer
Mixers: 60mL/2fl oz Scotch whiskey
30mL/1fl oz orange juice
30mL/1fl oz Benedictine
15mL/½fl oz green ginger wine

Method

Shake and strain into a champagne saucer, garnish with lemon peel and serve.

Snow Flake

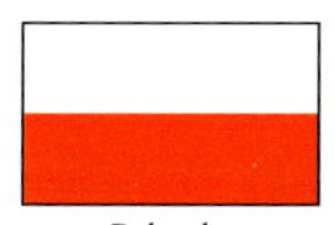
Poland

Ingredients

Glass: 300mL/10oz Hi-Ball Glass
Mixers: 30mL/1fl oz vodka
10mL/⅜fl oz Advocaat
15mL/½fl oz Galliano Liverno
1 dash cream
15mL/½fl oz Southern Comfort
20mL/⅝fl oz orange juice
lemonade (top up)

Method

Shake and strain into hi-ball glass, top with lemonade and serve with straws.

Something Swampy

Maldives

Ingredients

Glass: Brandy Balloon
Mixers: 90mL/3fl oz Blue Curaçao
30mL/1fl oz Parfait Amour
90mL/3fl oz vodka
30mL/1fl oz tequila
30mL/1fl oz Midori
lemonade (top up)

Method
Shake and pour over crushed ice in a very large brandy balloon. Top with lemonade. Garnish with jelly frogs, straws and serve.

Sonja

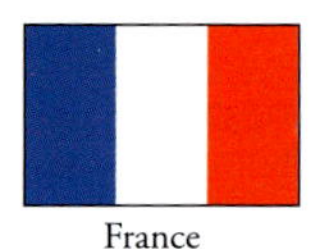
France

Ingredients

Glass: 90mL/3oz Cocktail Glass
Mixers: 30mL/1fl oz yellow Chartreuse
fresh cream (float)
15mL/½fl oz Blue Curaçao
15mL/½fl oz Galliano

Method
Stir Chartreuse, Blue Curaçao and Galliano and strain into cocktail glass. Float cream and sprinkle with nutmeg, garnish with cherry and serve.

Australia

South Pacific

Ingredients
Glass: 285mL/9½oz Hi-Ball Glass
Mixers: 30mL/1fl oz gin
15mL/½fl oz Galliano
top with lemonade
15mL/½fl oz Blue Curaçao

Method
Build over ice, then add the Blue Curaçao last.
Garnish with lemon slice, cherry, swizzle stick and straws.

South Seas

South Africa

Ingredients

Glass: 150mL/5oz Champagne Saucer

Mixers: 30mL/1fl oz Frangelico
60mL/2fl oz orange juice
20mL/⅝fl oz mango liqueur
½ banana

Method

Blend until smooth. Pour into a champagne glass and serve.

South Yarra Samurai

Australia

Ingredients

Glass: Brandy Balloon

Mixers: 30mL/1fl oz Midori
½ banana
30mL/1fl oz banana liqueur
30mL/1fl oz lemon juice

Method

Blend until smooth and pour into a brandy Balloon, garnish with strawberry and serve.

Southern Peach

U.S.A.

Ingredients

Glass: 150mL/5oz Martini Glass

Mixers: 30mL/1fl oz Cointreau
15mL/½fl oz brandy
15mL/½fl oz cherry brandy
15mL/½fl oz pineapple juice
15mL/½fl oz lemon juice

Method

Shake with ice and strain.
Butterfly a strawberry, place on side of glass, twirl cream over strawberry and sprinkle over flaked chocolate.
A magical cocktail that can be 'fluffed' up by adding egg white.

Soviet Cocktail

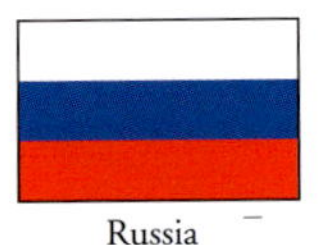
Russia

Ingredients

Glass: 90mL/3oz Cocktail glass
Mixers: 30mL/1fl oz vodka
10mL/3/8fl oz dry vermouth
10mL/3/8fl oz Amontillado

Method

Shake over ice and pour. Garnish with a twist of lemon.
Amontillado sherry has a medium dry taste and nutty flavor. May be substituted with Amaretto.

Spain

Spanish Moss

Ingredients

Glass: 150mL/5oz Old Fashioned
Mixers: 30mL/1fl oz Chambord
10mL/3/8fl oz Kahlúa
5mL/1/8fl oz green Crème de Menthe

Method

Shake with ice and strain over a cube of ice. Garnish with a green cherry.
Chambord is a raspberry flavored liqueur from France.

New Zealand

Splice

Ingredients

Glass: 210mL/7oz Hurricane Glass

Mixers: 30mL/1fl oz melon liqueur
15mL/½fl oz Galliano
15mL/½fl oz coconut liqueur
30mL/1fl oz pineapple juice
30mL/1fl oz cream

Method

Blend with ice and pour.
Garnish with pineapple wedge and leaves on side of glass.

Special Cream Chocolate

U.S.A.

Ingredients

Glass: 285mL/9oz Hi-Ball Glass

Mixers: 60g/2oz plain chocolate
½ teaspoon cinnamon
30mL/1fl oz brandy
150mL/5fl oz whipped cream (float)
300mL/10fl oz milk

Method

Heat chocolate, milk and cinnamon, add brandy and pour into hi-ball glasses. Float cream and serve with straws.

Springbok

South Africa

Ingredients

Glass: Cordial (Embassy)

Mixers: 20mL/⅝fl oz passionfruit syrup
10mL/⅜fl oz green Crème de Menthe
5mL/⅛fl oz ouzo

Method

Layer in order.

United Kingdom

Spritzer

Ingredients

Glass: 185mL/6oz Wine Goblet

Mixers: dry white wine, chilled
soda water

Method

Build, no ice.
"Wet the whistle" with a responsible alcoholic alternative. Ladies prefer the soda dilution although you may be asked for lemonade.

Sputnik

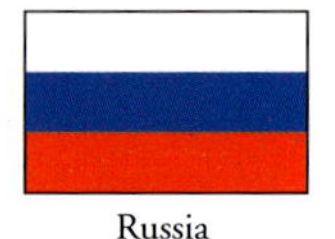

Russia

Ingredients

Glass: 150mL/5oz Cocktail Glass

Mixers: 75mL/2½fl oz vodka
10mL/⅜fl oz lemon juice
30mL/1fl oz Fernet Branca
½ teaspoon sugar

Method

Shake and strain over ice in cocktail glass and serve.

Squashed Frog

Australia

Ingredients

Glass: 90mL/3oz Sherry Glass

Mixers: 30mL/1fl oz Midori
30mL/1fl oz Baileys Irish Cream
10mL/⅜fl oz Advocaat
10mL/⅜fl oz cherry Advocaat

Method

Stir in Advocaat and cherry Advocaat. Float Midori and serve.

U.S.A.

Stars & Stripes

Ingredients

Glass: 300mL/10oz Fancy Cocktail

Mixers: 10mL/⅜fl oz Blue Curaçao
Blender 1
30mL/1fl oz Southern Comfort
30mL/1fl oz Frangelico
Blender 2
30mL/1fl oz strawberry liqueur
3-4 strawberries

Method

Pour Blue Curaçao into glass. Blend other ingredients with ice in 2 separate blenders and pour.

Garnish: sprinkle grated chocolate flakes over top and add a strawberry and USA flag to side of glass.

Steroid Blast

Canada

Ingredients

Glass: 150mL/5oz Cocktail Glass

Mixers: 30mL/1fl oz rum
30mL/1fl oz vodka
15mL/½fl oz tequila
30mL/1fl oz Benedictine
1 dash soda water

Method

Shake and strain into cocktail glass, top with soda water and serve.

Stimulation

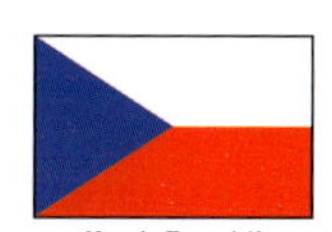

Czech Republic

Ingredients

Glass: 150mL/5oz Cocktail Glass

Mixers: 30mL/1fl oz Baileys Irish Cream
30mL/1fl oz Cointreau
30mL/1fl oz Malibu
15mL/½fl oz cream

Method

Layer in order in cocktail glass and serve.

Stinger

Switzerland

Ingredients

Glass: 90mL/3oz Cocktail Glass
Mixers: 30mL/1fl oz brandy
10mL/$\frac{3}{8}$fl oz white Crème de Menthe

Method

Stir over ice and strain.

U.S.A.

Stormy Monday

Ingredients

Glass: 210mL/7oz Fancy Hi-Ball
Mixers: 30mL/1fl oz Southern Comfort
30mL/1fl oz Malibu
120mL/4fl oz orange juice

Method

Build over ice.

Australia

Strawberry Blonde

Ingredients

Glass: 285mL/9½oz Hi-Ball Glass

Mixers: 30mL/1fl oz dark Crème de Cacao
top-up with cola
fresh cream, floated
splash of Grenadine

Method

Build over ice.
Garnish with a red cherry, swizzle sticks and straws.
Tasting this cocktail will reveal the secret of why 'blondes have more fun'. Placing ice in the glass after mixing the Crème de Cacao with cola will support the floating cream on top. A dessert cocktail. Ideal on a blind date.

Strawberry Colada

U.S.A.

Ingredients

Glass: 300mL/10oz Hi-Ball Glass

Mixers: 30mL/1fl oz white rum
30mL/1fl oz cream
30mL/1fl oz coconut cream
4 strawberries
30mL/1fl oz pineapple liqueur
90mL/3fl oz pineapple juice

Method

Blend ingredients and pour into a hi-ball glass and serve with a pineapple wedge as a garnish.

Strawberry Margarita

Mexico

Ingredients

Glass: 140mL Champagne Saucer

Mixers: 30mL/1fl oz tequila
5mL/⅙fl oz egg white
15mL/½fl oz Cointreau
2-4 strawberries
15mL/½fl oz strawberry liqueur
45mL/1½fl oz lemon juice

Method

Blend until smooth, pour into a salt rimmed glass with a half strawberry as garnish. Serve.

Strawberry Tongo

Zimbabwe

Ingredients

Glass: 150mL/5oz Cocktail Glass
Mixers: 30mL/1fl oz Tia Maria
10mL/⅜fl oz milk
30mL/1fl oz Kahlúa
2 strawberries
10mL/⅜fl oz Grand Marnier
30mL/1fl oz lemon juice

Method
Blend and pour into a cocktail glass and serve.

Strawgasm

U.S.A.

Ingredients

Glass: 210mL/7oz Colada Glass
Mixers: 15mL/½fl oz Malibu
3 strawberries
15mL/½fl oz strawberry liqueur
¼ small banana
15mL/½fl oz Galliano
45mL/1½fl oz cream
15mL/½fl oz Crème de Cacao

Method
Blend until smooth, pour into a colada glass and serve. Garnish with banana and mint leaves.

Summer Breeze

Australia

Ingredients
Glass: 300mL/10oz Fancy Cocktail Glass
Mixers: 60mL/2oz peach tree liqueur
15mL/½fl oz dark rum
15mL/½fl oz mango liqueur
15mL/½fl oz gin
60mL/2fl oz pineapple juice
60mL/2fl oz orange juice
1 fresh mango
1 fresh peach

Method
Blend with ice and pour.

Summer Sherbet

Singapore

Ingredients

Glass: 150mL/5oz Cocktail Glass
Mixers: 30mL/1fl oz mango liqueur
30mL/1fl oz lemon juice
30mL/1fl oz Galliano

Method
Shake and strain into a cocktail glass and serve.

Sundancer

Jamaica

Ingredients

Glass: 210mL/7oz Old Fashioned
Mixers: 45mL/1½fl oz dark rum
15mL/½fl oz lemon juice
30mL/1fl oz Amaretto
30mL/1fl oz orange juice
30mL/1fl oz pineapple juice
1 dash egg white

Method
Shake and strain into an old fashioned glass and serve.

Australia

Sunken Treasure

Ingredients
Glass: 140mL Cocktail Glass
Mixers: 30mL/1fl oz gin
15mL/½fl oz peach liqueur
top up with Champagne

Method
Garnish by placing a teaspoon of apricot conserve in the bottom of glass and then push a strawberry into conserve. Stir gin and peach liqueur over ice and strain, then top glass with champagne.

Sunkissed

Ingredients

Germany

Glass: 150mL/5oz Champagne Saucer

Mixers: 30mL/1fl oz Rubis
60mL/2fl oz blackcurrant juice
15mL/½fl oz Cointreau
1 tablespoon raspberries

Method
Blend until smooth and pour into a champagne saucer and serve.

Sunset Special

Ingredients

Egypt

Glass: 150mL/5oz Cocktail Glass

Mixers: 45mL/1½fl oz sweet vermouth
45mL/1½fl oz Cointreau
45mL/1½fl oz gin

Method
Shake and strain into cocktail glass, garnish with orange slice and serve.

Suntorian Star

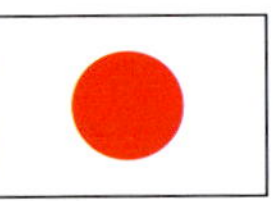

Japan

Ingredients

Glass: 150mL/5oz Cocktail Glass

Mixers: 30mL/1fl oz Midori
15mL/½fl oz banana liqueur
4 pieces fresh pineapple
½ passionfruit pulp
strawberries

Method
Puree strawberries and pour a twirl inside the glass. Blend Midori, banana liqueur and pineapple and pour into glass, topping with passionfruit pulp.

Surfers Paradise

Australia

Ingredients

Glass: 150mL/5oz Champagne Saucer

Mixers: 60mL/2fl oz vodka
15mL/½fl oz Blue Curaçao
45mL/1½fl oz dry vermouth
1 Maraschino cherry
20mL/fl oz Galliano

Method

Stir and strain into a champagne saucer, garnish with cherry and serve.

Surprise

United Kingdom

Ingredients

Glass: 210mL/7oz Old Fashioned

Mixers: 30mL/1fl oz gin
20mL/⅝fl oz apricot brandy
60mL/2fl oz orange juice

Method

Shake and strain over ice in an old fashioned glass and serve.

Sweden

Swedish Snowball

Ingredients

Glass: 210mL/7oz Old Fashioned

Mixers: 30mL/1fl oz Advocaat
15mL/½fl oz lemon juice
top up with soda water

Method

Build over ice then top up with soda. Garnish with a lemon slice.

Sweet Lady Jane

Thailand

Ingredients

Glass:	150mL/5oz Champagne Saucer
Mixers:	15mL/½fl oz Grand Marnier
	15mL/½fl oz orange juice
	15mL/½fl oz Cointreau
	15mL/½fl oz coconut cream
	30mL/1fl oz strawberry liqueur
	30mL/1fl oz fresh cream

Method

Shake with ice and strain.
Garnish with strawberry, mint and chocolate flakes.

U.S.A.

Sweet Maria

Ingredients

Glass:	150mL/5oz Old Fashioned
Mixers:	30mL/1fl oz bourbon
	30mL/1fl oz Tia Maria
	60mL/2fl oz cream

Method

Shake then strain into old fashioned glass.

United Kingdom

Sweet Martini

Ingredients

Glass: 90mL/3oz Cocktail Glass

Mixers: 45mL/1½fl oz gin
20mL/⅝fl oz rosso vermouth

Method

Stir over ice and strain.
Red cherry on toothpick in glass.
Sister to the "Dry Martini", the sweeter vermouth overwhelms the gin sting. A pre dinner cocktail which can be stirred and strained either:
"On The Rocks" - served in a standard Spirit glass over ice.
"Straight Up" - served in a 90mL/3 fl oz cocktail glass over ice.

Sweet Sixteen

New Zealand

Ingredients

Glass: 150mL/5oz Cocktail Glass

Mixers: 30mL/1fl oz gin
1 dash pineapple juice
15mL/½fl oz Malibu
1 dash coconut cream
15mL/½fl oz white Crème de Cacao
1 slice pineapple

Method

Blend until smooth and pour into a cocktail glass and serve.

Swiss Chocolate

Switzerland

Ingredients

Glass: 90oz/3oz Cocktail Glass

Mixers: 30mL/1fl oz anisette
fresh cream (float)
30mL/1fl oz cherry brandy
30mL/1fl oz green tea

Method

Pour ingredients into a cocktail glass, float cream, garnish with cherry and serve.

Talisman

Greece

Ingredients

Glass: 180mL/6oz Old Fashioned
Mixers: 30mL/1fl oz Midori
15mL/½fl oz lime juice
30mL/1fl oz orange juice

Method
Build ingredients in an old fashioned glass. Garnish with a lime slice in the glass and serve.

Temptation

Canada

Ingredients

Glass: 150mL/5oz Champagne Saucer
Mixers: 60mL/2fl oz rye whiskey
15mL/½fl oz Dubonnet
15mL/½fl oz Pernod
15mL/½fl oz white curaçao

Method
Stir and strain into a champagne saucer. Garnish with a twist of orange peel and serve.

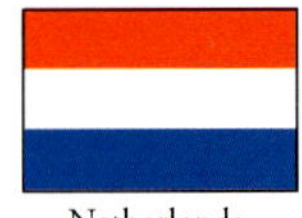
Netherlands

Tall Dutch Egg Nog

Ingredients
Glass: 300mL/10oz Beer Mug
Mixers: 30mL/1fl oz Bacardi
30mL/1fl oz orange juice
10mL/⅜fl oz dark rum
10mL/⅜fl oz Advocaat
120mL/4fl oz milk

Method
Blend over ice. Garnish with a sprinkle of cinnamon and egg.

Tennessee Manhattan Dry

U.S.A.

Ingredients

Glass: 90mL/3oz Cocktail Glass

Mixers: 45mL/1½fl oz Tennessee whiskey
20mL/⅝fl oz dry vermouth
2 dashes Angostura Bitter

Method

Stir and strain into cocktail glass. Garnish with twist of lemon peel and serve.

Tennessee Sour

U.S.A.

Ingredients

Glass: 150mL/5oz Cocktail Glass

Mixers: 60mL/2fl oz Tennessee whiskey
juice ½ lemon
dash of sugar syrup
soda water (top up)

Method

Shake ingredients except soda water. Strain into cocktail glass, top with soda. Garnish with lemon slice and cherry and serve.

Mexico

Tequila Slammer

Ingredients

Glass: 185mL/6oz Old Fashioned

Mixers: 30mL/1fl oz tequila
30mL/1fl oz dry ginger ale

Method

Build, no ice.
A one hit wonder - holding a coaster over the entire rim, rotate the glass clockwise on the bar 4-5 times. Lift and 'slam' the base of the glass down onto the bar, then drain in one shot. The carbonated mixer fizzes the tequila when slammed.
Usually bartenders splash only 5-10mL/⅛-⅜fl oz of dry ginger ale to aid the quick drinking process.

Tequila Sunrise

Mexico

Ingredients

Glass: 285mL/9½oz Hi-Ball Glass

Mixers: 30mL/1fl oz tequila
5mL/⅛fl oz Grenadine
top-up with orange juice

Method

Build over ice.
Sipping this long, cool cocktail at sunrise or sunset is magnificient.
To obtain the cleanest visual effect, drop Grenadine down the inside of the glass, after topping up with orange juice.
Dropping Grenadine in the middle creates a fallout effect, detracting from the presentation of the cocktail.
Best served with chilled, freshly squeezed oranges.

Tequila Sparkle

U.S.A.

Ingredients

Glass: 140mL/5oz Margarita Glass

Mixers: 20mL/⅝fl oz tequila
75mL/2½fl oz milk
30mL/1fl oz coffee liqueur
75mL/2½fl oz cream

Method

Frost the rims of a margarita glass with salt. Stir ingredients and strain into prepared glass and serve.

The Big Chill

Bermuda

Ingredients

Glass: 300mL/10oz Hi-Ball Glass

Mixers: 30mL/1fl oz Midori
30mL/1fl oz bacardi rum
15mL/½fl oz banana liqueur
90mL/3fl oz pineapple juice

Method

Build ingredients over ice in hi-ball glass and serve with straws.

Netherlands

The Dik Hewitt

Ingredients

Glass: 150mL/5oz Cocktail Glass

Mixers: 30mL/1fl oz Tennessee whiskey
30mL/1fl oz cognac
30mL/1fl oz Benedictine
glass of water (on the side)

Method

Shake with ice and strain.

The Time Warp

Australia

Ingredients

Glass: 150mL/5oz Cocktail Glass

Mixers: 20mL/⅝fl oz Midori
5mL/⅛fl oz Blue Curaçao
15mL/½fl oz Malibu
15mL/½fl oz pineapple juice
5mL/⅛fl oz raspberry cordial

Method

Shake Midori, Malibu, pineapple juice and strain into cocktail glass. Add raspberry cordial and Blue Curaçao, garnish with cherry and serve.

Third Degree

Saudi Arabia

Ingredients

Glass: 150mL/5oz Champagne Saucer

Mixers: 90mL/3fl oz gin
10mL/⅜fl oz Pernod
30mL/1fl oz dry vermouth

Method

Shake and strain into a champagne saucer, garnish with lemon peel and serve.

Third Rail

Ingredients

Italy

Glass:	90mL/3oz Cocktail Glass
Mixers:	30mL/1fl oz rum 20mL/⅝fl oz orange juice 20mL/⅝fl oz dry vermouth 20mL/⅝fl oz sweet vermouth

Method

Shake and strain into cocktail glass and serve.

Three Sisters

Ingredients

Australia

Glass:	150mL/5oz Champagne Saucer
Mixers:	45mL/1½fl oz brandy 1 dash Grenadine 45mL/1½fl oz Galliano 45mL/1½fl oz orange juice

Method

Shake and strain into a champagne saucer, garnish with cherry and serve.

Time Out

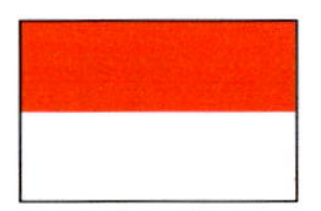

Indonesia

Ingredients

Glass:	285mL/9oz Fancy Hi-Ball Glass
Mixers:	30mL/1fl oz brandy 30mL/1fl oz Kahlúa 60mL/2fl oz orange juice 30mL/1fl oz cream peaches dash of Grenadine

Method

Blend with ice and pour.

Morocco

Tickled Pink

Ingredients

Glass: Whiskey Shot
Mixers: 45mL/1½fl oz white Crème de Cacao
5mL/⅛fl oz Grenadine

Method
Layer in order.

T.N.T

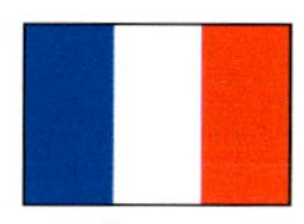

France

Ingredients
Glass: 140mL Cocktail Glass
Mixers: 45mL/1½fl oz brandy
20mL/⅝fl oz orange liqueur
dash of Pernod
dash of Angostura Bitter

Method
Stir over ice and strain.
A powder keg, really a cocktail to liven up the party. Drink in moderation, as this one can really cause a "bang."

Australia

Toblerone

Ingredients

Glass: 150mL/5oz Cocktail Glass
Mixers: 5mL/⅙fl oz Baileys Irish Cream
15mL/½fl oz Kahlúa
15mL/½fl oz white Crème de Cacao
30mL/1fl oz Frangelico
60mL/2fl oz cream
½ teaspoon honey

Method

Blend with ice and pour.
Sprinkle almond flakes and nutmeg over top.
To create a special effect drag a cotton strand over completed cocktail.

Tokyo Joe

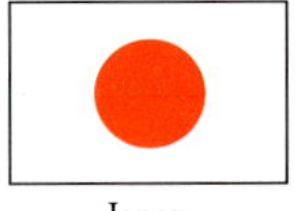
Japan

Ingredients

Glass: 90mL/3oz Cocktail Glass
Mixers: 45mL/1½fl oz vodka
45mL/1½fl oz Midori

Method

Layer in cocktail glass and serve.

Tokyo Rose

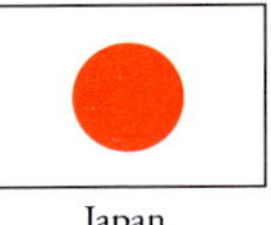
Japan

Ingredients

Glass: Cordial (Embassy)
Mixers: 10mL/⅜fl oz tomato juice
10mL/⅜fl oz vodka
10mL/⅜fl oz sake

Method

Layer in order.

U.S.A.

Tom Collins

Ingredients

Glass: 140mL Champagne Saucer
Mixers: 60mL/2fl oz lemon juice
60mL/2fl oz gin
soda water

Method
Put cracked ice, lemon juice, soda water and gin in a glass. Fill with soda water and stir. Serve with a slice of lemon and cherry for garnish.
Brandy, bourbon, rum or any whisky can be used instead of gin, the Collins is named after the liqour used, eg. Rum Collins.

---

2 B Slippery

Australia

Ingredients
Glass: 180mL/6oz Old Fashioned
Mixers: 30mL/1fl oz black Sambucca
30mL/1fl oz lime cordial

Method
Build over ice.

Top of the Crop

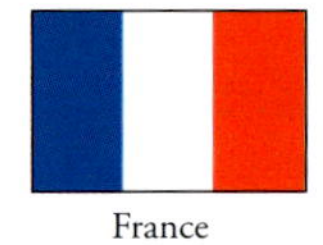
France

Ingredients

Glass: 300mL/10oz Hi-Ball Glass
Mixers: 30mL/1fl oz Pernod
ginger beer (top up)
30mL/1fl oz Blue Curaçao

Method
Quarter fill a hi-ball glass with cracked ice. Add Pernod and Blue curaçao, top with ginger beer, add straws and serve.

Topping

United Kingdom

Ingredients

Glass: 90mL/3oz Cocktail Glass
Mixers: 30mL/1fl oz gin
30mL/1fl oz dry vermouth
1 Maraschino cherry
15mL/½fl oz Crème de Violette

Method
Shake and strain into cocktail glass, garnish with cherry and serve.

Trader Vic's Rum Fizz

U.S.A.

Ingredients
Glass: 135mL/4½oz Tulip Champagne Glass
Mixers: 30mL/1fl oz dark rum
30mL/1fl oz lemon juice
10mL/⅜fl oz sugar
15mL/½fl oz cream soda
1 raw egg

Method
Shake over ice and pour. Garnish with an orange spiral.
From the range of cocktails for which the internationally renowned cocktail bar proprietor has become recognised.

Australia

Traffic Light

Ingredients

Glass: Tall Dutch Cordial
Mixers: 20mL/⅞fl oz strawberry liqueur
10mL/⅜fl oz Galliano
10mL/⅜fl oz green Chartreuse

Method

Layer in order, light, then straw shoot.

Traffic Stopper

India

Ingredients

Glass: Whiskey Shot
Mixers: 15mL/½fl oz banana liqueur
15mL/½fl oz Blue Curaçao
15mL/½fl oz Baileys Irish Cream

Method

Layer in order in a shot glass and serve.

Transplant

Mauritius

Ingredients

Glass: 300mL/10oz Hi-Ball Glass
Mixers: 30mL/1fl oz Bacardi rum
10mL/⅜fl oz Galliano
10mL/⅜fl oz Crème de Menthe
orange juice (top up)

Method

Place ingredients into a hi-ball glass and top with orange juice. Garnish with orange peel, straws and serve.

Triple Bypass

Portugal

Ingredients

Glass: 90mL/3oz Cocktail Glass
Mixers: 20mL/⅝fl oz Crème de Cassis
20mL/⅝fl oz white Crème de Menthe
20mL/⅝fl oz cherry brandy

Method

Layer liqueurs in order then float with cream.

Travelex

Ingredients

Austria

Glass: 90mL/3oz Cocktail Glass
Mixers: 20mL/⅝fl oz kümmel liqueur
15mL/½fl oz lemon juice
15mL/½fl oz Galliano
10mL/⅜fl oz vodka
10mL/⅜fl oz Crème de Banana

Method

Shake and strain into a cocktail glass, garnish with pineapple spear and serve.

Tropical

Ingredients

Philippines

Glass: 300mL/10oz Hi-Ball Glass
Mixers: 30mL/1fl oz vodka
60mL/2fl oz pineapple juice
30mL/1fl oz peach tree
1 dash cream
15mL/½fl oz Rubis
5 strawberries

Method

Blend and pour into hi-ball glass, add straws and serve.

Jamaica

Tropical Ambrosia

Ingredients

Glass: 285mL/9½oz Footed Hi-Ball Glass

Mixers: 1 mandarin orange
1 apple
150mL/5oz coconut milk
15mL/½fl oz lemon juice

Method

Blend over ice and pour. Garnish with an apple slice.

Tropical Delight

The Bahamas

Ingredients

Glass: 90mL/3oz Cocktail Glass

Mixers: 30mL/1fl oz dark rum
30mL/1fl oz cream
20mL/⅝fl oz orange juice

Method

Shake and strain into a cocktail glass, sprinkle with nutmeg and serve.

Tropical Field

U.S.A.

Ingredients

Glass: 150mL/5oz Cocktail Glass

Mixers: 30mL/1fl oz strawberry liqueur
15mL/½fl oz cherry brandy
30mL/1fl oz pineapple juice
30mL/1fl oz cream

Method

Shake and strain into cocktail glass, garnish with strawberry, cherry and serve.

Australia

Tropical Itch

Ingredients

Glass: 425mL/14oz Hurricane Glass

Mixers: 45mL/1½fl oz rum
45mL/1½fl oz bourbon
juice of half fresh lime
dash Angostura Bitter
top-up with pineapple juice and passionfruit
30mL/1fl oz rum, floated

Method

Build over ice.

Tropical Paradise

Cayman Is

Ingredients

Glass: 90mL/3oz Cocktail Glass

Mixers: 45mL/1½fl oz Bacardi rum
5mL/⅛fl oz lemon juice
45mL/1½fl oz peach tree
1 slice mango
20mL/⅝fl oz mango liqueur
1 dash mango nectar

Method

Blend and pour into cocktail glass and serve.

Tropical Sunset

Argentina

Ingredients

Glass: 300mL/10oz Hi-Ball Glass

Mixers: 30mL/1fl oz Bacardi rum
60mL/2fl oz orange juice
20mL/⅝fl oz Grand Marnier
1 egg yolk
30mL/1fl oz pineapple juice
1 dash Grenadine

Method

Shake and strain into a hi-ball glass, garnish with pineapple slice, straws and serve.

Turkish Delight

Turkey

Ingredients

Glass: 285mL/9½ oz Hi-Ball Glass
Mixers: 30mL/1fl oz Sabra
5mL/⅛fl oz Grenadine
15mL/½fl oz Parfait Amour
30mL/1fl oz cream
120mL/4fl oz milk

Method
Shake and strain into a colada glass, sprinkle with chocolate flakes, add straws and serve.

Twilight Zone

U.S.A.

Ingredients

Glass: 150mL/5oz Champagne Saucer
Mixers: 60mL/2fl oz Bacardi rum
15mL/½fl oz fresh cream
30mL/1fl oz Crème de Menthe
15mL/½fl oz Parfait Amour
15mL/½fl oz lime cordial

Method
Shake and strain into a champagne saucer and serve.

Finland

Two Stroke

Ingredients
Glass: Cordial (Embassy)
Mixers: 30mL/1fl oz chilled vodka
cracked pepper

Method
Layer in order.

V-Bomb

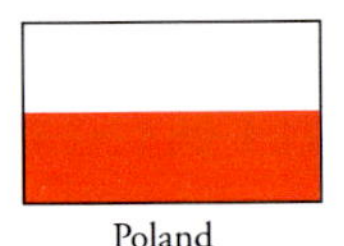
Poland

Ingredients

Glass: 300mL/10oz Beer Glass

Mixers: 60mL/2fl oz vodka
15mL/½fl oz lemon juice
sparkling wine

Method

Build over ice.

Valencia Smile

Spain

Ingredients

Glass: 150mL/5oz Champagne Flute

Mixers: 30mL/1fl oz apricot brandy
30mL/1fl oz orange juice
4 dashes apricot brandy
Champagne (top up)

Method

Shake and strain into a flute glass, top with champagne and serve.

Vampire's Passion

Romania

Ingredients

Glass: 150mL/5oz Cocktail Glass

Mixers: 30mL/1fl oz red Crème de Menthe
30mL/1fl oz black Sambucca
30mL/1fl oz Sambucca
30mL/1fl oz Baileys Irish Cream
15 mL (1/2 oz) strawberry liqueur

Method

Layer in order in cocktail glass and serve.

Australia

Velvet Hue

Ingredients

Glass:	210mL/7oz Old Fashioned
Mixers:	30mL/1fl oz Brandy
	30mL/1fl oz Kahlúa
	30mL/1fl oz Cointreau
	90mL/3fl oz cream

Method

Shake with ice, then strain into glass.

Velvet Hammer

U.S.A.

Ingredients

Glass:	150mL/5oz Cocktail Glass
Mixers:	30mL/1fl oz Cointreau
	30mL/1fl oz cream
	30mL/1fl oz Galliano

Method

Half fill a cocktail glass with crushed ice. Shake ingredients, pour over ice and serve.

Vermouth Cassis

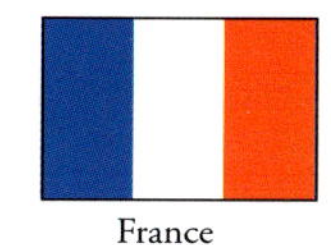

France

Ingredients

Glass:	180mL/8oz Wine Goblet Glass
Mixers:	90mL/3fl oz dry vermouth
	soda water (top up)
	45mL/1½fl oz Crème de Cassis

Method

Place a few cubes of ice in a goblet glass along with vermouth and Crème de Cassis. Top with soda water, garnish with lemon peel and serve.

Vicious Vernon

Chile

Ingredients

Glass: Whiskey Shot
Mixers: 15mL/½fl oz banana liqueur
15mL/½fl oz Baileys Irish Cream
15mL/½fl oz Kahlúa

Method
Layer in a shot glass and serve.

Violet Slumber

Czech Republic

Ingredients

Glass: 140mL Champagne Saucer
Mixers: 15mL/½fl oz Malibu
10mL/⅜fl oz orange juice
15mL/½fl oz Parfait Amour

Method
Layer in a shot glass and serve.

Viking II

Norway

Ingredients
Glass: Whisky Prism Shot
Mixers: 20mL/⅞fl oz Galliano
20mL/⅞fl oz Aquavit

Method
Layer in order.

United Kingdom

Virgin Mary

Ingredients

Glass: 285mL/9½oz Hi-Ball Glass

Mixers: 150mL/5fl oz tomato juice
15mL/½fl oz lemon juice
teaspoon Worcestershire Sauce
Tabasco Sauce
salt and pepper to taste

Method

Blend all ingredients together, then serve in salt-rimmed glass with ice, garnished with celery stalk, mint sprig and slice of lemon.

Virgin's Delight

Thailand

Ingredients

Glass: 150mL/5oz Champagne Saucer

Mixers: 20mL/⅝fl oz Cointreau
20mL/⅝fl oz cream
20mL/⅝fl oz Galliano
20mL/⅝fl oz orange juice

Method

Shake and strain into a champagne saucer, garnish with cherry and serve.

Virgin's Paradise

U.S.A.

Ingredients

Glass: 150mL/5oz Champagne Saucer

Mixers: 20mL/⅝fl oz gin
20mL/⅝fl oz cream
20mL/⅝fl oz Galliano
20mL/⅝fl oz orange juice
20mL/⅝fl oz almond liqueur

Method

Shake and strain into a champagne saucer, garnish with cherry and serve.

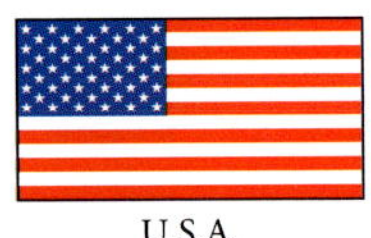
U.S.A.

Vodkatini

Ingredients

Glass: 90mL/3oz Cocktail Glass
Mixers: 45mL/1½fl oz vodka
10mL/⅜fl oz dry vermouth

Method

Shake and strain into cocktail glass, garnish with lemon twist.

Vodka Gibson

United Kingdom

Ingredients

Glass: 90mL/3oz Cocktail Glass
Mixers: 30mL/1fl oz vodka
15mL/½fl oz dry vermouth

Method

Shake and strain into cocktail glass, garnish with cocktail onion and serve.

Vodka Collins

U.S.A.

Ingredients

Glass: 300mL/10oz Hi-Ball Glass
Mixers: 30mL/1fl oz vodka
1 teaspoon sugar
1 slice lemon
juice 1 lime
soda water (top up)

Method

Shake and strain into hi-ball glass and top with soda water. Garnish with lemon slice, cherry and serve with straws.

Volcano

Japan

Ingredients

Glass: 300mL/10oz Hurricane
Mixers: 15mL/½fl oz Bacardi rum
15mL/½fl oz Blue Curaçao
15mL/½fl oz dark rum
green Chartreuse
orange juice

Method

Soak ½ lime wheel in a small amount of green Chartreuse. Shake Bacardi and rum with ice and strain into a hurricane glass. Top up with equal parts of orange and pineapple juices. Add Blue Curaçao and float the lime slice. Ignite the lime and serve with straws beside the glass.

Voodoo Cure

Haiti

Ingredients

Glass: 150mL/5oz Champagne Saucer
Mixers: 30mL/1fl oz Bacardi rum
½ banana
20mL/⅝fl oz banana liqueur
60mL/2fl oz orange juice
15mL/½fl oz Malibu

Method

Blend until smooth and pour into a champagne saucer and serve.

Voodoo Child

U.S.A.

Ingredients

Glass: 90mL/3oz Cocktail Glass
Mixers: 15mL/½fl oz melon liqueur
15mL/½fl oz black Sambucca
15mL/½fl oz Baileys Irish Cream
15mL/½fl oz Tia Maria
15mL/½fl oz cream

Method

Layer melon liqueur on black Sambucca in glass. Shake other ingredients with ice and strain.
Garnish with green and black jelly babies on a skewer, then place across top of glass.

Waldorf

U.S.A.

Ingredients

Glass: 120mL/4oz Cocktail Glass
Mixers: 30mL/1fl oz Bourbon
5mL/⅛fl oz Pernod
5mL/⅛fl oz sweet vermouth
2 dashes of Angostura Bitter

Method

Shake over ice and strain. Garnish with an orange twist.

Ward

Canada

Ingredients

Glass: 120mL/4oz Cocktail Glass
Mixers: 45mL/1½fl oz Canadian whiskey
15mL/½fl oz powdered sugar
30mL/1fl oz lemon juice
5mL/⅛fl oz Grenadine

Method

Shake and strain into cocktail glass and serve.

Ward Eight

Canada

Ingredients

Glass: 120mL/4oz Cocktail Glass
Mixers: 45mL/1½fl oz rye whiskey
10mL/⅜fl oz Grenadine
15mL/½fl oz orange juice
15mL/½fl oz lemon juice

Method

Shake and strain into cocktail glass and serve.

Water Bubba

Ivory Coast

Ingredients

Glass: Cordial (Embassy)
Mixers: 10mL/½fl oz cherry Advocaat
10mL/½fl oz Blue Curaçao
10mL/⅜fl oz Advocaat

Method
Layer in order, serve.

Westmooreland

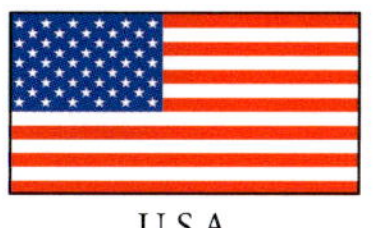

U.S.A.

Ingredients

Glass: 210mL/7oz Old Fashioned
Mixers: 90mL/3fl oz bourbon
1 tablespoon sugar
2 mint sprigs

Method
Crush half the mint with sugar and ice. Place in an old fashioned glass, add bourbon. Place remaining mint and ice into glass and serve with straws.

Barbados

West Indies Yellow Bird

Ingredients
Glass: 210mL/ Footed Hi-Ball Glass
Mixers: 30mL/1fl oz dark rum
15mL/½fl oz Banana Liqueur
15mL/½fl oz Galliano
45mL/1½fl oz pineapple juice
45mL/1½fl oz orange juice

Method
Blend with ice. Garnish with a pineapple wedge and cherry.

Wet Spot

Hong Kong

Ingredients

Glass:	150mL/5 oz Cocktail Glass
Mixers:	30mL/1fl oz Midori
	15mL/½fl oz Frangelico
	30mL/1fl oz apple juice
	30mL/1fl oz cream
	30mL/1fl oz passionfruit pulp, float

Method

Shake and strain all ingredients with the exception of passionfruit pulp. Pour into glass then float passionfruit pulp.

United Kingdom

Whiskey Sour

Ingredients

Glass:	140mL/5 oz Wine Glass
Mixers:	45mL/1½fl oz Scotch Whisky
	30mL/1fl oz lemon juice
	15mL/½fl oz sugar syrup
	½ egg white

Method

Shake with ice and strain.
Garnish with a red cherry at bottom of glass and slice of lemon on side.
A quaint appetizer before dinner. Shake vigorously so the egg white rises to a frothy head after straining. Some people prefer a 140mL/5 oz cocktail glass.

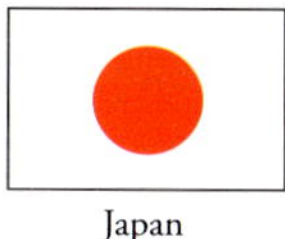
Japan

Whisper

Ingredients

Glass: 390mL/13oz Poco Grande Glass

Mixers: 45mL/1½fl oz strawberry liqueur
45mL/1½fl oz mango liqueur
45mL/1½fl oz lime juice
45mL/1½fl oz lemon juice
peaches

Method
Blend with ice and strain.

White Lady

U.S.A.

Ingredients

Glass: 90mL/3oz Cocktail Glass

Mixers: 30mL/1fl oz gin
15mL/½fl oz lemon juice
15mL/½fl oz sugar syrup
½ egg white

Method
Shake with ice and strain. A traditional pre dinner cocktail. Pure yet bland, change to either:
"Blue Lady" - substitute Blue Curaçao for sugar syrup.
or "Pink Lady" - substitute Grenadine for sugar syrup and add cream.

Widow's Kiss

Luxembourg

Ingredients

Glass:	90mL/3oz Cocktail Glass
Mixers:	30mL/1fl oz apple brandy
	10mL/⅜fl oz Benedictine
	10mL/⅜fl oz yellow Chartreuse
	5mL/⅛fl oz Angostura Bitter

Method

Shake over ice and strain. Garnish with a floating strawberry.

U.S.A.

Woodstock

Ingredients

Glass:	150mL/5oz Old Fashioned, sugar rimmed with maple syrup
Mixers:	30mL/1fl oz gin
	10mL/⅜fl oz lemon juice
	10mL/⅜fl oz maple syrup
	2 dashes Angostura Bitter

Method

Shake over ice and strain, then add cubed ice. Garnish with a straw.

X.T.C.

Australia

Ingredients

Glass: 90mL/3oz Cocktail Glass
Mixers: 30mL/1fl oz Tia Maria
30mL/1fl oz strawberry liqueur
30mL/1fl oz cream

Method

Shake with ice and strain.
Butterfly strawberry placed on side of glass, twirl thickened cream over strawberry and sprinkle over flaked chocolate.

Yorker

U.S.A.

Ingredients

Glass: 180mL/6oz Colada Glass
Mixers: 30mL/1fl oz Midori
30g/1oz avocado
30mL/1fl oz cream
60mL/2fl oz milk

Method

Blend ingredients and pour into a colada glass. Garnish with a strawberry and serve.

Zandoria

Jamaica

Ingredients

Glass: 140mL Champagne Saucer
Mixers: 30mL/1fl oz brandy
30mL/1fl oz Tia Maria
120mL/4fl oz fresh cream

Method

Shake and strain into cocktail glass.
Sprinkle with nutmeg and serve.

Zed

Ingredients

Belgium

Glass:	90mL/3oz Cocktail Glass
Mixers:	30mL/1fl oz gin 1 teaspoon sugar 30mL/1fl oz Mandarin Napoleon 90mL/3fl oz pineapple juice

Method

Shake and strain into cocktail glass.
Garnish with mint sprig and lemon.

Zipper

Ingredients

U.S.A.

Glass:	Cordial (Lexington)
Mixers:	10mL/3/8fl oz tequila 10mL/3/8fl oz Grand Marnier 10mL/3/8fl oz Baileys Irish Cream

Method

Layer in order in a shot glass and serve.

Zombie

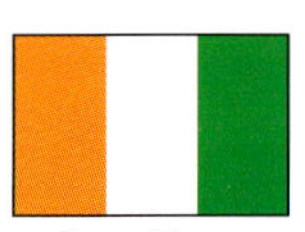

Ivory Coast

Ingredients

Glass:	300mL/10oz Fancy Cocktail Glass
Mixers:	45mL/1½fl oz Bacardi 30mL/1fl oz dark rum 30mL/1fl oz light rum 30mL/1fl oz pineapple juice 15mL/½fl oz lime or lemon juice 30mL/1fl oz apricot brandy 5mL/1/6fl oz sugar syrup

Method

Shake with ice and pour.
Garnish: Pineapple spear and leaves, cherry and mint leaves, swizzle stick and straws.

Zoom

Portugal

Ingredients

Glass: 150mL/5oz Cocktail Glass
Mixers: 45mL/1½fl oz brandy
20mL/⅝fl oz cream
15mL/½fl oz honey

Method
Shake and strain into a cocktail glass and serve.

Zorba the Greek

Greece

Ingredients

Glass: 150mL/5oz Cocktail Glass
Mixers: 60mL/2fl oz Bacardi rum
30mL/1fl oz orange juice
15mL/½fl oz ouzo
15mL/½fl oz Grenadine

Method
Shake and strain into a cocktail glass and serve.

Zimbabwe

Zulu Warrior

Ingredients
Glass: 210mL/7oz Old Fashioned
Mixers: 30mL/1fl oz Midori
30mL/1fl oz strawberry liqueur
30mL/1fl oz lemon juice
strawberries
rockmelon

Method
Blend with ice and pour.

Cocktail Index

A

B

C

D

E

F

G

H

I

J

K

L

M

N

O

P

Q

R

S

T

V

W

X, Y, Z

Great Vodka

Grey Goose
Kettle one

Wine (D-Liked)

Kenwood Zinfandel

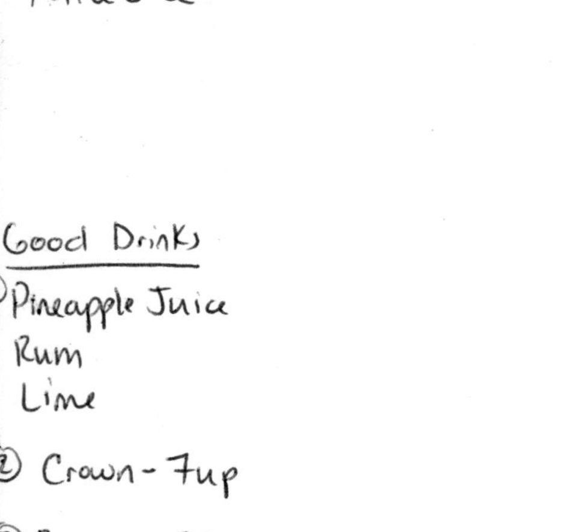

Good Drinks

1) Pineapple Juice
   Rum
   Lime

2) Crown - 7up

3) Beam - Coke

4) Mandrin oranje Vodka - 7up

5) Cran-apple, Vodka, lime